THE WRITING EXPERIMENT

Strategies for innovative creative writing

Hazel Smith

ALLEN&UNWIN

First published in 2005

Allen & Unwin
83 Alexander Street
Crows Nest NSW 2065
Australia
Phone: (61 2) 8425 0100
Fax: (61 2) 9906 2218
Email: info@allenandunwin.com
Web: www.allenandunwin.com

National Library of Australia
Cataloguing-in-Publication entry:

Smith, Hazel, 1950- .
The Writing Experiment: strategies for innovative creative writing.

Bibliography.
Includes index.
ISBN 978 1 7411 4015 6

1. Creative writing. 2. Creative writing (Higher education).
3. Creative writing - Handbooks, manuals, etc. 4. English
language - Writing. I. Title.

808.06

Set in 11/13 pt Minion by Midland Typesetters, Maryborough
Printed and bound in Australia by the SOS Print + Media Group.

10 9 8 7 6 5

Contents

Preface   iv
Introduction   vii

Part I: Introductory strategies   1
Chapter 1:   Playing with language, running with referents   3
Chapter 2:   Genre as a moveable feast   27
Chapter 3:   Working out with structures   48
Chapter 4:   Writing as recycling   65
Chapter 5:   Narrative, narratology, power   84
Chapter 6:   Dialoguing   110

Part II: Advanced strategies   131
Chapter 7:   Postmodern f(r)ictions   133
Chapter 8:   Postmodern poetry, avant-garde poetics   156
Chapter 9:   The invert, the cross-dresser, the fictocritic   192
Chapter 10: Tongues, talk and technologies   212
Chapter 11: New media travels   237
Chapter 12: Mapping worlds, moving cities   254

Conclusion: The ongoing editor   277
Acknowledgments   281
Index   283

Visit *The Writing Experiment* website at: www.allenandunwin.com/writingexp

Preface

The Writing Experiment is the culmination of my experience of teaching creative writing in the School of English at the University of New South Wales (UNSW) at both undergraduate and postgraduate levels from 1991 to 2001. It is dedicated with admiration and affection to the hundreds of students I taught during that period, and the breathtakingly good work they so often produced.

During my tenure at UNSW, I developed a method for teaching higher education students which combined three objectives: it theorised the process of writing; it was biased towards experimental approaches; and it was systematic and based on step-by-step strategies. As this method evolved, and as I transformed my teaching strategies in response to student and peer feedback, I felt that it would be valuable to document them in a book to make them more generally available. I also became aware that despite the heady and continuing rise of creative writing courses in American, Canadian, Australian and British universities during the last twenty years, there was a dearth of books in the area designed for specific use by higher education students, especially ones which also incorporated experimental and systematic strategies.

The book draws heavily on my own work as a writer, and my own interest in technique, experimental writing and analytical approaches to the creative process. I have engaged with nearly all the exercises in this book at one time or another, and many of them are central to my own creative practice. But the processes of writing and teaching have been symbiotic for me: my writing informed my teaching at every point, but teaching in turn took my writing into new areas. The book is also informed by my hybrid and intermedia approach to writing. My previous career as a professional musician, my collaborations with artists and musicians, and my love of film, the visual arts and music mean that I have constantly extended my writing beyond the purely literary, and have encouraged my students to do the same.

I would like to thank my previous colleagues in the School of English at the University of New South Wales, many of whom have contributed directly or indirectly to this book. In particular I would like to thank Anne Brewster, with whom I had the privilege to work closely and harmoniously for three years in the creative writing area. Her stimulation, advice and erudition have been immensely important, and she has given invaluable advice on drafts of this book. I am also indebted to Suzanne Eggins with whom for several years I jointly taught the first-year course 'Factual and Creative Writing': her precise and penetrating lectures on professional writing encouraged me to think through the importance of systematic approaches to creative writing. My warm thanks also to my current colleagues in the School of Creative Communication, University of Canberra, for providing a friendly, stimulating and innovative environment in which to complete this book, and particularly to Maureen Bettle for reading and commenting painstakingly on a draft of the manuscript.

I would like to thank my publisher Elizabeth Weiss for her excellent advice and enthusiastic support of this project; also my editor Karen Gee and the rest of the team at Allen & Unwin for all their cheerful assistance. I would also like to thank Laura Brown and Lisa McCarthy for helping me to contact ex-students; Kate Fagan for giving information on Lyn Hejinian's work; Joy Wallace for her advice and encouragement; and Roger Dean for reading the manuscript and making numerous suggestions. I also want to express my gratitude to all those authors and students who generously gave me permission to quote from their work, and to the UNSW student union for allowing me to reproduce work by students published in the magazine *Unsweetened.* But most of all I would like to thank the huge numbers of students—both those who are represented here and those who are not—who have stimulated me, kept me on my toes and given me invaluable feedback. As I put this book together I was increasingly frustrated by the fact that I had not kept a good deal of the wonderful work which students had produced over the years, and also that I would not have enough space to reproduce most of the examples in my possession. But I remembered with the greatest pleasure the lectures and tutorials in which I had laboured with students over the challenges and joys of creative work. I am extremely thankful for this unique experience, and know that it is the main dynamic of this book.

Hazel Smith
School of Creative Communication
Sonic Communications Research Group
University of Canberra

Introduction

Creative writing courses are an integral and indispensable part of university education, because they interconnect intellectual and creative exploration. *The Writing Experiment* is designed for university students enrolled in creative writing courses and for their teachers. Its aims are to suggest systematic strategies for creative writing, and to theorise the process of writing by relating it to the literary and cultural concepts which students encounter on other university courses. The book is based on the premise that creative writing can be systematically and analytically approached, and that successful work does not arise only from talent or inspiration. The following chapters attempt to *demystify* this process, and question many of the popular assumptions about the activity of writing.

A distinctive aspect of this book is that it breaks down complex tasks into easy-to-manage stages. Writers are taken through these steps—which are usually invisible in a finished text—by means of detailed examples and exercises. *The Writing Experiment* is based, therefore, on incremental strategies which recuperate, at a conscious level, the less accessible or unconscious aspects of the writing process.

This book has relevance to any kind of writing—from poetry to detective fiction. However, the strategies are biased towards explorative, innovative methods. The book avoids circumscribed technical advice about preconceived forms and suggests, instead, open-ended strategies with diverse outcomes. By adopting these, writers will learn how to explore alternative modes of working and find their own direction(s). The main take-home message from this volume is that it is possible to *work out* ways to write, and that experimentation is fundamental to creativity.

Although readers are advised to engage with the strategies provided, once they have finished the book they should also be able to devise their own.

As part of its experimental emphasis, this title also relates writing to other media and interweaves the verbal, visual and the sonic. Writing in the contemporary era needs to be redefined as a very broad category, which includes audiovisual projects, performance works, multimedia and hypermedia works, not just written texts. These kinds of creative endeavours are included, and encouraged, in this book.

The Writing Experiment is suitable for beginner and advanced writers, and is applicable both to undergraduate and postgraduate students. The opening six chapters (Part I) are particularly important for beginners, but advanced writers are likely to find many of the strategies in them helpful, or distinct from ones they normally use. The following six chapters (Part II) are more advanced and theoretical, and build on the strategies suggested in the first half. The book includes many examples of student work to demonstrate that it is based not only in theories about writing, but in the practice of teaching and learning in the university environment.

Although designed primarily for higher education students, this text can also be used by the more general reader. Such readers may wish to focus mainly on the exercises. They can skip over some of the more theoretical concepts if they wish, or increase their understanding of them with complementary reading.

FREQUENTLY ASKED QUESTIONS

The process of writing has traditionally been subject to extreme mystification. Secrecy has often been perpetuated by writers themselves, since published authors can be reluctant to reveal how they work—they may see this as giving away 'trade secrets'—and are often inarticulate about their writing methods. Many writers probably do not really know how they arrive at their texts, and mental events which occur during the creative process may be difficult to remember or describe. In addition, writers have historically had an ideological investment in the mystification of the creative process because it sustained a myth which was appealing to the public: that of the genius who is divinely inspired and individually endowed. However, this myth can be crippling to aspirant writers who feel helpless if they do not seem to have special talent, and cannot immediately match the work of their published peers.

In fact, writing does not arise out of a vacuum: there is always a process involved. Creative writers, at all stages of their careers, need to ask themselves questions about this process and the role of the author.

Some of these questions often initially include:

1. Do I have to have special qualities to be a writer?
2. Are there any rules or regulations which I must abide by when I am writing?
3. Will my writing be better if based on my personal experience?
4. Can I write if I don't have any good ideas, or any ideas at all?

These questions are all highly significant ones which are central to this book, and I will discuss each of them in turn.

1. Do I have to have special qualities to be a writer?

The popular belief is that writers have a special talent that is innate, that good writing is something that 'just happens', and that most aspects of the writing process are inaccessible both to the writer and to outsiders. However, this belief is fundamentally flawed, since talent partly arises out of the learning of particular skills, and awareness about the choices available in the process of writing. The main special qualities writers must have are perseverance, motivation, the willingness to search for methods which suit them, energy to push themselves out of their own comfort zones and avid reading habits. Failure to produce creative work is often due more to lack of stamina or insufficient commitment to the process, than a paucity of talent.

Self-awareness about the writing process is therefore crucial. Writers who develop this awareness will be able to intervene more effectively to develop their work or change direction. It is important to try a wide range of different techniques, since a writer who achieves average results with one technique may obtain excellent results with another.

2. Are there any rules I must abide by in writing?

There are no rules and regulations for creative writing, and no blueprints for a good piece of writing. Anyone who is looking for a formula for exciting work will not find it, and writers who rely on formulae usually produce dull results. However, strategies and techniques can be learnt: these are different from rules in that they set writing in motion rather than delineating correct methods. They are explorative and dynamic, and demonstrate a variety of means for generating and structuring material.

This book promotes experimental strategies rather than rules and regulations. Most broadly, an experimental approach to writing means retaining an open-ended and open-minded attitude, and pursuing new, diverse modes of textual exploration. As a consequence, experimental texts usually work against and beyond familiar literary codes and conventions. To write experimentally is to adopt a subversive and transgressive stance to the literary, and to break up generic and linguistic norms. This formal transgression is significant because it can be a means to rethink cultural mores: for example, to shake up ideas about sexual identity, class or race. Experimental texts, because they loosen linguistic and formal conventions, also have the advantage of being highly **polysemic**: that is, they suggest many different meanings and encourage conflicting interpretations. Such an approach to writing allows the exploration of political, psychological and philosophical ideas without reducing them to the level of dogma, description or propaganda.

At the same time experimental work can also develop its own codes and conventions over time, and become part of a 'tradition of the new'—a term famously coined by American art critic Harold Rosenberg (1965). Some forms of experimental poetry and fiction have turned into recognisable ways of working with language and genre which subsequent writers consciously adopt. This paradox—that any mode of experimentation is initially an appeal to the new but can become conventional over time—is one that is negotiated throughout this book.

Many traditionally accepted ideas about writing have also been exploded by literary theory. For example, theory has undermined the idea that literature unproblematically reflects the world. Semiotics, stemming from the linguistic theories of Ferdinand Saussure, asserts that words have an arbitrary rather than a natural relationship with the things to which they refer. Words are signs which stand for objects, events or ideas, but have no necessary connection with them. Consequently language refers to the 'real' world, but also constructs, transforms and mediates it. Some types of literary text (particularly those which belong to the genre of realism) may be so powerful and 'lifelike' that we forget that they are artificial linguistic constructs, but this is illusory. We can challenge this illusion by exploring experimental forms of writing which do not present language as 'natural'.

Finally the book suggests strategies which are experimental, but the outcomes can be of any type. It encourages you to be eclectic. It does not suggest sole identification with one type of writing or another, but mediation between them, and openness to all possibilities.

3. Will my writing be better if based on my personal experience?

Many people are motivated to write because they want to speak about their own experiences, and many writers use autobiographical experience as material, either directly or indirectly. But writing does not have to be based on personal experience, and frequently is not. To write is always to construct something, to create a fiction. There is a considerable difference between 'real life' and 'text life' though the two may be interconnected. Even where personal experience is used it is always mediated by language and sometimes transformed out of all recognition. Furthermore, it is arguable that success as a creative writer depends more on the ability to explore ideas and feelings through language, than on personal characteristics or experience. In fact, writing only autobiographically can be limiting, because it keeps us within the confines of our own particular world.

Many readers and writers automatically assume that a text is the expression of an author's personality. However, critical theory has tended to question the idea of the text as direct personal expression. Roland Barthes's essay, 'The Death of the Author' in *Image-Music-Text* (1977, pp. 142–8), asserts that texts are a result of what the authors have read rather than what they have experienced: the author's subjectivity is always diffused and transformed through language. Important here is the concept of **intertextuality**: the idea that any text is composed of other texts. Language always bears the traces of former uses, other contexts and discourses. In this sense language is never entirely personal and individual, but always has a public, social and political aspect.

Another prevalent belief is that a writer has a particular voice and style, and that learning to write is a matter of finding that voice as if it were pre-existent. In fact a writer does not have one voice but several, and these contrasting voices may emerge in different texts, at different times, or sometimes in the same text. One of the objectives of this book is to help writers extend their range by trying new approaches. Experimentation of this kind is very important because it is easy to write only in the way that seems to come most easily, and which does not require any extension of skill or outlook. However, without new approaches, writers are usually only utilising a very narrow part of their creativity. They will soon reach a limit in their work, a point beyond which it is difficult to develop.

4. Can I start to write if I don't have any good ideas, or any ideas at all?

It might seem that the only way to start writing is to have an idea to write about. Many would-be writers feel crippled because they think they do not have any good ideas: numerous aspirant writers have never written the great novel that they would like to write because they do not know how to begin. But in fact this does not have to be the case. Writing can start from an idea, but an equally valid way of approaching the activity is by playing with words on the page: as the words form patterns they suggest ideas.

Techniques of this kind are an important feature of this book. They can be a means of arriving at unusual ideas which might not arise by a more direct thematic approach.

At the same time you can stimulate your creativity by becoming aware of current intellectual debates and social issues, and participating in the world around you. Most interesting creative work is concerned with either psychological, political or philosophical issues, and in most cases the relationship between all three. Reading the newspaper, watching the television, surfing the Internet, and talking to friends—as well familiarising yourself with cultural theory and activity across the arts—can stimulate creative writing. In other words an active engagement with all aspects of the world around you should lead to a plethora of ideas for creative work.

CREATIVE WRITING, EDUCATIONAL ENVIRONMENTS

Creative writing used to be treated like the poor relation to literary studies within higher education. Literary texts were the prime object of attention, and students were given no opportunity to write such texts themselves. Even for the study of literature this was unfortunate, because it is possible to learn a great deal about literary texts by creating them. To understand the activity of writing is to appreciate more the way writers work, the choices they make and their use of language. Writing is often a means to becoming a more informed reader.

At the root of all the preceding questions are quite fundamental issues about writing, the role of the author, the way the writer engages with language, and the interface between real life and text life. These issues are explored in depth in literary theory in the work of such authors as Ferdinand Saussure, Roland Barthes, Jacques Derrida, Roman Jacobson and Julia Kristeva. This book makes a connection between the analytical ideas of some major literary theorists and the process of creative writing, and puts theory into practice. In this way it connects creative practice with a **poetics of writing**: that is, ways of analysing and theorising literature. The book also connects with many of the ideological and political issues at stake in the work of cultural theorists, such as Michel Foucault, Jacques Lacan or Michel de Certeau, and behind them the towering figures of Marx and Freud who have influenced so much intellectual thinking in the twentieth and 21st centuries. It is these thinkers who will help you to explore the psychological (through psychoanalytic theory) and the political (through cultural theory). *The Writing Experiment* sometimes engages with the work of these theorists implicitly rather than explicitly.

The aim of the book is not to expound the work of particular theorists, or to elucidate theoretical concepts in depth. Rather it is to show ways in which theoretical understanding might be adapted to the process of writing, and to help you develop a poetics of writing which you can apply to your own work.

The Writing Experiment also relates creative writing to the study of literature in higher education. It draws examples from contemporary Australian, British, American, New Zealand and Canadian writing, and non-English speaking and indigenous cultures. Writing and reading cannot be separated, and your own creative endeavours will help you understand the work of published writers you are studying on other courses, while extensive reading will help you to improve your creative work. In addition, *The Writing Experiment* connects with performance and hypermedia studies, since it emphasises off-the-page, as much as on-the-page, writing, and includes a chapter on the way writing is changing in response to new technologies. Again, because this is a book about *doing* writing, it does not give detailed accounts of literary movements, or individual writers, which can be found elsewhere.

More generally, the ability to think creatively is a very important part of academic work, and can complement analytical thinking. Some of the strategies in this book can also be used in academic work to generate ideas and forge connections between them. In expository, as well as creative, writing, analytical and creative thinking are intertwined and have a symbiotic relationship.

HOW TO USE *THE WRITING EXPERIMENT*

The book is divided into two sections. Part I, **Introductory strategies** consists of six chapters and explores basic approaches and techniques for writing. Readers are given the most help in this section, and the writing process is broken down into easy-to-manage and entertaining stages. Although these are introductory strategies, they can be used in the creation of sophisticated texts, and some challenging exercises are included which may be of equal interest and value to more advanced writers. Part II, **Advanced strategies**, also comprised of six chapters, explores more complex methods (or combinations of strategies learnt in the first section). It also includes background and historical information—particularly about the postmodern and experimental movements to which many of the exercises in the book relate. The book is written in a progressive and accumulative manner: an idea mentioned in passing in the first half is sometimes developed in much more detail, and theorised more extensively, in the second half. The book will probably be most effective if read and used in order as each chapter builds on strategies and approaches of the previous chapter(s). However, some readers might want to scan the book and read sections that appeal to them, or seem particularly relevant, and some strategies in Part II can be introduced at an earlier stage if desired.

In Part I, Chapter 1 **Playing with language, running with referents** introduces two approaches which are fundamental to the book. They are language-based strategies which use words as a form of text generation, and referent-based strategies which enable writers to build texts on a particular subject, idea or theme. Chapter 2 **Genre as a moveable feast** stresses the flexibility and malleability of genre and its importance as a tool of representation. It shifts between the modes of realism, surrealism and satire, and also demonstrates how prose can be transformed into poetry. Chapter 3 **Working out with structures** focuses on the importance of structure and the notion of structuring principles, both formally and ideologically. It also contains a section on adapting cultural (non-literary) forms to literary texts. Chapter 4 **Writing as recycling** uses the concept of intertextuality to move through collage, found texts and the rewriting of classic texts. Chapter 5 **Narrative, narratology, power** experiments with narrative technique and theory. Through this process it suggests ways in which narration affects the ideological status and import of the narrative. Chapter 6 **Dialoguing** explores dialogue in prose, performance texts and poems. It includes realistic and non-realistic dialogue, dialogue as a form of communication and power struggle, polylogues and contemporary forms of dialogue. It also promotes collaboration as dialoguing.

In Part II, Chapter 7 **Postmodern f(r)ictions** focuses on aspects of the postmodern novel. It explores the subversion of plot and character, the rewriting of history, and the construction of new worlds. Chapter 8 **Postmodern poetry, avant-garde poetics** is in two parts: the first shows how the 'postmodern lyric' questions many of the premises of the traditional lyric; the second emphasises the importance of linguistic innovation in avant-garde poetry, and discusses its political and poetic objectives. It encourages readers to play with language in ways which overturn conventions of grammar, syntax, vocabulary and structure. Chapter 9 **The invert, the cross-dresser, the fictocritic** engages with postmodern reinventions and subversions of genre, including the synoptic novel, discontinuous prose, mixed-genre writing and fictocriticism. It also suggests the cultural consequences of such subversion. Chapter 10 **Tongues, talk and technologies** centres mainly on oral performance in a contemporary context. It includes strategies for speech-based and sonic poetry, and basic improvisatory techniques in performance. It also mobilises intermedia work, which combines text with image and sound.

Chapter 11 **New media travels** is dedicated to writing and new technologies. Readers become 'cyberwriters' who are initiated into the creative possibilities of hypertext, hypermedia, animation and codework. Chapter 12 **Mapping worlds, moving cities** introduces the concept of postmodern geography, and projects place as dynamic, multiplicitous and socially produced. It enters the city as a site of difference, and includes the walk poem and an exercise in time-space compression. The book ends with **The ongoing editor**, which questions the notion of editing as a necessarily discrete stage in the writing process, while suggesting that many of the approaches in the book can be applied as strategies to critique and polish work.

The exercises, which are the major focus of the book, are outlined in each chapter following the introduction. These exercises are quite broad, but detailed advice about how to approach them is given throughout the chapter where they are referenced again. Any new theoretical or technical terms which they contain are explicated as the chapter proceeds. In most cases the reader is taken through a number of stages in the creative process, and examples are given of published and student writing. Chapters 10 and 11 are supported by examples of performance and new media work which can be accessed from *The Writing Experiment* website at www.allenandunwin.com/writingexp. The website should be used in conjunction with reading the relevant chapters and working on the exercises. In other places website addresses are sometimes given for the work of interesting performers or web artists. Such addresses are, of course, subject to change, but if they move they can usually be found again at their new location through a Google search in an Internet browser.

The Writing Experiment does not aim to cover all forms of writing or the creative process. It does not dwell a great deal on strategies which are thoroughly and effectively documented elsewhere, and can be used in conjunction with other stimulating books about writing, such as Lance Olsen's *Rebel Yell* (1999), John Singleton and Mary Luckhurst's edited volume *The Creative Writing Handbook* (1996) and Brenda Walker's edited volume *The Writer's Reader* (2002). However, *The Writing Experiment* does aim to inculcate a special way of thinking about writing which can be widely, even comprehensively, applied.

REFERENCES

Barthes, R. 1977, *Image-Music-Text*, Fontana, London.
Olsen, L. 1999, *Rebel Yell: A Short Guide to Writing Fiction*, 2nd edn, Cambrian Publications, San Jose, California.

Rosenberg, H. 1965, *The Tradition of the New*, McGraw-Hill, New York.

Singleton, J. and Luckhurst, M. (eds.) 1996, *The Creative Writing Handbook: Techniques for New Writers*, Macmillan, London.

Walker, B. (ed.), 2002, *The Writer's Reader: A Guide to Writing Fiction and Poetry*, Halstead Press, Sydney.

PART I
Introductory strategies

CHAPTER ONE
Playing with language, running with referents

In the Introduction I emphasised that you do not have to have an idea to start writing, but can generate ideas by manipulating words. So this chapter initially encourages you to play with language, without necessarily having any particular idea or theme firmly in mind. When you play with language you are engaging with **language-based strategies**. The fundamental premise on which such strategies are based is that words suggest other words. Start with one word—any word—and it will lead you to many others, until you have formed a whole text. These methods invite you to explore the sounds and meanings of words as a way of finding ideas, rather than starting to write from a preconceived idea. If you soak up these approaches, you need never suffer from writer's block, because words will serve as automatic triggers for writing.

A very important idea in literary theory, on which language-based strategies are constructed, is that language creates the world rather than the other way round. Reality is not simply 'out there' independent of words and unchanged by them. Rather, the way we use language makes the world how it is. Playing with language allows us to construct our own world, and question some of the ways in which reality is normally perceived.

In talking about language-based strategies, I am distinguishing them from **referent-based strategies**. Referent-based strategies help you to 'run' with a particular subject, theme or idea you have in mind, and to build a text upon it. In the second half of this chapter we will take the mirror as a referent, and see how far we can run with it.

Language-based and **referent-based strategies** are the two most fundamental approaches to writing. All writing engages with one of them, and most writing includes a combination. Here we explore them separately to show how each can be a powerful tool in your writing.

exercises

1. Play with language and build up three short texts using the following techniques in turn:
   a) word association
   b) phrase manipulation
   c) combining words from a word pool. You can add words such as 'is' or 'of' to combine the words into short phrases. Try to make your combinations unusual and striking.
2. Write a short creative text using one of the following referents: the mirror, the map or the machine.

PLAYING WITH LANGUAGE

Language-based strategies encourage you to think in ways which are non-linear, and to make unconscious connections. They coax the associative modes of thinking which are pivotal to creative endeavour. These exercises are fun to do, they play games with language, but they can also produce challenging and unusual texts.

It is essential to have some language-based strategies at your disposal, and all good writers do. Language-based strategies tend to be very fundamental; if you start with language you are immediately concentrating on the medium in which you have to express yourself. As you play with words, new lines of thought may begin to reveal themselves. If you start with an idea it still has to be converted into language, and that is the difficult part—because you can have the most amazing idea in the world, but it is not always easy to find the right words to express it or fully convey its complexity.

Language-based strategies sharpen your sensitivity to language and help you to be discriminating, imaginative and unconventional in the way you use it. Inexperienced writers sometimes fall back on clichés like 'his heart throbbed' or 'her eyes were full of tears': these exercises will help you avoid them. So even if you end up writing in a way which is very different from the style induced by these exercises, you will find them a useful technical resource.

Language-based strategies exploit the relation between the **signifier** and the **signified**. According to the linguist, Ferdinand Saussure, the signifier is the material form of the word—its visual and aural dimension, the way it looks and sounds—and the signified is the concept, the meaning. In normal conversation we tend to concentrate on the signified rather than the signifier, but your writing, particularly poetry, can be enhanced if you stress the signifier as much as the signified. (For more explanation and detail about Saussure's ideas see *Structuralism and Semiotics* (Hawkes 1977), *Saussure* (Culler 1976), *Critical Practice* (Belsey 2002) and *The Theory Toolbox* (Nealon & Giroux 2003).

These exercises encourage you to take account of the sounds of the words. In them sound is used as a generative process (a way of making one word suggest another). The objective of the exercises, however, is not to encourage you to write traditional rhymed verse. This type of writing now seems somewhat anachronistic because it was mainly predominant in pre-twentieth century poetry, though it is retained in some popular forms such as rap. Rather, playing with language helps you to explore other ways of using sound. And since rhyming verse is a technique with which you are probably already familiar, I suggest that you avoid it completely for the moment, in order to widen your scope and steer your creativity in other directions.

WORD ASSOCIATION

The word association exercise (Exercise 1a) is a commonly used strategy, but my version of the exercise is different from others in the emphasis it puts on sound as well as sense. This exercise has many functions. First, it sensitises you to language, making you aware of its plasticity: the way language is like clay in your hands. Second, it can be used to develop strings of ideas. Writers often use word association to trigger thoughts on a particular topic, and it is a good way to dredge up unconscious connections through language. Third, it can result, with some care and manoeuvring, in an experimental text which is stimulating to read in itself. Such texts are often powerful because they are **polysemic**: that is, they have many different meanings and these fly out in several directions at once. In the following examples I break down the process of word association into several stages.

So let's take a word and see how we can spawn others from it by association. Our purpose here is to eventually produce a large block of words—half a page or more—combining different types of association. Examples of this kind of writing can be seen in Examples 1.6 to 1.10, but we will start with a breakdown of the process into preliminary strategies. You may want to try all these strategies in turn, either starting with the same word I have used or thinking up one of your own.

First, we will see what happens when we take one word and forge others from it which are similar to it in sound. In doing this I am playing with the signifier. In order to make it clear how all the words relate to that first word, I will repeat it each time.

Example 1.1: Association by sound (playing with the signifier)

green ghost	truth token
green grate	truth ruthless
green grist	truth truck
green guard	truth rucksack
green grain	truth roof
green real	truth suit
green read	truth soup
green needle	truth ute
green scene	truth time
green knee	truth tool
green agreeable	truth tower
green aggravate	truth uterus
green oversee	
green industry	

Here I have improvised pairs of words in which the second word always bears a sonic relationship to the first. To do so, I have employed strategies such as alliteration, assonance or half rhymes. The second word may be quite distant initially in meaning, but the meanings of the two words become related through sound. In this way connections between words can be produced by sound that would never occur by a primarily semantic route. As you can see, some of these combinations suggest unusual images, for example that truth is token or a soup.

Now let's see how I can produce word association by meaning:

Example 1.2: Association by meaning (playing with the signified)

green blue	truth falsehood
green sick	truth real
green grow	truth fiction
green inexperienced	truth language

Here I have generated each second word in the pair by meaning (even though a combination like 'truth falsehood' works by antithesis). And you will notice how I am exploiting the different senses of the word 'green': the way we associate it with colour, or with naivety, or environmentalism.

Let's look now at two other strategies, dissociation and leapfrogging:

Example 1.3: Dissociation

green falsehood	truth nest
green milk	truth lamp
green impulse	truth petal
green puddle	truth bird

In this example I have generated words largely by dissociation, by writing down a second word which seemed to have no immediate connection with the first. But it is surprising how once you place unrelated words side by side a connection between them can suddenly be forged. You can see that there is some mileage in the notion of 'a nest of truths', or 'a bird of truth', or a 'green impulse'.

Example 1.4: Leapfrogging

greenpeace
peace talk
talkback
backdrop

In this group I am doing what I call leapfrogging: that is, making the end of one word the beginning of the next, and through this process building up new words.

So in all the above examples I am playing with the relationship between sound and sense, sometimes homing in more on the sound, sometimes more on the sense. I am also, in these examples, trying to divide the sound from the sense but, of course, the two often go hand in hand. If you say 'green grow' you arrive at a combination of words which is linked by sound, but also intimately connected by sense.

In the next example I have used a multisyllabic word. This gives more scope than a word of just one syllable. I have also employed a mixture of strategies here for generating the second word. Decide for yourself what strategies are at work here:

Example 1.5: Mixed strategies

energy synergy
energy generate
energy genesis
energy emphasis
energy gene

energy dynamism
energy exercise
energy electricity
energy aerobics
energy pen
energy light

Let's go further now: instead of confining ourselves to the first word we will keep breeding new words all the time by different forms of association or dissociation. For example, if we start with the word 'truth', instead of retreating back to it each time we can strike out with a whole stream of other words:

Example 1.6: Moving away from the first word
truth ruthless mucus mindplay playback falsehood hoodwink wisecrack crackdown whitewash cycle circle syntax tax free freedom phantom furtive fistful fightback backdown

You can see here how I have used a mixture of association, dissociation and leapfrogging to produce this passage. When you create such a text, you can keep referring back to the first word and use that as the basis for association. Or you can take each new word as the basis for association. Or you can go back to any previous word. One of the effects of the passage is to make truth, which we tend to think about as an absolute, a contested concept, since it is juxtaposed with such ideas as falsehood, hoodwink and whitewash. Moving away from the base word in this way is the mark of a fully-fledged word association.

You are now ready to try a word association of your own, combining these strategies. However, before you do so, it may be helpful to look at some examples of this approach in action by both students and published writers. The following example of word association, by student Elisabeth Crawford, is very effective because it draws on a wide range of different tactics to keep the surface of the language fresh, and doesn't overdo any particular approach. Here the author extends the technique by allowing some of the words to gather into phrases and familiar sayings, and then dissolve again into word association. The piece is also striking because playing with language allows Elisabeth to move through a range of disparate ideas which are nevertheless connected by their political relevance (including environmental concerns and queer politics). Her text therefore engages (but in a very flexible way) with current **ideology**—that is, beliefs about our society and the manipulation of those beliefs within the prevailing power structures and institutions:

Example 1.7
greengage plum apple eve mother earth ground zero green to smithereens Granny Smith baby smith Adam Smith USA AID LDC rainforest green revolution foreign debt IMF greenbacks green fronts greenpeace greenhouse green room All the world's a stage a part alone a mortgage green belt green lawn true blue lily white no yellowbellied reds blacks greenies blue for boys pink for girls girlies poofters faggots burn 'em at the stake barby tinny junky HIV AIDS AZT reprieve hope faith love God good evil right left forsaken my god my god why? there is a green hill valley shadow of death life limb bobby telly soapy sudsy squeaky clean lean mean machine sewing reaping crop harvest paddock damn just give me a home among the gum trees with lots of plum trees

'word association' (Crawford 1992)

In the next example, by student Michele Sweeney, word association conveys a short narrative, but one in which sensory impressions and feelings are more loosely connected, condensed and rapidly transforming than in a conventional narrative. Notice here how the impression of verbal speed created by the word strings (without the usual grammatical connectives) mimics the movement of travel, and the quick shifts of daydreaming and desire:

Example 1.8
Travel air bus cab plane to see sight see eyes sore feet walk climb rock mountain view sunset night lights dance move around the world bag port of call yell your name out and about what why am I here? There you get souvenirs tacky shopping duty free ride hitchhike and die in truck full of baggage empty inside hotel bed sleep awake to coffee Paris romance fall in love again on a Greek isle church roam around Spanish steps inside your mind wandering where to go to nearest embassy rules out Tokyo sukiyaki eat not in Bombay weave through crowds in London lost in a pickle yummy cakes patisserie puff like a balloon hot air plane glide through my dreams

'word association' (Sweeney 1993b)

It is important, however, to realise that this technique (or other closely related techniques) is also to be found in the work of published authors. The following extract is from a piece by Australian writer Ania Walwicz, who was born in Poland and whose work shows considerable European influence. The text is not entirely driven by word association, but we can see that generating words through their connection in sound is an important element in the text—for example in the verbal string 'person parson ardent emperor wilhelm potsdam jesa jesus'. Look at the way word association also keeps the piece open: the meaning does not close itself off. The prose poem continuously extends itself, weaving together childhood memories and fantasies, fairytale utopias and (seemingly more adult) erotic desires:

Example 1.9

tips waves up big dipper fires wings lift me up roll out entry for prince of shiny press into me furbelows bows on tip toes cartwheels in lovely head lamp glower put on her dots dot in dot dotter dot dottie lain in finer blades naps cherubs i'm all wreathed in tulle tulle skirts fly up thighs tight wrap in tunnel of love need a belt please a chord bang in big peaks up top plaits comes along so fast to me on my lay press with holds but not against me at all let flow engaged embraced in carriage of gold to weddings of mine in ornate halls i'm bride bridely a merry mary she shouts in van makes me happy prince aloise la belle cadix i'm on my way to become somebody else relay to longest i'm fiancée of person parson ardent emperor wilhelm potsdam jesa jesus in yearn honeymoons caress one doesn't know who one has touch glory goddess of shining gold i can change places with any move through all orchid pearls arias top speed epic lushy lush ermines bares my breasts swell forth in my stream of pours from her in heady welcomen adored faithful prays and pardons my empress of roses mayerling pulses gives me so much to walk on flames at top powers

From 'wonderful' (Walwicz 1989, p. 249)

The second example employs word association much less consistently and only as one element amongst many others. But it is intriguing to see how, in Example 1.10, Christine Brooke-Rose, one of Britain's leading experimental novelists, incorporates word association into her idiosyncratic prose style. Interspersed with more formal sentence structure, it creates a highly evocative impression of an academic meditating on how she might lose her job because her expertise is considered redundant:

Example 1.10

I shall soon be quite redundant at last despite of all, as redundant as you after queue and as totally predictable, information-content zero.

The programme-cuts will one by one proceed apace, which will entail laying off paying off with luck all the teachers of dead languages like literature philosophy history, for who will want to know about ancient passions divine royal middle class or working in words and phrases and structures that will continue to spark out inside the techne that will soon be silenced by the high technology?

From *Amalgamemnon* (Brooke-Rose 1994, p. 5)

PHRASE MANIPULATION

Just as we can start to build a text from a word, we can also forge a piece of writing from a phrase. In Exercise 1b you are asked to generate a text through phrase manipulation. To do this you take a phrase as a starting point, and then make lots of other phrases from it. The initial phrase may have a verb in it, but it doesn't have to. The important point is that it is short and only has a few words in it.

A phrase contains more possibilities than a single word to grow and mutate. We can change the word order, substitute one word for another, subtract and add words. Let's have a look at these various strategies in turn.

Phrase permutation

Here the position of the words in relation to each other is changed within the phrase or short sentence, usually radically transforming the sense. For example:

Example 1.11
The death of the author
the author of death

Or:

Example 1.12
a rolling landscape
the landscape rolls away

You can see how effective this technique is in the following poem by Australian poet Myron Lysenko. Particularly important is the twist in the last stanza:

Example 1.13
They stood
under the big tree
and talked slowly

Under the tree
they stood
and slowly talked big

The big tree
stood slowly
and under they talked

They stood big
and slowly talked
the tree under

The big tree talked
and they slowly
understood

'Under The Tree' (Lysenko 1998, p. 27)

Substitution

Another way of changing the phrase is by substituting one word for another. In the following example either the word 'death' or 'author' is replaced by another word:

Example 1.14
the death of the author
the death of autumn
the death of the daughter
the death of the century
deleting the author
the author's orbit
death authorised
the demise of the orchestra

Most writers work with substitution as a way of improving on words which are linguistically weak. However I am attempting here not simply to find synonyms of the words, but to alter the sense of the phrase, to allow language to lead the way. It's important when undertaking this kind of exercise not to stick with a preconceived meaning, but to allow the words themselves to offer new directions. Also do not expect the phrases to follow on from each other, or necessarily to make obvious sense. The idea of the exercise is to become absorbed in the process, not to arrive immediately at a finished product.

Addition and subtraction

Words can also be added or subtracted from the phrase, taking it in a new direction:

Example 1.15
reversing the death of the author
death in the fist of the author

In the next example, which works outwards from the more poetic phrase 'silence is a searchlight', a mixture of strategies is employed. The word searchlight is broken up as part of the linguistic play:

Example 1.16: Mixed strategies
silence is a searchlight
the light searches out the silence
the search for silence lights the day
daylight certifies our secrets
bright light reverses time
the silence wilts
the silence ignites
silence is litmus
silence plucks out its own eyes
silence is an island
lying is an island
lying is an enigma
lying trumps up a licence

Once you have generated your phrases you can, if you wish, order them into a persuasive succession. You can arrange the text as poetry or prose. Let's again look at two student examples of phrase manipulation which do this. The first is by Michele Sweeney:

Example 1.17
Travel is exciting
Excitement in travel
is there exciting travel?
Travel is titillating
Travel is tickets
To travel is to trek
Excitement is over-rated
Excitement is a word

To travel is unkind
To travel is wicked
To travel is a gum nut
To travel is a lie
To travel is insular
Travellers are hair nets
Shiny is new
Diamonds are forever.

'phrase manipulation' (Sweeney 1993a)

Note how in the first stanza Michele works by permutation of the phrase and then substitution. She returns to the idea of excitement at the end of the first section, but drops the idea of travel. Notice also how the assertions become wilder as the poem progresses. They take several new turns, and end with the familiar saying 'diamonds are forever', which seems quite far removed from the original travel. However, the last two phrases do relate to the rest of the piece, because they raise the question of whether the excitement of travel brings enduring value, or simply stimulates the need for novelty.

The second piece, written by another student, Canadian Gabrielle Prendergast—now a professional film scriptwriter—uses phrase manipulation to build a poetic meditation on the subject of time. The second section permutes the first by substituting, adding and subtracting words. Sometimes, as in the last line, permutation occurs by simply moving the position of a full stop, thereby changing the way the words are grouped and consequently the sense:

Example 1.18
Time
bends backward. clocks explode. coiled springs into sets of wings.
flying falling to another lover another life. elements burn soak bury

and chill the way. sadly brother time gives no clues but a shadow.
celluloid rushes side by side, nature baptises back alley temples.
trembling fingers and shivering flesh. coward! the truth is so steadfast and sharp. uphold me time. the enemy refuses to budge.

I'm
bending backwards. spine explodes. a coiled spring into white wing
and falling flying to another life another lover. figments burn soak
bury and chill my way. sister sadly I'm finding no clues but a shadow.
celluloid rushes end to end. nature's baptism in back alley temple.
trembling fingers touch shivering flesh. courage so sharp steadfast
and true. uphold me. time the enemy is refusing to budge.

'White Christmas Eve' (Prendergast 1991)

Richard James Allen is a poet who has lived and worked extensively in both
Australia and America. His prose poem, 'Interviews for the Freedom of
Dreams' (of which an extract is given below), might also seem to be generated through phrase manipulation. Each phrase is a striking image, an
evocative little world in itself. But all the phrases also network together to
produce a panorama of ideas about history, language, society and identity:
this would be difficult to achieve in a poem committed to a sharp but
narrower focus. Notice how the phrases surge relentlessly forward, partly
through substitution of some words and retention of others. Note also
how sound, though used unobtrusively, is an important factor: 'bill' suggests 'bizarre', 'clearing house' suggests 'conspiracy'. This creates cohesion
between the phrases and makes them seem less disparate:

Example 1.19
a beginning that now seems arbitrary, an end that will seem
arbitrary. a bill of hope. a bill of tragedy. a bizarre series of
countries we keep passing through like mirrors. a carnival of mixed
messages. a clearing house for the emotions. a conspiracy of legs.
a course in applied moods. a family of books. a flag flapping
against the prose. a halo of history. a halo of words. a history of
imagination. a history of sewerage. a history of thunderclaps.
a hotel in the mouth. a magical connection to unhappiness. a
mathematical land where the pieces add up. a memory of ladders.
a peach in the road. a prolonged disassociation of the naming
capacity. a revised history of paradise. a theory that includes itself.
a walk through footage. a symphony of pure minds. a truly lonely
book. an alphabet stairway. an encyclopedia of images. an

unadorned and unpropitious work. an uncomfortably colourful world. another concept of imagination. another crucifixion in terms. another day in this pretty world of ours. are we sharing the same century? at the end of character, what begins? battles across the marne, the toy soldier game, the uglinesses of his childhood coming back, little blotches of unsatisfied time, pockets of emptiness, an enormous gap to be filled, hours to cross like miles, he was searching for a mission, yes, a cause, and made a kind of cause of himself. bethlehem attachments. beware of angels. bizzare little prophets. casting memories. catapults of language. children vomiting in books out of jealousy because their national hero is not getting published. climbing out of the valley of the ordinary. competing for the thoughts of god. competing for the house of the past. copyright in paradise. courting fallen angels. dancing in the future. dead or a string quartet. do dreams have assets? does jimmie have boundaries? does jimmie think late night tv staves off death? dream images of a hundred white generals pulling an enormous black leg. dreaming about having sleep as a job. dreams with huge casts of strange, strange characters. each book only the beginning of what it is necessary to say. each step closer to the world, the more it blurs. erase all distinguishing marks.

From 'Interviews for the Freedom of Dreams' (Allen 1993, p. 29)

The following piece, an extract from a collaboration *Neither the One nor the Other*, between British poets Frances Presley and Elizabeth James, is again based on phrase manipulation: it employs many of the strategies already discussed to witty effect, using the initial sentence as a base but also working away from it. The technique allows the poets to take words closely related in sound (past, pastoral, aporia, parsnip, etc.) to produce meanings to do with history, language, religion and the environment. These accumulate in such a way as to effectively question (though not through linear argument or logical sequence) the supremacy of the pastoral tradition in literature:

Example 1.20
We need to approach the pastoral with care and remember that it's not a convenient utpoa

(out-take)

we need
we need to approach

we need to approach the past
to approach the past we need we need
to approach the pastoral
we need to approach the pastoral in a car
o approach the pastoral with care
we read to poach the pastor
to cart toward aporia
approach the waste and pare the weed to the core
to catch a parsnip

and remember that it's not
and remember that it's not a convent
and remember that it's a con

ut poesia pastoralis

From *Neither the One nor the Other* (Presley & James 1999, no pages)

WORD POOLS

Exercise 1c asks you to create a pool of words and then combine the words into unusual and striking combinations. The words that make up the pool do not necessarily have to relate to each other, in fact the exercise will probably work better if they are unconnected in meaning. Choose some verbs, nouns and adjectives which are colourful or strong. Begin by creating a pool of about 15–20 words:

Example 1.21: Word pool
Time

clock   excrement
step   vomit   bicycle
word   fidget
blood   drift
mouth loss   squat

sense   wail   ladder

Once you have done that, juggle the words into combinations which seem to be evocative, unusual and striking. By this I mean forge phrases such as 'time squats', or 'sense wails', which create a metaphorical effect. You may use joining words such as 'of' or 'is' which bind the words together into a phrase, or employ the word 'like' to form a comparison. It often works well if you follow a noun with a verb but there are many alternatives:

Example 1.22: Combinations from the word pool
time squats
sense wails
sense vomits
blood words
the clock's drift
words fidget
time's excrement

As you move through these language-based exercises, you may find that a poem, or piece of prose, is emerging which leads you off on a tangent from the exercise. By all means do submit to this process as it may lead towards a really committed piece of writing. But also try, in other pieces, sticking strictly to the exercise, so that you develop expertise with that technique.

You may also want to combine two of the exercises, such as word association and phrase permutation. Again begin by keeping them separate, and then mix them if you wish.

RUNNING WITH THE REFERENT

So far we have been exploring language-based strategies, but sometimes you will want to start with a specific idea, or event, as the basis of your creative text. This is what I call a **referent-based** strategy (see Exercise 2). Referent here means the object or event to which the text refers. The referent for a creative text can be an object, event or mood on which the text is based. So if you write a poem about your unhappy love affair, you are using the love affair as a referent. Some different types of referent are:

- object
- event
- idea
- emotion
- political issue.

You can see from this that anything can be a referent, even the most mundane object. Once you realise this, it is very liberating because it means that anything, however ordinary, can form the basis for your writing. You can then 'run' with the referent: that is, let it suggest all sorts of different directions, some of which you will follow, some of which you will discard.

Let us think about each kind of referent listed above in turn, though these categories in practice overlap (and referents will generally run into each other, like different coloured clothes which have been washed together). An object referent might be a tree or a book; an event, a quarrel or a lunch-party; an idea, the essence of time or the status of truth; an emotion, anger or joy; a political issue, environmental pollution or the treatment of refugees. And, of course, you might create a poem or fiction based on several referents. In fact a central issue in literary theory has been the notion that any text is intrinsically political, because it is always written from a particular ideological position. In other words, all texts—because they are ideological—have a political referent, even if it is not very overt.

Exercise 2 asks you to write a creative text based on the mirror, the map or the machine (all of which are object referents). Your creative text can be a poem, a description or a short sketch: the form you feel will most suit your ideas. This exercise is designed to show you that almost any referent can be milked for ideas. Of course, when you are running with a referent, you will also need writing technique to shape your text. As I said before, most writing is a combination of language-based and referent-based strategies. If you play with language it produces ideas which you can then consider, if you begin with an idea it has to manifest itself in language, so you may find yourself moving backwards and forwards between the two strategies. For example, you might come up with an idea and work with that on one page, and then you might play with language on another page, and then bring the two together.

THE MEDIUM IS THE MIRROR

The mirror is a powerful referent because it has many symbolic, cultural and philosophical resonances. We look in the mirror and see ourselves reflected back, but not always in a way we expect or want. There is a mismatch between ourselves and our mirror images: they are never identical to each other. This produces a 'split self', the implications of which are theorised in more detail in Chapter 8. The mirror also projects society's expectations of how we (women in particular) should look: expectations we can never fully meet. But the concept of the mirror is also influential much more broadly, for example, in the way we think about history, since different eras often reflect each other (though this mirror may also be a distorting lens). And the mirror is haunted by the relationship between illusion and reality, since the image both reflects and intercepts the real. The mirror, then, has many different connotations, and any text may engage with several of these meanings at once.

Some possible aspects of the mirror you might want to emphasise could be:

- as a metaphor for identity
- the inversion of the image in the mirror
- body image
- looking in the mirror as a form of introspection
- a distorting mirror
- a room of mirrors
- memory as a series of mirrors
- history as a series of mirrors
- the gendered mirror
- working by association. Ideas related to the mirror such as shadows, echoes, reflections, twins and likenesses (you may be able to work outwards from the idea of the mirror into related concepts).

As you 'run' with the referent you might make a list of possible ideas you could follow up, or jot down phrases or words that come to mind, but still feel unable to cohere them into a creative text. Here are some of the ways that you can mobilise the ideas in broad outline:

- using the mirror as part of an incident
- describing the sensation of looking in the mirror
- using the mirror as a metaphor.

The referent can therefore be employed as a means of exploring psychological or political content. Through the mirror we might probe the fluid or unstable nature of identity; through the map, the complexities of migration; through the machine, the problems of mechanisation in contemporary society. The interest of the map or the mirror, in particular, is that they lend themselves to metaphor. The mirror, for example, can become a metaphor for subjectivity.

Let's look at some examples of using the mirror as a referent, firstly Rhyll McMaster's poem 'The Mirror'.

Example 1.23
I look into the mirror of my life
and see my mother.

She glares back at me
warningly.
She says, 'I'm bitterly disappointed.'

Then she says,
'You're lucky.'

I turn my eyes.
Even sideways I still catch glimpses
of clenched jaws, pursed lips
hurt senses.

'I'm most upset.
You can't survive,' she says
'without deep resentment.'

'The Mirror' (McMaster 1994, p. 121)

In this (fairly conventional but strong) poem the mirror is used as a way of thinking about identity and our genetic and familial heritage. The speaker looks into the mirror of her life hoping to see herself, but only finds the dominating presence of her mother and her own unwelcome likeness to her. The poem exploits the mirror image to convey the power struggle between mother and daughter, and to challenge the ideological assumption that such relationships are close and harmonious. But the mirror also symbolises the tension between the burden of our heritage and the potential of what we can achieve.

The mirror image often appears in novels. In the following extract from American writer Carson McCullers's *The Heart is a Lonely Hunter*, the mirror symbolises the ambivalence of memory, and Biff's reassessment of his identity, when the death of his wife ends their dull, limited yet secure marriage:

Example 1.24

Biff uncorked the bottle. He stood shirtless before the mirror and dabbed some of the perfume on his dark, hairy armpits. The scent made him stiffen. He exchanged a deadly secret glance with himself in the mirror and stood motionless. He was stunned by the memories brought to him with the perfume, not because of their clarity, but because they gathered together the whole long span of years and were complete. Biff rubbed his nose and looked sideways at himself. The boundary of death. He felt in him each minute that he had lived with her. And now their life together was whole as only the past can be whole. Abruptly Biff turned away.

From *The Heart is a Lonely Hunter* (McCullers 1981, p. 198)

Here the mirror is integrated into the narrative with other symbolic elements, such as the scent of the perfume. The passage follows the sentence 'He seldom thought of her', and precedes a paragraph in which we are told how Biff has 'done over' the bedroom which before had been 'tacky and flossy and drab', and made it much more attractive, bright and modern, 'luxurious and sedate'. We are informed that 'in this room nothing reminded him of her', though at the same time Alice's scent bottle constantly brings back the past, and some of its more positive aspects, such as the period before they were married. Looking in the mirror symbolises the balance between commemorating the past and moving on from it.

American writer Don DeLillo's novel *The Body Artist* also deals with the relationship between death and self. In this passage the mirror image is a way of re-membering and re-embodying the mourned person. The passage also suggests that the mirror has a life of its own and that different mirrors present the same reality in their own distinctive way:

Example 1.25
When she could not remember what he looked like, she leaned into a mirror and there he was, not really, only hintingly, barely at all, but there in a way, in a manner of thinking, in some mirrors more than others, more than rueful reproduction, depending on the hour and the light and the quality of the glass, the strategies of the glass, with its reversal of left and right, this room or that, because every image in every mirror is only virtual, even when you expect to see yourself.

From *The Body Artist* (DeLillo 2001, pp. 112–13)

In British novelist Julian Barnes's novel *Love, etc*, Oliver contemplates a past incident involving his wife Gillian. He meditates, in his own effusive and exaggerated voice, on how useful it would be if we all had a rear-view mirror to keep track of the past and its impact:

Example 1.26
So there I was, two-wheeling out of your sight past glinting steel silos crammed with the crushed blood of the Minervois grape, while Gillian was doing a fast-fade in my rear-view mirror. A gauche

term, don't you find—rear-view mirror—so filled with plod and particularity? Compare the snappier French: *rétroviseur*. Retrovision: how much we wish we had it, eh? But we live our lives without such useful little mirrors magnifying the road just travelled. We barrel up the A61 towards Toulouse, looking ahead, looking ahead. Those who forget their history are condemned to repeat it. The *rétroviseur*: essential for not just road safety but the race's survival. Oh dear, I feel an advertising slogan coming on.

From *Love, etc*, (Barnes 2001, pp. 18–19)

In my own prose poem 'Mirror' the metaphor of the mirror keeps changing:

Example 1.27
The mirror hangs slightly crooked on the wall, thin and long like a mask. Sometimes it seems to be part of the wall, sometimes it seems to stand out from it. One day you look it in the eye. The next day you sit where you can avoid it.

There have been days when you have taken the mirror off the wall and carried it across your back like a cross, sagging under its weight. There have been times when the mirror seemed to dissolve and you dipped your hand in it and smeared it over you. These are the worst.

There is a man in the mirror who tries to speak but he cannot make sounds. There is only a fish mouth darting and hands frenetically gesticulating.

Once you hung a cloth over the glass as if it were in disgrace. And you often smooth over the edges trying to bend them. You try to teach your friend tricks, how to draw rabbits out of a hat. Or you play love games with her, putting your hand behind her neck and stroking her.

There are moments when the mirror is made of layers you can peel away, labels from their sticky backs. Sometimes you smear the sheet with blood, or toothpaste, or chalk words on it. You long to walk through the looking-glass, but you do not dare to take the risk.

You feel good when you move the magnet and it cannot move without you. But it can screen a stranger's thoughts or the mirror image of a dream.

Once you cut your finger on the uncompromising edge.

Sometimes you turn the mirror to the wall, or you look into the mirror and see nothing, or you mistake a new reflection for your face.

'Mirror' (Smith 2000, p. 11)

Here the mirror is a way of exploring the tension between what we are and what we would like to be; the instability of identity (and gender); and the fusion of reality and illusion. The mirror is a fluid image and appears in the poem in various guises, for example as 'a glass', 'a magnet' and a 'cross'.

'Mirrors' by Australian writer Richard Lunn is an experimental short story about an upper-class, monied woman who is having an adulterous affair. The piece is written in sections, and realistic scenes are juxtaposed with highly symbolic passages about a mirror maze, in which the woman and her lover feel trapped, but which they also find erotically stimulating. When the man and woman try to fight their way out of the maze the man 'dies', and the woman is left to struggle on her own. At this point the text forcefully conveys the woman's confrontation with the mirrors, and her struggle to control the images which threaten to multiply, fragment and overpower her:

Example 1.28
A slow, cold anger takes hold of her and hurls her like a stone through corridors of glass. A mirror crazes around her fist and breaks apart. Another follows, then another, but hunger and exhaustion too are fists, which beat inside her as she moves until, as if she were a shattering reflection amongst a host of shattering reflections, she stumbles to the floor. Unconscious hours pass in which her memories fragment and merge with fantasies, as multiple reflections might break apart and merge into reality. For when she wakes there is no past that she recalls, no thought or feeling but the anger that hurls her down the corridors. Emptied of memories, devoid of fear or regret, she marches through the gleaming chambers. Her images swagger beside her, raise bloodied arms and smash themselves to tinkling shards. She lies on floors in jagged puddles of reflections and rushes up glass tunnels in a headlong herd of selves. She feels at times as if she's nothing but a moving consciousness, a disembodied, many-bodied anger, nowhere and everywhere, conquering whole armies of herself. Her body streams with red medals. She lifts her fist to smash a mirror. It tinkles into splinters and reveals a man face down upon the floor.

From 'Mirrors' (Lunn 1986, p. 9)

All these passages, then, explore different approaches to writing about the power of the mirror. Now try your own!

CONCLUSION

Playing with language and running with referents are fundamental approaches to writing, and can be used by beginners and more advanced writers alike. Although these strategies are introductory ones, they will form the bread and butter of your writing as it develops, and you will be able to add many more such techniques to your repertoire. You may use them to generate finished texts, or simply as ways of starting the process of writing. Over a period of time, they can be integrated into your writing with various degrees of complexity, for example a text will usually run with several referents at once, while language- and referent-based strategies are not mutually exclusive and will often be used together. This book builds on these fundamental strategies and they are implicit throughout, but sometimes return more directly. Chapter 8, for example, suggests many more exercises for playing with language, while Chapter 12 helps you to develop a particular referent, the city, in considerable depth.

REFERENCES

Allen, R. 1993, 'Interviews for the Freedom of Dreams', *Hope For a Man Named Jimmie & Grand Illusion Joe*, Five Islands Press, Wollongong, pp. 27–34.

Barnes, J. 2001, *Love, etc*, Picador, London. First published in 2000 by Jonathan Cape.

Belsey, C. 2002, *Critical Practice*, 2nd edn, Routledge, London. First published in 1980 by Methuen.

Brooke-Rose, C. 1994, *Amalgamemnon*, Dalkey Archive Press, Normal, Illinois. Originally published in 1984 by Carcanet Press, Great Britain.

Crawford, E. 1992, 'word association', unpublished.

Culler, J. 1976, *Saussure*, Fontana Press, London.

DeLillo, D. 2001, *The Body Artist*, Picador, London.

Hawkes, T. 1977, *Structuralism and Semiotics*, Methuen, London.

Lunn, R. 1986, 'Mirrors', *Transgressions: Australian Writing Now*, (ed.) D. Anderson, Penguin Australia, Ringwood, Victoria, pp. 3–11.

Lysenko, M. 1998, 'Under The Tree', *Winning and Losing*, Hit & Miss Publishers, Brunswick, Victoria.

McCullers, C. 1981, *The Heart is a Lonely Hunter*, Penguin, Harmondsworth, Middlesex. First published in 1943 by The Cresset Press.

McMaster, R. 1994, 'The Mirror', *Flying the Coop: New and Selected Poems 1972–1994*, Heinemann, Sydney.

Nealon, J.T. and Giroux, S.S. 2003, *The Theory Toolbox: Critical Concepts for the Humanities, Arts, and Social Sciences*, Rowman & Littlefield Publishers, Inc., Lanham, Maryland.

Prendergast, G. 1991, 'White Christmas Eve', unpublished.

Presley, F. and James, E. 1999, *Neither the One nor the Other*, Form Books, London.

Smith, H. 2000, 'Mirror', *Keys Round Her Tongue: Short Prose, Poems and Peformance Texts*, Soma Publications, Sydney.

Sweeney, M. 1993a, 'phrase manipulation', unpublished.

—— 1993b, 'word association', unpublished.

Walwicz, A. 1989, 'wonderful', *Boat*, Angus & Robertson, Sydney, pp. 249–52.

CHAPTER TWO
Genre as a moveable feast

In this chapter we experiment with genre through fundamental prose and poetry techniques. Genre is the French term for a type, species or class of composition. The term genre is used to distinguish a broad range of different kinds of writing from the non-literary to the literary. In literary studies it is primarily used to distinguish poetry, fiction and drama. Genres are characterised by different codes and conventions: these change with historical circumstances. The term genre, however, can also apply to recognisable types of writing within a particular genre (such as the detective or science fiction novel), or different *modes* of writing within a genre such as realism, satire or surrealism.

The first part of this chapter focuses on prose, the second on poetry. In the first part we build up a short realist prose passage, and then revamp it in **surrealist** and **satirical** modes. We see how genre is a moveable feast: subtle changes in the way we use language effect changes in genre. In the second half of the chapter we again move, this time from prose to poetry. We convert a single sentence into a poem, and look at the many different ways in which that sentence can be rearranged and transformed to emphasise its poetic qualities. We are concerned throughout with issues of **representation**: how we convey the world in words, in which genre is an important factor. Although this chapter works separately with poetry and prose, some strategies are relevant to both. This is particularly true of metaphor, which is addressed in the poetry section but is also important in prose.

exercises

1. Create a realist prose passage in which you construct a person-in-action. Your text should be a detailed sketch, not a story.
2. Rewrite the previous passage in:
   a) a surreal mode
   b) a satirical mode.
3. Create a short poem (between four and 30 lines) on any subject. Consider lineation, typography, metaphor, syntax, and also how these technical features affect the meaning(s) of the poem.

PROSE CHANGES CLOTHES

The following sections help you construct a realist prose passage and then rewrite, or 'dress it up', in surrealist and satirical modes. These modes are not necessarily totally discontinuous from each other: rewriting the same passage in different ways will show you how they interface.

A TOUCH OF REALISM

Realism can be powerfully used in writing to convey psychological and social realities, and it is the mode with which you are likely to be most familiar. Some of the techniques for writing realist prose we will explore will probably be ones you already adopt in your writing automatically. That does not mean that they are desirable for all types of writing, and other genres and modes may require you to work against these principles.

In fact an important idea in this chapter is that realism is only one type of writing amongst a range of alternatives. Realism is the dominant fictional mode in our society, because it seems to mirror our world. It is important to remember, however, that realism constitutes a set of conventions which give the appearance of reality, it does not convey that reality directly. Realism depends on maintaining an *illusion* of reality. As Catherine Belsey says, 'Realism is plausible not because it reflects the world, but because it is constructed out of what is (discursively) familiar' (2002, p. 44). As a result, Belsey argues, realism is basically a conservative form:

> The experience of reading a realistic text is ultimately reassuring, however harrowing the events of the story, because the world evoked in the fiction,

its patterns of cause and effect, of social relationships and moral values, largely confirm the patterns of the world we seem to know.

(Belsey 2002, p. 47)

Realism is therefore an important and powerful mode of writing, and one which has many different manifestations. But it has its limits if used to the exclusion of all other modes of writing. As we will see in Chapter 7, post-modernist fiction has often subverted the conventions of realism.

Animating a person-in-action

Exercise 1 asks you to construct a person-in-action in a realist mode: that is, in a lifelike way. I use the word construction, rather than description, to emphasise the dynamic nature of the process. For you may start this exercise by immediately recalling someone you have observed, but you do not have to have anything in mind when you start, you can build your person-in-action from the words in the exercise. One way of doing this is by using a constructivist approach where you gradually build up the passage. So you begin by writing down the words 'person' and 'actions'. These words serve as a prompt which sets your mind in motion. Even if you do not approach the exercise consciously in this way, you will probably be making such creative moves semiconsciously. Start with just the two words:

Example 2.1
    person
    actions

Then start to connect the two words:
    parts of the body
    actions involving parts of the body

Then lay out alternatives:
    legs, arms, neck, face
    washing up, walking, singing, talking, eating
    playing an instrument

And narrow it down to one possibility:
    matchstick thin legs and arms
    erratic eating, opening and closing the fridge door
    anorexic behaviour

Let's start to develop these lists into sentences. The sentences can be quite simple at this stage:

Example 2.2
She is very thin and her arms and legs are like matchsticks. She opens the fridge door and closes it. She walks away then turns back. She opens the fridge door, takes out a yoghurt, and shuts it again.

After you have written down a skeleton of the passage, you can gradually develop it, using the techniques of **addition** and **substitution** to amplify and focus it. This kind of technique is often used by published writers: Peter Carey, for example, describes a process called 'cantilevering' (Grenville & Woolfe 1993), in which he starts a passage over and over again, each time building and modifying the passage. This process is like the one I will be taking you through here. So the passage might become:

Example 2.3
She is becoming thinner by the day. Her arms and legs are so frail you can see the veins stand out and her face is hollow and creased. She is losing her hair, it sprouts only in tufts. She paces up and down outside the fridge and then opens the door. Inside are rows of plain and fruit-flavoured yoghurt, egg sandwiches and cartons of milk. She closes the fridge door abruptly. She walks away, then turns back and opens it again. She looks around. She takes out a yoghurt, peels off the lid, and quickly swallows a spoonful. Then she shuts the door, feeling acutely anxious and repelled by her behaviour.

This process of transformation mainly involves **amplification** and **refinement** of the individual sentences. So you fill in details and flesh out the piece, but you also try to focus the whole passage and shape the language, to show more clearly how the woman looks and feels.

As you construct the passage make sure you use some strong verbs. This is quite difficult in my passage, because it is about somebody acting hesitantly. However, in the following version I have made some adjustments to the verbs which I have underlined:

Example 2.4
She is becoming thinner by the day. Her arms and legs are so frail you can see the veins, and her face is hollow and creased. She is losing her hair, it sprouts only in tufts. She circles in front of the fridge and then opens the door. Inside are rows of plain and fruit-flavoured yoghurt, egg sandwiches and cartons of milk. She slams the fridge door abruptly. She edges away, then turns back and opens it cautiously again. She glances from side to side. She slides out a yoghurt, peels off the lid, and quickly

swallows a spoonful. Then she lets the door go, feeling acutely anxious and repelled by her behaviour.

Now let's look in more detail at the considerations involved in constructing a person-in-action.

(i) The visual aspect

In realist writing it is usually important to create a strong visual impression. Think of yourself as a filmmaker as well as a writer. Can you visualise what you are writing? We can learn a great deal from filmmakers, because film has in some respects superceded writing as the primary form of realist representation.

You can also draw on the other senses as well as vision, and this will make your piece even stronger. Use all five senses if you can. Maybe we need to hear or smell certain aspects of the scenario. For instance, in my example, we can hear the woman slamming the fridge door. Perhaps I could also evoke the smell of the food.

(ii) A sense of movement

I suggested that we construct a person-in-action, rather than simply describe someone, because description can often be rather static. I want you to create a sense of movement or change, of something actually happening in time. Use strong verbs to do this: that is, verbs which animate the action.

Let's look at three published examples of a person-in-action. The first one is by British writer Angela Carter:

Example 2.5

She pulled open drawers and cupboards and tipped out the contents in heaps, attacking them with her strong hands. She dug into boxes and jars of cosmetics and perfume, daubing herself and the furniture and the walls. She dragged mattress and pillows from the bed and punched them and kicked them until springs twanged through the brocade mattress cover and the pillows burst in a fine haze of down. The telegram was still clenched between her teeth, gradually darkening with saliva. She neither saw nor heard anything but wrecked like an automaton. Feathers stuck in the tears and grease on her cheeks.

From *The Magic Toyshop* (Carter 1981, p. 25)

This passage is effective because Carter uses strong verbs such as 'dug' and 'dragged', 'punched' and 'kicked'. Note also how the girl's movements activate motion in the objects around her, 'the pillows burst in a fine haze of down'.

The next passage is by Canadian novelist Margaret Atwood:

Example 2.6
At the right moment Miss Flegg gave me a shove and I lurched onto the stage, trying to look, as she had instructed me, as much like a mothball as possible. Then I danced. There were no steps to my dance, as I hadn't been taught any, so I made it up as I went along. I swung my arms, I bumped into the butterflies, I spun in circles and stamped my feet as hard as I could on the boards of the flimsy stage, until it shook. I threw myself into the part, it was a dance of rage and destruction, tears rolled down my cheeks behind the fur, the butterflies would die; my feet hurt for days afterwards. "This isn't me," I kept saying to myself, "they're making me do it"; yet even though I was concealed in the teddy-bear suit, which flopped about me and made me sweat, I felt naked and exposed, as if this ridiculous dance was the truth about me and everyone could see it.

From *Lady Oracle* (Atwood 1982, p. 50)

Here there is a considerable build-up of strong verbs in the sentence beginning 'I swung my arms . . .' but the passage is also effective because the actions indicate the girl's feelings, her embarrassment and anger: 'it was a dance of rage and destruction'.

The third passage is by American novelist Paul Auster, and is a fictional account of a movie star from the silent-film era:

Example 2.7
Hector can charm you with any one of a thousand gestures. Light-footed and nimble, nonchalant to the point of indifference, he threads himself through the obstacle course of life without the slightest trace of clumsiness or fear, dazzling you with his backpedals and dodges, his sudden torques and lunging pavanes, his double takes and hop-steps and rhumba swivels. Observe the thrums and fidgets of his fingers, his deftly timed exhales, the slight cock of the head when something unexpected catches his eye. These miniature acrobatics are a function of character, but they also give pleasure in and of themselves.

From *The Book of Illusions* (Auster 2002, p. 33)

In this passage Auster uses nouns and adjectives, as much as verbs, to suggest the smoothness and skill of Hector's actions. This is evident, for example, in the phrase 'his double takes and hop-steps and rhumba swivels'. The narrator also directs us how to watch his movements on the screen, 'Observe the thrums and fidgets of his fingers, his deftly timed exhales, the slight cock of his head when something unexpected catches his eye.'

(iii) The inclusion of detail

As you can see from the previous examples, detail is an important aspect of realist writing. If you just say 'she was lethargic', and leave it at that, your writing will be rather bland. If you say 'she walked in a ponderous way, pulling her feet and throwing her weight awkwardly forward', you will be evoking mood and feeling through a visual impression. When you are constructing or evoking a person, object or action, generate as many details as you can. If stuck, you can make lists of characteristics by association. For instance, if you were describing a person you could start with red hair, then lead on to green eyes and turned-up nose (like building an identi-kit picture). You do not need to have a picture in your mind's eye, you can gradually assemble it.

At the same time some general statements like 'she looked tired' or 'she seemed upset', if used sparingly, can help to summarise an impression. They can be accompanied by details which amplify the more general statement. So the words 'she looked tired' might be followed by a phrase such as 'she had bags under her eyes'; this gives more specificity, and helps to create a precise visual image. How much of the emphasis is on details and how much is on generalities will vary from writer to writer.

Closely connected to this is negotiating the relationship between part and whole. In my text, the sentence 'She is becoming thinner by the day' refers to the whole person, but the reference to veins in the arm, and hollow cheeks, focuses us on parts of the body. If you were describing someone washing up, you might move between focusing on their hands and their whole body. Mediating between a sense of the whole, and individual parts, implying what the whole is like from the parts, and how the parts fit together to make the whole, is central to any kind of realist representation. In the Angela Carter example, the focus in the first sentence shifts from the whole person to the hands:

Example 2.8

She pulled open drawers and cupboards and tipped out the contents in heaps, attacking them with her strong hands.

The process is analogous to that of a filmmaker who takes a mixture of long shots of a scene, where we see the action in its entirety, and then close-ups, where we see only one aspect in detail. You will obtain the best results by mixing your shots, shooting from different angles, and moving between parts and wholes. And you are engaging here with a complex amalgam of part and whole: of the person, of their actions, and the environment in which, or on which, they are acting.

SURREALISM STRIKES OUT

Exercise 2 explores ways of writing which deviate from realist conventions, and which construct reality rather differently. One of the paradoxes of writing is that you can say a great deal about social and psychological realities when not writing in a wholly realist vein. One way of deviating from realism is to adopt a mode which is either surreal or satirical. While realism constructs modes of being which are usually more familiar to us, surrealism **defamiliarises** the world, that is, makes us see it as if for the first time. So try now to write a surreal text (see Exercise 2a) by rewriting your previous text. You may find, if you rewrite your piece, that the person-in-action becomes a person who is acted upon.

A surrealist writer is normally less interested in representing the external world than in conveying psychological and social reality by **presenting** the world in an abnormal way. A surrealist text usually creates a physically impossible situation, it transgresses normal physical laws: it conjures up a situation that doesn't exist in reality.

For example, the well-known story by Franz Kafka, *Metamorphosis*, deals with the transformation of a person into an insect. This situation is physically impossible, but it obviously has a lot of far-reaching psychological ramifications (for example, fears of transgressing boundaries). Similarly, the extract from a short story by American writer Donald Barthelme, in Example 2.9 below, describes an expanding balloon: this grows and grows, and eventually covers a vast expanse of the city. Again this is an image which defies physical reality:

Example 2.9
The balloon, beginning at a point on Fourteenth Street, the exact location of which I cannot reveal, expanded northward all one night, while people were sleeping, until it reached the Park. There, I stopped it; at dawn the northernmost edges lay over the Plaza; the free-hanging motion was frivolous and gentle. But experiencing a faint irritation at stopping, even to protect the trees, and seeing no

reason the balloon should not be allowed to expand upward, over the parts of the city it was already covering, into the "air space" to be found there, I asked the engineers to see to it. This expansion took place throughout the morning, soft imperceptible sighing of gas through the valves. The balloon then covered forty-five blocks north-south and an irregular area east-west, as many as six cross-town blocks on either side of the Avenue in some places. That was the situation, then.

From 'The Balloon' (Barthelme 1993, p. 53)

So how can you generate a surrealist image? Let us think about our original diagram, which involved a person and a set of actions. A realistic action might be 'she crossed and uncrossed her arms at the table several times'. A surrealistic action would have to work against physical possibility and so could be 'she watched her legs crossing and uncrossing at the other side of the room'. This is impossible physically, but it is quite suggestive psychologically, as we are all familiar with the sensation of watching ourselves performing actions which don't seem quite to belong to us. So let's now turn my passage into a surrealist text (Exercise 2a):

Example 2.10: Surrealist rewriting
As she looked vacantly at the fridge door it burst open. A dark brown chocolate cake bounced on the floor and proceeded to shuffle across it. It was followed by a large unopened carton of cream. The cake waited in the middle of the room for the cream carton, then they simultaneously leapt onto the table.

The main strategy I am using here is one of **inversion**. I am making objects active and people passive. I am also attributing impossible actions to objects: chocolate cakes do not have a will of their own.

Although this passage is built on the premise of physical impossibility, it does seem to inscribe a psychological reality. We all know the feeling that food is acting of its own accord. But this way of conveying psychological reality is very different from the kind of observation we find in realist writing, where objects are usually subservient to human behaviour.

Another surreal scenario would be if the woman opened the fridge and found a child sleeping in it. In that situation the woman would be still acting, but she would be encountering a physically impossible situation. So the surreal often hinges on the unexpected and inconceivable becoming real.

SATIRE BITES BACK

It is also possible to break out of realism through satire, and this is the focus of Exercise 2b which asks you to rewrite your passage in a satirical mode. In satirical writing the author is usually making a comment about society: he or she is critiquing that society by 'sending it up'. There is often a sense that the characters are 'types', that they represent certain strata of social behaviour. Satirical writing is characterised by exaggeration, incongruity and deflation. In Example 2.11, my original passage is rewritten in a satirical vein. Through rewriting, the passage becomes a satire on food and contemporary society:

Example 2.11: Satirical rewriting
She was worshipping in the mirror, when the worm inside her stirred. She hobbled from the bedroom on her high-rise backless heels. A higher power was directing her. Her nostrils started to dilate before she opened the door. The high crept up on her: it was a Yoplait just like the one in the ads. She intoned the jingle like a mantra. Then she seized the door, grabbed the Yoplait, and with a mixture of guilt and pleasure voraciously licked the lid.

Here we have a portrait of a person caught between two contemporary religions: beauty and food. The passage satirises both by exploiting religious metaphors, and by depicting the woman's behaviour in an exaggerated way. There is an abundance of incongruity—she is trying to be elegant but she hobbles. There is a pun on high, playing on the verbal connection between religious higher powers, and the euphoria which can result from taking drugs. The piece points to contemporary society through the reference to high-rise buildings. These buildings tend to symbolise alienation and loneliness in our society, and their attendant psychological problems.

We also feel that the woman is a certain 'type'. We are less interested in her as an individual than as a representative of a particular category of behaviour. In addition, the point of view has changed from the original passage: the narrator is more distant from the subject matter.

A good example of satirical writing is this extract from *White Noise* by Don DeLillo, about an American university which includes a Hitler Studies department:

Example 2.12
There is no Hitler building as such. We are quartered in Centenary Hall, a dark brick structure we share with the popular culture department, known officially as American environments. A curious

group. The teaching staff is composed almost solely of New York émigrés, smart, thuggish, movie-mad, trivia-crazed. They are here to decipher the natural language of the culture, to make a formal method of the shiny pleasures they'd known in their Europe-shadowed childhoods—an Aristotelianism of bubble gum wrappers and detergent jingles. The department head is Alfonse (Fast Food) Stompanato, a broad-chested glowering man whose collection of prewar soda pop bottles is on permanent display in an alcove. All his teachers are male, wear rumpled clothes, need haircuts, cough into their armpits. Together they look like teamster officials assembled to identify the body of a mutilated colleague. The impression is one of pervasive bitterness, suspicion and intrigue.

From *White Noise* (DeLillo 1986, p. 9)

This passage is characterised by exaggeration, 'The teaching staff is composed almost solely of New York émigrés, smart, thuggish, movie-mad, trivia-crazed'; incongruity, 'an Aristotelianism of bubble gum wrappers'; and caricature, 'All his teachers are male, wear rumpled clothes, need haircuts, cough into their armpits'. It satirises universities, implying that some academics make a living by turning the popular culture they enjoy into an elitist academic discipline. The passage partly relies on 'types' to create a certain effect. Overall it deflates academic pomposity, since academics are shown up to be very conformist.

WHEN PROSE TURNS TO POETRY

In the second half of this chapter, which focuses on Exercise 3, we will experiment with different aspects of poetry so that you can create a short poem. There are countless types of poem, and any writer will employ some tactics at the expense of others. The language-based strategies in the first chapter (word association, phrase permutation and word pools) can help you to build poems. In this section I am going to explore a few more poetic techniques, but they are still only a fraction of the alternatives available. In your poem you are not expected to experiment with all the possibilities—just some of them. You may want to combine some of these techniques with others from the first chapter.

In order to analyse some of the strategies, I will look at all the different operations we can perform on a sentence to turn it into a poem. The poem 'The Red Wheelbarrow' by American poet William Carlos Williams is made out of a single sentence. It becomes a poem, rather than a sentence, because of the way Williams arranges the words on the page, and because of its strong visual focus on a single object (Williams 1976, p. 57). So I will take a sentence and look at the way we can draw out its poetic and semantic qualities by rearranging the words, or turning them into a metaphor, or by playing with the syntax. This does not mean when you create your poem that you have to be restricted to a sentence, it is just a means of laying the techniques bare. What these strategies do is to defamiliarise that particular sentence, make us look at it with fresh eyes. Defamiliarisation, compression and the polysemic play of language are all ways that we can distinguish poetry from prose. However, it cannot be said too often that poetry and prose sometimes share the same characteristics, and that we may often find ourselves writing poetic prose or prose poems.

Lineation

One of the possibilities that poetry presents is to write in lines (this is only a possibility because prose poems are not lineated). The unit of the line can perform many functions. For example, if you put a single word on a line it tends to give it a certain emphasis. Similarly, the line can act as a form of punctuation: many contemporary poets hardly punctuate their poems, instead they use the line ends for that purpose. The meaning of the words can be radically altered by the way you lineate the poem, creating ambiguities which make the poem richer. However, it is also possible to carry the sense across the line, and this can be a way of making the poem move relentlessly forwards. Many inexperienced writers do not consider lineation very carefully, but it can be a very potent means of both controlling and freeing up the meaning in poetry.

How can you experiment with lineation? Let us take a sentence and see if it can be turned into a poem by breaking it up into lines. The sentence is 'she stood in front of the door, wondering whether to open it'.

Example 2.13
>   she stood
>   in
>   front of
>   the door
>   wondering whether
>   to open
>   it

Here the lineation opens up possibilities that might not have seemed present in the original sentence: 'she stood in' becomes an independent phrase, as well as one which relates to the rest of the poem, and takes on the connotation of 'she stood in for something'. It thereby acquires another level of meaning, which is superimposed upon the overall meaning it has as part of the sentence. We can also read 'wondering whether to open' as an independent configuration. So the poem becomes about a woman wondering whether to open herself up, as well as wondering whether to open a door. By lineating the sentence we are creating several levels of meaning; these co-exist with each other.

Spacing and typography

You may want to play not only with the lineation, but also with spacing and typography:

Example 2.14
>   **she stood in front of the**
>   **door**
>   wondering
>
>   *whether*
>   to open
>   IT

Here the spacing of the words, and the use of different font styles, reflects the hesitation that the woman feels. In the next example the words are spaced differently again, and some words are edited out, making the poem more elliptical. In this case the reader has to do more work, because she or he has to fill in the context:

Example 2.15
>   THE DOOR
>
>   to
>   open
>   or

This is a **minimalist** poem in which the emphasis is on extreme compression.

It is also possible to activate an **acrostic** or **mesostic** structure. In an acrostic the vertical word is on the extreme left-hand side and each letter forms the start of a line, as in Example 2.32 later in this chapter. In a mesostic the vertical word hangs down the middle of the poem. So the word 'door' becomes a hook for other words (this can be quite effective with names), with the result that the poem functions on both a horizontal and vertical axis:

Example 2.16

she stoo**D**
in front **O**f the door
w **O**ndering
whethe**R**

Or you may want to turn your poem into a visual object:

Example 2.17

D O O R
O   O
O   A
R O A R

Example 2.18

　D O O R
　D O O R O
D O O R　O A
　O R O A R
　R O A R
　　A R
　　R

These are both examples of a **concrete** poem: that is, a poem in which the visual aspect largely carries the meaning(s). In Example 2.17 the poem becomes iconic, that is, it looks like the object or event to which it refers. It also implies, through the configuration of door/roar, the confrontational aspect of standing in front of the door. In Example 2.18 the poem becomes an intricate and visual play of letters which conveys the woman's agitation in a more abstract way. It is very important here that the form of the poem marries with the meaning.

Simile and metaphor

One of the ways in which you can enrich the language of your poem is through metaphor and simile. The basis for metaphor is one of transfer. You describe one object in terms of another, so the metaphor *time is a river* describes time in terms of a river, and the reader has to work out the similarities between the concept of time and the object of the river. In a simile we say that something is like something else. Metaphor and simile are ways of extending the range of language and the way we perceive the world; they forge new connections between seemingly unrelated objects and events. Metaphor helps to add extra levels to the text, although in Chapter 8 I will point out some of its pitfalls and limitations.

Inexperienced writers often want to create metaphors but do not know how. As we saw in the last chapter, using a word pool can result in some unusual metaphors, and you can certainly employ the word pool when you are writing poems. You can, for example, think up a central idea and then find combinations of words from the pool that fit well with it. Often, activating the word pool will make the idea unfold in new directions. However, another way of creating metaphors is to focus on the process of transfer: seeing one object or event in terms of another. Let's look at some strategies for doing that.

The sentence 'she stood in front of the door wondering whether to open it', if read in the context of poetry, can be perceived as a metaphor in itself. It could suggest, for example, that the woman is on the verge of a major personal or political decision. The door could be the threshold between the conscious and the unconscious, the personal and the political, and so on.

It would, therefore, be perfectly reasonable to leave the wording of this sentence as it is. It was William Carlos Williams who famously coined the phrase 'no ideas but in things'. What Williams meant was that we don't necessarily need to create metaphors, because objects and events resonate with meanings beyond themselves anyway. You may decide that constructing metaphor is rather artificial, and that you prefer a more direct approach to writing: we will see in Chapter 8 that there are many other alternatives. However, understanding how to create metaphors is a fundamental strategy that is useful to know about, whether you decide to implement it or not.

So another way of saying 'she wondered whether to open the door', would be, 'she asked herself the question whether she should open the door'. If we turn the door into a question mark, or compare the door to a question mark, we can create a metaphor or simile:

Example 2.19
the door hangs
like an unanswered question

A variation on this would be:

Example 2.20
the door calls
but she cannot find
her reply.

Here the door becomes animate. In the next example the animation of the door is combined with wordplay on call. It exploits different meanings of the word as in the phrase 'call and response', and also as in visit.

Example 2.21
the door calls
but fails to collect her

In Example 2.22 the door becomes a person and one who is sending out contradictory signals:

Example 2.22
the door
beckons
repels her

Example 2.23 suggests a hand of cards and also extending a hand:

Example 2.23
the door shows
the hand that it hides

In Example 2.24 'flaunt' is substituted for 'shows' to make the metaphor more evocative:

Example 2.24
the door
flaunts
the hand
that it hides

The following example hinges on association. The question arises: what is a door like? It is like a frontier:

Example 2.25
she stalls at the frontier
new space eludes her

In the next example the idea of the frontier is revisited with antithetical results. And using the question is more confrontational:

Example 2.26
frontier or front line?
gold or gunfire?

In Example 2.27 the doubt is likened to flying a kite. The door has disappeared, but again association is important, producing the image of doubt flapping about in the breeze:

Example 2.27
a wind kicks up
she flies her doubts high

In Example 2.28 the door is made active again, but the doubt becomes a colour which both intensifies and retreats. Notice also the compression in the last two lines:

Example 2.28
the door
poses
a question
darkens and pales

In the following example the word 'mark' derives from the image of a question mark. I have then transferred it to the phrase 'the mark of a thought': a thought which is preventing her going through the door. This shows how metaphor can become self-generative, so that one 'transfer' suggests another:

Example 2.29
the mark of a thought
on the handle

The next example transfers the features of the door to the doubt:

Example 2.30
doubt
swings
on its hinges

In Example 2.31 the door disappears from the equation: the idea of opening and closing is transferred to the metaphorical selves. This version spells out the psychological aspect, which is implicit in other examples:

Example 2.3 I
she searched out
her selves
wondering
whether
to open
one

In Example 2.32 we no longer have only one metaphor. There are several in the poem: sowing seeds, weather and wind imagery. There is also a pun on whether/weather and draught/draft:

Example 2.32
    Dreams blow their draughts
    On the wastes of decision
    Only the whether sows
    Rites become reasons

Once you start developing metaphors the process is self-generative: one metaphor leads to another. Sometimes you find the metaphor takes you down a new path, and the poem starts to grow in an unexpected fashion. In fact it can be liberating and creative to let the metaphors evolve in their own way. Do not force all the metaphors to 'agree' with each other, the assumption that metaphors should neatly fit with each other in the poem is sometimes put forward as a 'rule' writers should follow, but very few poems adhere to it. In fact the poem may be more dynamic if you allow the metaphors to fly out in several directions at once.

Example 2.33
a tall door

a question which pales

the mark of a quest which dismantles

Here the unified sentence has prised itself apart, and become a series of images which are almost independent of each other. The reader can make them cohere into a series of events or thoughts, but the construction is looser than in other examples.

You can see from the above examples how it is possible to either relentlessly pursue one metaphor through a poem, or introduce a number of them. Some poems, like Michael Dransfield's 'A Strange Bird' (1991, p. 354), hinge on a single metaphor. Others like Sylvia Plath's 'Words' (1981, p. 270) develop through a number of different metaphors which are interconnected. There is a network of comparisons running through this poem, rather than just one central comparison. In more experimental poems there is often a greater diversity, and flexibility, of metaphor, and this matter will be dealt with in more detail in Chapter 8.

Grammar and syntax

Finally, you can experiment with unconventional grammar and syntax:

Example 2.34
Opening fronts door
whether wondering

In this example the words are compressed, the subject is absent, and the words are not ordered or joined together in the normal way. This results in a more abstract impression. There is less emphasis on a clear visual image, and cause and effect are loosened. The lines become a rapid succession of impressions from which the central agent 'she' is removed: this also releases several meanings simultaneously (fronts in this context makes us think of confronts). Much experimental poetry adopts compression, and abnormal grammar and syntax, in order to achieve greater multiplicity of meaning. Again, this kind of linguistic experimentation will be explored at greater length in Chapter 8.

You are now ready to write a short poem: you may want to use only a sentence or make the poem longer. Try, however, to apply some of these strategies I have outlined to organise, lay out and develop the poem. The following poem by student Amy Tan combines the mirror referent from the previous chapter with some of the strategies from this one. Note the use of imaginative layout of the poem, and the way she has followed through the metaphor:

Example 2.35: Student example
i come to You
You have me under
               control
i do not live a day without
You

You
    reign as master and i
            Your slave

You look at me
i desire Your daily assessment
Your gaze seizes
            me

I bare myself before You
You inspect
me
You have me under
           control

MIRROR You reign as **MASTER**
          and i **your** *slave*

'Mirror' (Tan 1998)

CONCLUSION

In this chapter we have explored how changes to language cause shifts in genre. We have moved not only between prose and poetry, but also between generic modes such as satire and surrealism. This has given us a sense of the flexibility of genre, and the way that exciting writing often pushes productively at its edges. In fact turning genre on its head is a major experimental strategy, and one of the ways in which our writing can question how we represent the world around and within us. Genre will therefore be shifted even further in later chapters. For example, Chapter 5 both delineates and 'moves' narrative as a genre; Chapters 7 and 8 explore the redrawing of generic boundaries in postmodern fiction and poetry; and Chapter 9 inverts, subverts and crosses over genres. In Chapters 10 and 11 we also will see how genre resituates and extends itself even further in performance and cyberspace.

REFERENCES

Atwood, M. 1982, *Lady Oracle*, Virago Press, London. First published in 1977 by André Deutsch Limited, Great Britain.

Auster, P. 2002, *The Book of Illusions*, Henry Holt & Co., New York.

Barthelme, D. 1993, 'The Balloon', *60 Stories*, Penguin, Harmondsworth, Middlesex, pp. 53–8.

Belsey, C. 2002, *Critical Practice*, 2nd edn, Routledge, London. First published in 1980 by Methuen.

Carter, A. 1981, *The Magic Toyshop*, Virago, London. First published in 1967 by William Heinemann.

DeLillo, D. 1986, *White Noise*, Picador, London.

Dransfield, M. 1991, 'A Strange Bird', *The Penguin Book of Modern Australian Poetry*, (eds) J. Tranter and P. Mead, Penguin Books Australia, Ringwood, Victoria.

Grenville, K. and Woolfe, S. (eds) 1993, *Making Stories: How Ten Australian Novels Were Written*, Allen & Unwin, Sydney.

Plath, S. 1981, 'Words', *Collected Poems*, Faber & Faber, London.

Tan, A. 1998, 'Mirror', unpublished.

Williams, W.C. 1976, 'The Red Wheelbarrow', *Selected Poems*, Penguin, Harmondsworth, Middlesex.

CHAPTER THREE
Working out with structures

Anybody who enjoys some form of music, and nearly all of us do, shows appreciation of structure. Many pop songs, for example, are based on a structure in which the melody is repeated over and over again in successive verses. When we talk about structure we are referring to the relationship between the elements of the text, and the kind of pattern they form. One of the important aspects of a structure is that it can bring together separate chunks of text, so that they resonate with each other and belong to an overall design. These blocks may remain as sections, or may be fused together into a new whole.

Structures normally originate with one or more **structuring principles** or methods of organisation. For example, the basis of a structure may be repetition: this could be its structuring principle, though most large-scale works would be based on several such principles. The advantage for the writer in thinking in terms of structural principles is that such an approach enhances control and flexibility. It allows you to organise your material in suggestive ways, and create complexity by combining principles. Once you become used to experimenting with structures, you can start to invent your own by juggling the elements of the text and bending them in every direction.

Structures are very important because they help you to design your work in unusual or unexpected ways. This will mean that your texts will be more stimulating to read and more original. More significantly, how you organise your material impacts on what you have to say. The same words may create quite a different impression if they are arranged in another fashion. A cunning structure may, for example, help you to simultaneously project contrasting aspects of a political issue, or contradictory psychological states.

Obviously there are many different ways of making structures. You might map out a plan quite carefully before you start to write, and this skeleton design might help you to generate ideas. More commonly, as a piece of writing develops, a particular type of textual patterning and organisation starts to emerge. Decisions about structure are ideological as well as formal, not only because the shape of the text affects the content, but also because some types of structure are more conservative than others. While conservative structures are more **closed**, adventurous ones tend more towards **openness**. They broaden the scope of the writing and maximise the plurality and complexity of the meaning: its psychological and political import. The structural principles discussed in this chapter can lead to open forms of writing if used effectively.

An interest in, even reverence for, structure was central to the movement known as **structuralism**. This was a revolutionary, putatively scientific methodology for analysing texts, which became very influential in the 70s and early 80s. One of the central tenets of structuralism is that any literary text is made up of smaller units (that is, every macrostructure is made up of micro-elements) and that these acquire shape and meaning through their relationship to each other, the way they are arranged in the text. Structuralist analysis (see Hawkes 1977; Eagleton 1996) tends to highlight the relationship between different elements of the text, for example in repetitions, variations, oppositions, symmetries and parallelisms. It is this kind of relationship between constituent parts of the text that we will be exploring in this chapter in terms of creative practice. However, we will also be keeping a firm eye on the semantic and cultural consequences of such structural decisions: these were often underplayed in structuralist analysis.

In the first half of this chapter we will work out with a few different types of structuring principle: the eventual aim is that you will start to invent your own. In the second half of the chapter we will explore the adaptation of culturally significant, non-literary forms—such as advertisements, lists or recipes—to literary texts.

exercises

1. Create a text based on one or more of the following structural principles:
   a) linearity
   b) repetition

c) variation
d) simultaneity
e) multilayering
f) number.
2. Create a literary text using a culturally specific but non-literary form.

STRUCTURE IN PRINCIPLE

In this section we will look at six different types of structuring principles: linearity, repetition, variation, simultaneity, multilayering and number. You may want to 'work out with' all structural principles in turn, or choose one or two that particularly interest you.

In the following examples the structure of the texts are summarised: they represent the skeleton outline or structural components of the texts, not the whole text.

Linearity

A linear structure (Exercise 1a) comprises a series of events or ideas: it is based on the concept of a sequence. Linearity is the simplest form of structure, because it does not demand rearrangement of the material. A linear structure might be a narrative or a logical argument. An example of a linear structure is as follows (this is not an actual poem but an outline of the structure):

Example 3.1
a) woman approaches the door
b) puts her hand on the handle and hesitates
c) enters the room
d) finds something unexpected

In this example the four lines might be the beginning lines of four different stanzas. This, however, is less important than the fact that the structure hangs on a short linear narrative.

Linearity is one of the least adventurous types of structure because there is no real reorganisation of the material. The other structures here all, to varying degrees, disrupt linearity. In Chapter 5 we will see how longer narratives are usually non-linear in organisation.

Repetition

A linear structure depends on a chronological or logical sequence. Repetition (see Exercise 1b) is usually more **non-linear** because it involves circling round an idea rather than advancing through it. A repetitive structure can be effective for exploring different (including contradictory) aspects of a particular idea or subject. It can also create a very rhythmic and insistent effect, which is persuasive at a visceral level. One example of such a structure is where a repeating phrase or construction is used to bind sections of the text together. This repeating pattern then functions as a hook on which ideas or images can be hung:

Example 3.2

> she wondered whether
> a
> she wondered whether
> b
> she wondered whether
> c

In Example 3.2 the phrase 'she wondered whether' starts each section of the text.

Let's now look at an example of a repeating structure in a published poem 'Pause' by Australian poet Alison Croggon:

Example 3.3

Within the undivided moments
A train stops on a bridge
A woman's finger touches the rim of a man's mouth
A child hides in his secret place and counts his collection of stones
A general tells his soldiers that justice is not possible

Within the undivided moments
A woman decides to speak the lie she has always told before
A man decides to publish the lie he has always published before
A lie becomes a truth and then a history
A student turns off the desk light and stares out of the darkening window

Within the undivided moments
A baby tastes an orange for the first time
A soldier stamps on the hands of a little boy
A man loses his mind in the endless garden

Within the undivided moments
A twig falls in an empty pathway
A moth rests in a margin of light beside the darkening window
A spider shakes its web behind the cupboards in the hospital
A beetle pauses and turns at the edge of a puddle of blood
And above the vanishing lovers
Magnificent lords of cloud reveal again
Beauty no one can see

'Pause' (Croggon 1997, p. 6)

This poem has what I call a hook, a binding phrase 'Within the divided moments' on which the other phrases hang, and which helps to sectionalise the poem. However, the structure is not predictably regular (there are different numbers of lines in most of the sections). Structure means shape, but not necessarily symmetry or regularity. In fact, too much emphasis on symmetry and regularity can lead to monotony and predictability of form and content.

'Within the undivided moments' is a striking and engaging hook phrase: it suggests that these chosen moments have an integrity, a special quality, which is possibly lacking in other moments. But this hook phrase also has the power to transform the way we interpret the 'hanging' images in the poem. Some of the moments seem quite unique or intense, but others are more mundane (a train stops on the bridge). These everyday moments seem to be 'undivided' because of the way they are perceived. But the poem also suggests that most moments—because they are part of the process of life itself—have a special quality to them, which usually goes unnoticed. The poem, therefore, uses a relatively simple structure to complex and ambiguous ends. The repeating line pulls together a cluster of images which are quite dissimilar, but with a particular and heightened focus.

Variation

Closely related to the idea of repetition is variation (Exercise 1c). You can build a structure in which several blocks of texts are variations on the same idea or the same technique. Instead of one word association, for example, you could produce three which are interrelated:

Example 3.4
a) word association based on green
b) word association based on red
c) word association based on blue

One way to do this is to create three texts which start with a different colour, and use word association as a means of development. The three passages will consequently be similar in style and focus, but will all be different in the way they evoke and contextualise a particular colour. When you have written the three passages you can join them together into a seamless web, or keep them separate: an advantage of keeping them apart is that the structure—what the building blocks are and how they are arranged—will be strongly apparent. In this chapter I am laying the mechanism bare, but in practice writers often cover over the joins in the structure so that they are not so apparent.

You can see that this is a more complex structure than just one word association on its own, because the reader is being asked to consider the relationship between the separate blocks of text. Similarly, you could build a structure on three different persons-in-action:

Example 3.5
a) person a in action
b) person b in action
c) person c in action

Another type of variation, one which is evident in both the macrostructure and the microdetail of the poem, can be seen in 'Poem: "In the stump of the old tree . . ."' by British poet Hugh Sykes Davies:

Example 3.6
In the stump of the old tree, where the heart has rotted out,/there is a hole the length of a man's arm, and a dank pool at the/bottom of it where the rain gathers, and the old leaves turn into/lacy skeletons. But do not put your hand down to see, because

in the stumps of old trees, where the hearts have rotted out,/there are holes the length of a man's arm, and dank pools at the/bottom where the rain gathers and old leaves turn to lace, and the/beak of a dead bird gapes like a trap. But do not put your/hand down to see, because

in the stumps of old trees with rotten hearts, where the rain/gathers and the laced leaves and the dead bird like a trap, there/are holes the length of a man's arm, and in every crevice of the/rotten wood grow weasel's eyes like molluscs, their lids open/and shut with the tide. But do not put your hand down to see, because in the stumps of old trees where the rain gathers and the/trapped leaves and the beak, and the laced weasel's eyes, there are/holes the length of a man's arm, and at the bottom a sodden bible/written in the language of rooks. But do not put your hand down/to see, because

in the stumps of old trees where the hearts have rotted out there are holes the length of a man's arm where the weasels are/trapped and the letters of the rook language are laced on the/sodden leaves, and at the bottom there is a man's arm. But do/not put your hand down to see, because

in the stumps of old trees where the hearts have rotted out/there are deep holes and dank pools where the rain gathers, and/if you ever put your hand down to see, you can wipe it in the/sharp grass till it bleeds, but you'll never want to eat with/it again.

'Poem: "In the stump of the old tree . . ."' (Davies 1964, pp. 227–8)

When we read the beginning of this poem (which was written prior to World War II in 1936) we are unlikely to see where it is going: it seems to be a poem about the environment. However, it develops through variation, and builds up to a very unpleasant climax where it is a man's arm—presumably the remnant of a battle—which is in the tree stump. It is distinct from many of the war poems written in the 1930s, some of which descend into banal war propaganda. This poem not only projects the brutality of war, but it is political in a subtle, accumulative way which is largely a consequence of the varying structure.

Student Isabelle Gerrard's short prose piece 'A World, A Girl, A Memory: act one' also uses a varying structure ('there is dirt'/'there is a sky'/'there are ants'/'there is a girl') with some repetition ('there is a world'):

Example 3.7
there is a world: and in this world a little girl. It is a small world, a lumpish round world, a world with dirt and sky and ants.

there is dirt; and it sticks to her knees as she kneels. Tiny red craters mark her legs and her palms where the dirt has pressed into her flesh. She kneels, solitary, surrounded by piles and wells.

there is a sky; and it drifts hesitantly above. A self-conscious sky, fidgeting with questions: 'Why Has This Solitary Girl Not Gazed Upwards To Admire?' Afraid, this sky of pale mauve-grey refuses to meet the horizon.

there are ants; and they invade with a fury that time does not diminish. Theirs is the task of reclamation, to reclaim the piles from the wells and the wells from the piles. All around the horizon is rising and falling as if beneath a tumultuous wind. But the air is still; the sky hovers.

there is a girl; and her determination matches the ants'. She is a cartographer; and has a love for maps, for pale blue grids, for curving tendril lines that denote and describe. In this changeable landscape her mapping tools lie closeted, her pale grid empty.

there is a world; and the girl must still this world. And so she kneels, patiently, gently lifting each ant between forefinger and thumb. Beside her is a little perspex farm, ready and filled with dirt. It is empty. On her other side is a little ant pile, growing higher with little mangled ant bodies. She sighs and frowns as she works, releasing slow and single tears.

there is a world; and in this world a little girl. It is a lumpish round world with a skittish sky. It is a world with an empty map, a pile of ants, and a well filled with solemn tears.

'A World, A Girl, A Memory: act one' (Gerrard 1999, p. 59)

This piece is ostensibly based on an incident about a girl playing with soil and insects. But Isabelle does not use a progressive or narrative structure. Rather she dislocates and fractures the incident and then restructures it. That way she makes us focus on one element at a time, using a varying structure as her basis. An effect of this is to reduce the representational aspect of the scenario, and strongly emphasise the symbolic and ritualistic elements.

Simultaneity

Some kinds of structure allow several things to happen at once, rather like a number of people talking at the same time. I call these simultaneous structures (Exercise 1d). One type of simultaneous structure consists of two or more vertical columns on the page, so that there is a continual choice about whether to read across or down. This exercise is both stimulating and fun, and leads to many different meanings jostling together at once.

A simultaneous structure is usually most successful when the piece reads well both horizontally and vertically. The poem should acquire different dimensions depending on how it is read spatially. The following is a very good realisation of this exercise:

Example 3.8

90s market

she said	he said
give me the world	to live
in that unseemly	impoverished
style of yours	is ugly
i want	beauty
compensation	remains
at issue	all aloof
is the truth	not daring
close enough	to give
is not	its insecurity
good enough	to trust
but	then
he said	she said
trust me	to live
a good life	it's nothing
it's better	to die
angry	young
men are	famous
everywhere	it's something
don't you want	to make a name
to be different	just be yourself

'90s market' (Lyons 1996)

Notice how alternative scenarios and versions arise from reading down or across the columns. This creates different perspectives not only on the relationship between the two people, but their views on materialism/anti-materialism, and the importance/dangers of individualism. The personal and social interweave but in a way which is fluid and multivalent. In fact, there are more than three versions: as we read down and across, there seem to be almost an infinite number of narrative and poetic possibilities.

Multilayering

A structure in which different kinds of textual material alternate and recur is what I call a multilayered structure (Exercise 1e).

An example of a multilayered structure would be:

Example 3.9
Text A: word association (a)
Text B: person-in-action (a)
Text C: referent-based text (a)

Text A: word association (b)
Text B: person-in-action (b)
Text C: referent-based text (b)

Text A: word association (c)
Text B: person-in-action (c)
Text C: referent-based text (c)

A multilayered structure is rather like a multidecker sandwich in which there is a layer of bread, a layer of tomato, a layer of bread, then a layer of egg, a layer of bread, a layer of tomato again, and then another layer of bread. So a multilayered structure alternates contrasting kinds of text, over and over again, though with some variation. In Example 3.9 three distinct types of text alternate, but each time the material comes back it will have developed further. A structure can be multilayered in many different ways, it can alternate stories or images or themes. This type of structure is often used by novelists when they want to narrate several stories at once, or poets when they wish to create complex relationships between different sets of ideas or themes. A good example of a multilayered text is T.S. Eliot's 'The Waste Land' (1963) which interconnects by this means a wealth of historical and literary allusion. But multilayered structures are also popular in TV soap operas, where the action often cuts backwards and forwards between two or three different storylines.

Number

Numerical structures are built on an arithmetical count or limit, and this is the focus of Exercise 1f. The number can be the basis of the sections in a text, or the lines in a stanza, or the words or syllables in a line. For example, you might decide to create a poem in which the first stanza is three lines long, the second five lines, the third seven, and so on. Or you might decide to create a poem which had twelve sections, each composed of twelve sentences. One example might be increasing numbers of words per line in each stanza:

Example 3.10
stanza one: 3 lines and 3 words each line
stanza two: 5 lines and 5 words each line

stanza three: 7 lines and 7 words per line
stanza four: 9 lines and 9 words per line

Alternatively:

Example 3.11
stanza one: 2 lines
stanza two: 5 lines
stanza three: 8 lines
stanza four: 11 lines
stanza five: 7 lines
stanza six: 3 lines

In this second example the number of lines per stanza goes up by the addi-tion of the number 3, and then descends by subtraction of the number 4.

Numbers have often been important in writing. A traditional Japanese haiku is written to a numerical system, and conventional poetic metrics have a numerical base. However, here I am proposing that you create your own arithmetical bases for composition, rather than fitting into traditional schemes.

Using a numerical method is a fascinating way of approaching writing, because it gives you a limit to work against, and it is often boundaries, rather than total freedom, that trigger the most exciting creative work. This sense of a limit was one of the advantages of a conventional rhyme and metric scheme, but it can be anachronistic to return to the metrical structures of the past, which were culturally specific to that time. Writing tends to be most effective if it has contemporary relevance in both form and content: we need to find an up-to-date way of using numbers. Also we do not want to be tied down to rules which are a straightjacket, so much as define self-imposed limits against which we can creatively push. This defining of self-imposed limits is sometimes known as **procedural** writing (Perloff 1991, pp. 134–70).

A number of contemporary writers have worked with numerical struc-tures to intriguing effect. American poet, Ron Silliman, has written many pieces based on them. For example, his 'I Meet Osip Brik' is in thirteen sections, each of which consists of thirteen sentences (Silliman 1986). Sometimes writers have favoured systems which are well known in math-ematics, such as the **fibonacci** series (1, 1, 2, 3, 5, 8, 13, 21) in which each number is the sum of the previous two: this is used by Silliman in his prose poem *Tjanting* (1981). Sometimes they have used a number which seemed to be strongly related to the subject matter. *My Life*—an alternative and anticonventional autobiography by American poet Lyn Hejinian (1987)—

was originally written in 1978 when she was 37: it has 37 sections with 37 lines in each section. When Hejinian became 45 she revised *My Life*, adding eight sections to the book and eight extra sentences to each section. She did not add these sentences to the end of each section, but interspersed them at irregular intervals. She has continued to revise the work, by adding sections: the most recent additions have been published as *My Life in the Nineties* (2003). Numerical structures were also fundamental to the very important French group Oulipo, (Ouvroir de Littérature Potentielle, or Workshop for Potential Literature) founded in 1960, and discussed in more detail in Chapter 8.

Think up a numerical system that interests you and base a text on it. Perhaps you want to shape a poem on a rising or descending arithmetical sequence; a number or set of numbers which has particular significance for you; or any type of mathematical series you are familiar with.

NON-LITERARY FORMS, LITERARY TRANSFORMATIONS

Exercise 2, at the beginning of this chapter, suggests that you might like to write a text based on a culturally specific, but non-literary, form or genre. This will extend your range of forms and structures. But it is also a way of questioning the supremacy of the literary as a category. Are literary texts, after all, so different from other genres of writing which are prominent in our culture such as newspaper articles or popular songs? Contemporary cultural theory has tended to see all writing as text, and to question the ideological distinction between the literary and the non-literary. An advertisement, for example, can have linguistic interest comparable to a poem and may have as much cultural relevance.

So a text of this kind can throw the 'literary' world into relief as well as satirising contemporary modes of communication. It might take one of the following forms:

- a tourist guide
- a recipe
- a how-to manual
- a newspaper article
- an advertisement
- a diary entry
- a list.

By adapting the literary to the non-literary, you can bring forms of popular culture into your writing: many contemporary writers have incorporated such elements into their work. Bernard Cohen's novel *Tourism* (1992), which is discussed further in Chapter 12, is structured like a tourist manual. However, the entries about Australian cities are very unlike those you might expect to find in such a book, and tend to be abstract and philosophical, rather than specific and commercial.

Over the years I have seen a great deal of entertaining and perceptive work produced by students employing these methods. One student created a text in which he attempted to sell death through the form of an advertisement. Another rewrote a section of a Shakespeare play as a recipe.

At this point I am not asking you to base a whole text on such a principle. But many published authors insert non-literary forms into longer works. For example, Australian writer Jan McKemmish includes postcards in her novel *A Gap in the Records* (1985), while British novelist Mark Haddon's *The Curious Incident of the Dog in the Night-time* (2003) is full of mathematical formulae, diagrams, maps and lists. Use of letters or diary entries are commonplace in novels from the nineteenth century to the present day. The insertion of such texts into fiction can be useful in breaking up the narrative and producing more generic variety. Non-literary texts can also be part of mixed-genre pieces, as we will see in Chapter 9.

The following passage uses the advertising style on websites (the claim to be able to accomplish almost anything in a digital environment) to satirise the limits of consumerism. We can't buy apologies 'ready-made', if we could they would be worthless: nor can apologies wipe out the past. The passage alludes particularly to Australian Prime Minister John Howard's refusal to apologise to indigenous people in Australia for the historical injustices they have suffered (including massacres, torture and the removal of children from their parents):

Example 3.12
Fellow-consumers—visit our web-site! Download any of our 10 million virtual apologies! Listen to a stereo byte or two in the voice of your choice. Wipe out all those guilt feelings! Cleanse the past! Choose any phrasing you like, or let our resident writers pick the most soothing words. The essence of all our apologies is that they don't have to be what they mean, *or think what they say*. We have every kind of apology you could desire: beginner and advanced, family and national, racist and multi-cultural, new age, site-specific, low-fat, easy-care, quick fix, superglue and slow-release. All with state of the art graphics and available on instant demand.

Remember: our apologies can be made-to-mood—also cut-price sets available if you buy now, complete with automatic renewals.

Staff choice and bargain of the month: an apology to indigenous people, carefully worded to avoid any real expression of regret.

If we haven't got the right style for you in stock, all we can do is say how terribly sorry we are, and advise you next time to place your order several altercations in advance.

And please do business with us again.

From 'ProseThetic Memories' (Brewster & Smith 2002, pp. 200–1)

Note here how the text mimics the language and posturing of advertising: the idea of staff choice, items being individually 'made-to-mood', 'cut-price' options and so on. I have also adopted a stance, familiar from consumer culture, which suggests that the goods under question can do anything under the sun.

The piece 'Untitled' (see Example 3.13 on page 63) is by Japanese poet Yuriya Kumagai, formerly a student in one of my postgraduate classes. The advertisement for the lost voice satirises the notion, deeply embedded in capitalist society, that we can gain or regain anything if we pay a price for it. But it also plays on the relationship between voice and body. Particularly ironic is the way it suggests that it might be possible to find the voice without also locating the embodied owner.

All these texts have a satirical edge, and are commenting on contemporary culture, but exploiting its forms. Sometimes these forms are taken from advertising, where the purpose is to coerce us into buying something, whether we really want it or not. At other times they may be media based, and their objective may be to persuade us of a particular view of the world which is politically biased.

Non-literary textual elements can also be integrated into literary texts. Iranian poet Mohammad Tavallaei's 'School of English', written when he was a postgraduate student, begins with an extended version of the information that we have to give on a passport or visa form. However, the cultural discrimination, of which the poet feels he is an object, rebounds on him in the form of self-denigration. The passport details reinforce the feelings of alienation the poet suffers as a consequence of the western, non-western divide (on which he subsequently expands):

Example 3.14
Age: 49
Sex: Male
Height: 165 cm

Weight: 63 kg
Hair: Black and White
Face: Wrinkled and Ugly
Nose: Fleshy
Eyes: Myopic, with Double Vision

Is it not strange that these features
Of an imported material
From far and exotic places
For acculturation—
Monkey-like mimicry of alien sounds and signs,
Academic ass-licking and smiling in awkward situations—
Transform into sites of antagonism
Between the circumcised and the uncircumcised?

Why does lack of foreskin
Prefigure so predominantly in their minds?

Their language:
the zone of my silence,
A Post-Babylonian Babble
hurting more than colonial history and geography.

'School of English' (Tavallaei 1996, pp. 57–8)

CONCLUSION

Working out with structure means juggling and rearranging our material to have maximum formal and cultural impact. Structures are sometimes clearly visible on the page (a repeating structure may be apparent at a glance) and the visual layout on the page may reinforce the effect. However, sometimes structures are so complex that we may only begin to grasp them after several readings. This chapter deals with relatively simple structures, but as your writing develops you will become more and more aware of different kinds of structuring principles, and how to combine several at once. Structure is also very important in many of the chapters ahead, and most often consists of the disruption of a linear sequence: this is a feature of most kinds of writing, but is most extreme in experimental texts. In Chapter 5, for example, we see how narrative linearity may be broken up to give maximum effect to the narrative content. Likewise, Chapters 7, 8 and 9 all deal with various types of disruption to the linear sequence, and alternative forms of restructuring in postmodern poetry and prose. Finally, Chapter 11 takes us into the web-like, branching and recursive structures of cyberspace.

Example 3.13: 'Untitled' (Kumagai 1995, p. 12)

LOST

ONE PROFOUND VOICE

OF GREAT SENTIMENTAL VALUE

LAST HEARD

IN THE DEPARTURE LOUNGE

OF AN INTERNATIONAL AIRPORT

REWARD

$1953 FOR THE VOICE

$1995 FOR THE OWNER OF THE VOICE

-

PLEASE CONTACT

LIFE☎LINE: 1-800-28-1117

REFERENCES

Brewster, A. and Smith, H. 2002, 'ProseThetic Memories', *Salt.v16. An International Journal of Poetry and Poetics: Memory Writing*, (ed). T.-A. White, Salt Publishing, Applecross, Western Australia, pp. 199–211.

Cohen, B. 1992, *Tourism*, Picador, Sydney.

Croggon, A. 1997, 'Pause', *The Blue Gate*, Black Pepper, North Fitzroy, Victoria.

Davies, H.S. 1964, 'Poem: "In the stump of the old tree . . ."', *Poetry of the Thirties*, (ed.) R. Skelton, Penguin, Harmondsworth, Middlesex.

Eagleton, T. 1996, *Literary Theory*, 2nd edn, University of Minnesota Press, Minneapolis.

Eliot, T.S. 1963, *Collected Poems 1909–1962*, Faber & Faber, London.

Gerrard, I. 1999, 'A World, A Girl, A Memory: act one', *Unsweetened*, (eds) R. Caudra and A. Phillips, UNSW Union, Sydney.

Haddon, M. 2003, *The Curious Incident of the Dog in the Night-time*, David Fickling Books, Oxford.

Hawkes, T.S. 1977, *Structuralism and Semiotics*, Methuen, London.

Hejinian, L. 1987, *My Life*, Sun & Moon Press, Los Angeles.

—— 2003, *My Life in the Nineties*, Shark Books, New York.

Kumagai, Y.J. 1995, 'Untitled', *Her Space-Time Continuum*, University Editions, Huntingdon, West Virginia.

Lyons, G. 1996, '90s Market', unpublished.

McKemmish, J. 1985, *A Gap in the Records*, Sybylla Cooperative Press & Publications, Melbourne.

Perloff, M. 1991, *Radical Artifice: Writing Poetry in the Age of Media*, University of Chicago Press, Chicago.

Silliman, R. 1981, *Tjanting*, The Figures, Great Barrington, Massechusets.

—— 1986, 'I Meet Osip Brik', *The Age of Huts*, Roof Books, New York, pp. 76–8.

Tavallaei, M.N. 1996, 'School of English', *New Literatures Review*, vol. 32.

CHAPTER FOUR
Writing as recycling

In this chapter we will look at ways in which you can recycle texts in creative writing. By recycling texts I mean enriching your own writing by incorporating texts by other people. Relevant here is the concept of **intertextuality**. This is a term coined by Julia Kristeva, Roland Barthes and others to highlight the way that no text is ever completely new, original or independent: writers are always, to some degree, reinventing what has already been written (Wolfreys 2004, pp. 119–21). Writing is rather like recycling paper, you give the texts you have read another life through the way you reshape them. Or to put it another way, when we write we are constantly scavenging from what we have read in the past, either directly or obliquely. We pilfer (though in the most law-abiding way), not only from literary texts, but non-literary ones such as newspaper articles and a wide range of visual and oral media such as TV or radio.

Recycling texts is a way of milking this relationship between the text that you are creating and those that other people have written. It's also a way of building ideas without having to depend only on your own thoughts. Just as everything that goes on around you—everything you observe or imagine—might be material for your writing, so everything that you have read is potentially grist for your mill, and can be reinvented in your own work.

Many writers have recycled texts in this way, and it can be a resource for you. Of course I'm not suggesting that you stop generating your own texts, and exclusively use those written by other authors. Rather it's another technique to add to your bag of tools to use along with others. It can also be a very effective way of triggering writing: for example, you can sift through newspapers, articles or novels and use them as a springboard, jotting down striking phrases here or there. In fact this happens to most writers, both consciously and unconsciously: while they are reading a book, a striking phrase stimulates them to write, either at that moment or subsequently. However, when you are recycling texts you need to fully acknowledge your sources so that it is clear you are not plagiarising the work of others.

There are a number of strategies for recycling texts, including making collages, discovering found texts, and rewriting classic fictions from another point of view. There are also numerous extensions of, and variations upon, these techniques. For example, there is a process known as 'writing through' which has been explored extensively by the American poet Jackson Mac Low. It involves using one text as a 'core', and taking words from it on a systematic basis (say every fifth word) to form another piece of writing: Mac Low uses this kind of approach in *The Virgina Woolf Poems* (1985). This volume is a 'writing through' of Woolf's novel *The Waves* (though the original novel is hardly recognisable from Mac Low's text). Another intriguing example is *A Humument: A Treated Victorian Novel* by British artist Tom Phillips (1980), which is a makeover of a Victorian novel by William Mallock called *A Human Document*. Phillips transformed the novel by painting over large sections of each page. But he allowed rivulets of words to remain: these convey very different meanings from the ones they would produce in their original context. In the process Phillips creates another novel which is superimposed on Mallock's. The central character is Bill Toge (the name Toge is made out of the words 'together' and 'altogether' when they appear in Mallock's novel).

All these techniques, to a greater or lesser extent, overlap. We will concentrate on three: collage, found texts and the rewriting of a classic text.

exercises

1. a) Make a collage by cutting and pasting texts with scissors and glue.
   b) Rewrite the collage as a poem or other kind of creative text.
2. Create a found text.
3. Rewrite a classic text, fairytale or myth from a contemporary point of view.

CUTTING IT WITH COLLAGE

What is a collage?

Exercise 1 focuses on making a collage. A collage is an amalgamation of extracts from pre-existing texts usually by several different authors. Collages often bring together textual fragments from unrelated sources. These fragments are removed from their original contexts and pieced together into new formations.

Collage became prominent in the visual arts and in literature in the early part of the twentieth century. Part of the modernist movement, it was a technique used by the artists Braque, Picasso, Kurt Schwitters and others in the early 1900s, and was also taken up by modernist poets such as Ezra Pound and T.S. Eliot. Some of Schwitters works, for example, are 'assemblages', containing objects such as rail tickets, stamps or newspaper cuttings. Collage has continued to be important in postmodernist writing, though somewhat transmuted into quotation, pastiche and intertextual reference.

A literary collage usually brings together chunks of writing drawn from a number of different sources and juxtaposes them. It lifts texts, or parts of texts, out of their original environments, and places them together to form a new context. In a collage we are usually conscious of certain discontinuities between the elements, but also of new continuities produced by the interface between them. The main characteristic of this kind of technique is therefore **juxtaposition**, whereby unconnected texts can be put side by side in such a way that a relationship between them is forged. Juxtaposition is enormously important in experimental writing, because it allows ideas to resonate with each other without necessarily being seamlessly joined together. This discontinuous structure means the connections between the texts retain a greater fluidity, so that the meanings interact with each other in multiple ways.

Sometimes the collage consists of a text which is primarily written by the author, but into which quotations from other authors are inserted. Sometimes the author withdraws entirely from the scene of the writing, so that none of the words are his or her own. However, even in this case, the author plays an all-important role in the rearrangement of the texts. Collage, therefore, encourages you to approach creative writing through other means than personal experience. Your creativity is expressed through your choice of texts, the way you structure their relationship, and the degree to which you transform them.

Many twentieth-century writers have used collage techniques. For example, T.S. Eliot's long poem 'The Waste Land' (1963) is a kind of collage, because Eliot inserts words and references from mythological, literary or religious texts into his own writing. Here collage mainly takes the form of quotation, but Eliot also rewrites some passages (for example, recasting the famous speech from Shakespeare's *Anthony and Cleopatra* 'The barge she sat in, like a burnish'd throne' into a decadent contemporary setting). The writing is principally Eliot's own, but the poem is, nevertheless, partly a constellation of other texts. Another example of collage is *Paterson* by American poet William Carlos Williams (1983). In *Paterson* Williams takes textual materials—such as a passage from a letter or part of a historical document—and juxtaposes them with passages of his own writing.

COLLAGE IN CLOSE-UP

The Ash Range, by Australian writer Laurie Duggan (1987), uses diaries, journals and newspaper stories—including accounts by early Australian pioneers, to chart the history of Gippsland, Victoria—and patches them together, sometimes reorganising them in ways which suit his poetic purpose. As we read *The Ash Range*, the early days of colonial Australia emerge through the voices of the invaders. But this is different from the author telling us directly what he thinks about these historical events; instead he is acting as a facilitator, so that ideas emerge almost magically from the material itself. This approach demonstrates the significance of which voices are, or are not, heard: the history of indigenous people can normally only be guessed at through colonial reports.

In this extract you can see how Duggan draws on accounts from early explorers, their response to the landscape, and their condescending attitude towards indigenous Australians:

Example 4.1: Juxtaposition of textual chunks

Passed through a chain of clear downs to some very extensive ones, where we met a tribe of natives, who fled at our approach, however, we soon, by tokens of kindness, offering them biscuits etc. together with the assistance of a domesticated native of our party, induced them to come nearer and nearer, till by degrees we ultimately became good friends; but on no account would they touch or approach our horses, of which they were from the first much more frightened than of ourselves. We learned that the clear country before us was called Monaroo.

Mark
Currie
4/6/1823

Extensive plains   James
  gently undulating   Atkinson
    destitute of timber   1826
extend, with interruption
  to Maniroon Plains
    south of Lake George,
large portions
  occupied in grazing.
                The silence and
solitude that reign in these wide spreading untenanted
wastes, are indescribable.
                No traces of the works or
even the existence of man are here to be met with,
except perhaps the ashes of a fire on the banks of
some river.
              From the contemplation of this vacancy
and solitude the mind recoils with weariness.

Near Mr Rose's station is a lofty table-mountain,   George
forming the commencement of a mountainous range,   Bennett
extending in a south-west direction,   1834
                named 'Bugong',
from the circumstance of multitudes of small moths
congregating at certain months of the year about
masses of granite. November, December and January
the native blacks assemble to collect the Bugong; the
bodies of these insects contain a quantity of oil, and
they are sought after as a luscious and fattening
food.
        12th of December, at dawn, accompanied by a
stock-keeper and some of the blacks, I commenced my
excursion.
              The view from the second summit of
Bugong was open to the southward.

From *The Ash Range* (Duggan 1987, pp. 33–4)

The texts in *The Ash Range* are mainly structured by the passage of time,
and particular periods, such as the Gold Rush. However, collage can often
be effective when it involves texts which are radically different, and are
thrown into unexpected relationships with each other. The following

passage, written by Anne Brewster, is taken from a longer collaboration about memory (Brewster & Smith 2002). Here the author intercuts a nineteenth century text from Thoreau, which celebrates male achievement; a text about hysteria and recovered memory syndrome by Marita Sturken; and a text from Gertrude Stein. These are all from strikingly different sources (two are literary but are from contrasting periods and perspectives, while one is non-literary):

Example 4.2: Textual intercutting
Stein, Sturken and Thoreau: A collage

hysterics suffer mainly from reminiscences. naturally I would then begin again. he is blessed over all mortals who loses no moment of the passing life in remembering the past. I did not begin again I just began. the object has not perhaps actually died, but has been lost as an object of love. then I said to myself this time it will be different and I began. above all we cannot afford not to live in the present. in the case of women's recovered memories, the question of belief is crucially tied to the history of disbelief. then I said to myself this time it will be different and I began. he is blessed over all mortals. the victor can afford to forget. and after that what changes what changes after that. can we have a theory of experience that allows for the suggestibility of memory, but which does not label women as hysterics? there was an inevitable beginning of beginning. preserving the love or idealization of the object. I went on and on to almost a thousand pages of it. naturally one does not know how it happened until it is well over beginning. this trackless initial forgetting.

From 'ProseThetic Memories' (Brewster & Smith 2002, p. 204)

This piece shows how collage can rub different discourses together, that is, alternative modes of speaking and writing, sometimes on the same theme or themes. Different discourses convey divergent ideologies, and collages often pit these contrasting perspectives against each other, creating productive tensions. Collage can, therefore, create an interface between conflicting political views, texts from different periods, different aspects of a particular topic, and the personal and the political. In this passage the more technical/theoretical psychoanalytic language of 'the object has not perhaps actually died, but has been lost as an object of love' or 'can we have a theory of experience that allows for the suggestibility of memory, but which does not label women as hysterics?' is from Sturken. It is juxtaposed with the poetic repetition of 'I would then begin again' and 'I did not begin again I just began' from Stein, and Thoreau's nineteenth-century and masculinist rhetoric 'he is blessed over all mortals who loses no moment of the passing life in remembering the past'. The contrasting texts and their respective registers suggest that different forms of remembering are available to men and women.

An important aspect of this collage is the way it intercuts so rapidly between unrelated sources. This is also true of Amanda Stewart's performance poem '.romance (1981)':

Example 4.3: Textual intercutting
.romance
Ist date Ist kiss Ist kiss Ist
fuck Ist/ Ist/ Ist/ relived
                        to be roses/candles/
moons/waves/beaches/idiosynchronize/
presents/chocolates/early morning
lust/walks/fires/song/dance/hold hands/
press close/meetin the eyes/hands/movement/hands/
move/lips/eyes/shoulder/nape/eyes/lobes/ears/eyes/
'till death us do part
                ing is such sweet sor
                                ry to s
                                        ay i
love y
        ou are the way the truth and the l
                                ight of the
silvery moon rose is a rose is a rose is a way to s
                                                        ay i
love y
        ou are my love is love is love is love is love
.is love

'.romance (1981)' (Stewart 1998, p. 13)

As we move into the second part of the poem, a number of well-worn phrases are collaged together, but merged so that they overlap. The poem includes a biblical quotation "till death do us part', some lines from old popular songs including 'by the light of the silvery moon', and a quotation from Gertrude Stein 'a rose is a rose is a rose', all of which are drawn from diverse social and artistic contexts. Welded together they suggest the commodification and commercialisation of romance in contemporary society: important again here is the tension between the old context from which the quotations are taken and their new juxtaposition. The popular songs, for example, exploit stereotypical images of 'romance', but Amanda Stewart is ironising them, subverting their original purpose.

Creating a collage

So how can you make a collage? There are many methods, but try one first which focuses on cutting and pasting texts with scissors and glue (see Exercise 1a). This is an adaption of William Burroughs's **cut-up method** which he developed together with writer Brion Gysin: it became well known and widely used during the twentieth century. Burroughs would cut up texts (often his own) and then rearrange them to make new ones which would not have arisen through 'normal' writing.

The following process will help you to experiment with collage:

I. Equip yourself with a large piece of paper and a pair of scissors. Sift through texts you have been recently reading, such as newspaper articles, extracts from books, material from websites (or texts you are particularly fond of that you have read in the past). Photocopy the sources (you need to do this because you will be cutting them up). You may find it easiest to decide on a topic such as war, ethnicity or the body, and then search for a range of texts which refer to this in varying ways. However, excellent effects can also be obtained by welding together materials on unassociated topics, especially with a good deal of intercutting between the texts. Whichever way you approach the collage, try to draw on a number of contrasting sources. You may want to research for your collage, or use favourite texts you have read in the past, or cut up your own poetry/fiction/essay material (a collage doesn't have to consist entirely of borrowings from other people).

You may also wish to include photographs or drawings in your collage. The visual images may be interspersed amongst the texts, but you may also want to cut up the photographs. And you may want to play with the idea of captions: for example by cutting out a photograph from the newspaper and giving it a new heading.

2. Cut up the texts you have amassed into small chunks, or cut out chunks that are particularly interesting to you. A small chunk may be a word, a phrase or several sentences. Although very provocative collages can be made from longer passages, you are likely to obtain the best, and the most radical, results initially if you use a more intensive intercutting technique—that is, juxtaposing smaller fragments of text. This allows the texts to resonate with each other more closely, and is likely to result in a greater transformation of the original material. Reading long extracts cut out of newspaper articles, for instance, can become tedious, but small fragments, if they are elided and worked together into a new text, can create connotations which could not have been predicted from the original sources. The more you intercut between sources, the more the new text becomes a unique item and your 'own'.

3. As you arrange your pieces, try to breed stimulating connections between different ideas or points of view. If you place together an extract from the newspaper about refugee camps, a section from an official historical document which contains racist views, some fictional dialogue between two politicians about immigration, and an account of a detainee in a refugee camp, an effect will be created which is quite distinct from perceiving each text on its own. The piece will resonate with a number of voices and registers which either contradict or complement each other, and your collage will be more multidimensional than if you wrote a continuous text. Similarly, if you bring together two or three pieces of text which don't seem to have any relationship at all—like an entry from a computer manual and an advertisement for a coffee machine—connections may be forged which could never have arisen any other way. Such a text might trigger ideas about mechanisation or contemporary marketing.

One approach to working on the texts is to weld them into a continuous whole, so the seams are not apparent. But an equally valid way of tackling the exercise is to retain a strong sense of several disparate sources, because one of the benefits of a collage is that it helps both writer and reader to explore the relationships between previously unconnected pieces of writing: this is more evident when the seams are visible. An important aspect of a collage can be (and perhaps should be) **multiplicity**, many themes and ideas placed simultaneously together, to create a rich tapestry of ideas.

4. Don't initially stick down the words on the page, unless you are certain where you want them to go. Move them around, try out various different relationships between them, consider cutting back some of them further.

Although you may want to put your texts together in rows to mimic prose, you can also add another dimension to your collage by considering its spatial design. Try one which is not entirely regular (you can place the texts upside down, or at an angle, or scatter them around the page rather than putting them in rows). Consider alternative ways of aligning texts: two textual fragments might be put side by side because they reinforce or contrast sharply with each other.

5. When you have decided where you want the pieces to go, stick them down. Remember, as with any other kinds of writing, there will always be a range of possibilities, and there is no right or wrong way to design the collage. If you want to explore alternatives, you can always photocopy the pieces and try a number of alternative arrangements.

6. The paste-up may turn out to be a complete work in itself and you may want to stop there. Or it may seem to you to be somewhat preliminary. Whichever, try next rewriting your collage as prose or poetry (Exercise 1b). You may find you can follow the order of the texts as they appear in the collage, or you may have to radically rearrange them. The spatial design may suggest a structure for the page: texts at the edges of the collage, for example, might be used to frame the beginning or end of a poem or narrative. Don't be afraid to transform the piece, editing out or adding in words, or even whole sections. In some cases you may work close to the original material; in other cases you may move a considerable distance from it. On occasion, you may even return to texts that you excluded from the original paste-up!

When you are writing up the collage, you can play various 'tricks' with it. Try, for example, reading and writing horizontally across two separate pieces of text which are placed side by side, and see what happens, or try doing this through the whole collage. Overall, remain open to new possibilities. Do not worry if the rewritten collage does not always make 'sense' in the normal way. This may be productive, because it means you are opening yourself to new directions and types of meaning.

At the end of this exercise you should have two collages—the original and the rewritten one—and you can decide which one is more striking. One kind of approach to collage is not better than the other, but may be more effective for you.

You may want to use collage techniques strictly in your writing. But you may also decide to use them loosely or partially, so that, for example, only a fraction of a text is conceived in this way. Or you may activate a collage technique to start off a text and then deviate from it very substantially, so that the original sources are largely discarded. While some writers do employ a 'pure' collage technique, others approach collage much more loosely: we might call this 'applied' collage. In fact, when you hear or read phrases and then draw them into your writing, you are using an applied collage technique, without being fully aware of it.

SHAKING THE (FOUND)ATIONS

Another mode of recycling is to create a text from 'found' material (Exercise 2). A **found text** is a pre-existent piece of writing with a non-literary function. We all know the sensation of looking at a notice, an instruction, a recipe or an advertisement and thinking that it would make a good poem: authors of found texts act upon such impressions. The author finds a text which is not intended for literary purposes, and then makes the audience conceive of it as a literary object. When you are creating a found text, you leave the text exactly as it is, or modify it slightly to emphasise its literary potential (for example by adding line breaks to make it more like a poem).

Using found material as the basis for an artwork has been even more common in the visual arts than in literature. The American artist Robert Rauschenberg, for example, in the 1960s and 70s, would often include 'real' objects in his artworks, such as a bed.

Found objects and found texts shake up many of our fundamental assumptions about artistic practice. For a start, found texts radically blur the dividing line between everyday culture and high art. They raise vital questions about what constitutes an art object, and why we value some objects as art and not others. Marcel Duchamp's gesture of placing a urinal in an art gallery, signing it R. Mutt, and calling it a work of art is a particularly provocative example of found art which raises questions about what we class as aesthetic.

In addition, found texts, like collage, challenge the whole notion of what it means to be an author. Can an author simply put his or her name to something which already exists? In fact, it seems as if such texts are around us all the time anonymously but we have not yet 'found them out'.

Let's look at a found poem by Canadian gay activist and poet Ian Young. It is called 'Poem Found in a Dime Store Diary'.

Example 4.4: Found poem
Place these slips inside your diary
   in the appropriate place

....

Tomorrow is my wife's birthday

....

Tomorrow is my husband's birthday

....

Tomorrow is my wedding anniversary

....

Tomorrow is my mother's birthday

....
Tomorrow is my father's birthday

....
Tomorrow my Holidays start

....
Tomorrow is

....
Tomorrow is

....
Tomorrow is

'Poem Found in a Dime Store Diary' (Young 1972, p. 190)

This text is a list of slips that the manufacturer has designed for diary owners to put in their diaries to mark off important days. However, if we look at it through literary rather than practical eyes, we can see that the structure and layout could be viewed as quasi-poetic (the text is in lines with a repetitive structure which binds them together). Furthermore, presenting the text as a poem turns it into a parodic comment about contemporary values. The critic Stephen Matterson has suggested, for example, that the poem explores what society expects of an individual. Individuals are assumed to have a husband or wife, and to celebrate birthdays and anniversaries. They will be married, in employment and family conscious. Being single, gay, unemployed, illegitimate or alienated from the family are by implication deviant forms of behaviour (Matterson 1990).

These ideas are given significance by presenting the diary slips as a poem. We subject the text to the metaphorical and semantic scrutiny that we would normally bring to a literary work. Such an approach may well open up the text to multiple interpretations. For example, even if we agree with Matterson's interpretation of the poem, we might want to qualify it by pointing out that the last few slips are left blank for the owner to fill in. This could mean that they point tentatively to a space for social and cultural difference. In other words, we could also find some ambiguity in the piece.

Matterson points out that the reiteration of 'Tomorrow is' at the end of the poem echoes Macbeth's 'To-morrow and to-morrow and to-morrow' speech in Shakespeare's play (Matterson 1990). Presumably the words 'tomorrow' and 'tomorrow' are not designed in the original text to be deliberate echoes of Macbeth, but the author has cleverly chosen his found text and framed it as a poem, so that this kind of intertextual connection can be made.

When you are creating found texts you have to be observant as well as imaginative. Many texts that you read during your daily existence (like instructions on tins of food) could be the basis for a found poem, if you focused on their language, structure and possible meanings rather than simply on their utility. Letters and other forms of communication may also be potent as found texts. Moya Costello's 'Covering Letters (A Found Story)' (1994, pp. 115–18) are letters from and to the editors of literary journals, and are based on her experience as an editor and writer. In close juxtaposition they both illuminate and satirise the frustrating process of trying to get into print (for the writer) and wading through a pile of indifferent submissions (for the editor).

Start looking at the texts around you, and see whether you can turn them into a found text.

RECYCLING AS REWRITING

Exercise 3 engages with the rewriting of a classic text, fairytale or myth from a contemporary point of view. To do this you need to take a text (usually a familiar one) such as *Jane Eyre*, or *Hamlet*, and rewrite it from a new perspective. This would usually be a contemporary perspective, but it might also be a feminist or postcolonial one. Bringing the story up to date is crucial (there is not much point if you start with an archaic fairytale and then produce another one in the same mode). Modernising the story can be very illuminating because classic texts such as *King Lear* or *Middlemarch* are part of our cultural heritage; they are familiar to many of us, and it's very easy to accept them without really questioning the assumptions on which they were built. They were also written in the past, so rewriting them can be a way of examining how attitudes—both about writing and about history—have changed. The process makes us rethink the text, and rewriting can bring out certain elements which were suppressed in the original. *Wide Sargasso Sea*, by British/West Indies writer Jean Rhys (1966), for example, is a feminist and postcolonial rewriting of the novel *Jane Eyre*.

'The Bloody Chamber', a story by Angela Carter (1981), is a rewriting of the classic Bluebeard fairytale. In the fairytale Bluebeard, who is old and ugly, gives his young wife a bunch of keys and tells her expressly not to use one of them, which opens a forbidden chamber. The young wife, however, cannot resist the temptation to open the locked room: when she does she finds the bodies of Bluebeard's previous wives, whom he has murdered.

The key she has used becomes bloodstained, and is a telltale sign that she has opened the room: she cannot remove the stain because the key is bewitched. Her husband consequently finds out she has disobeyed him and plans to murder her, but just in time her brothers arrive and kill Bluebeard, she inherits all his money, and it all ends 'happily ever after'. Obviously there is a moral tale here about good triumphing over evil. But there is also another patriarchal and sexist moral, which is that if a woman disobeys her husband she may end up in difficulties. In this case disobeying the husband turns out to be acceptable because he is evil, but the story still reinforces the law of marital obedience.

Angela Carter keeps close to many aspects of the original fairytale, and she certainly repeats the same story about the wife entering the forbidden room, finding the former dead wives, and being left with a blood-stained key. But she rewrites the narrative in a contemporary world: Bluebeard is a rich and powerful man who travels on business, and his new bride chats to her mother on the telephone. At the same time Bluebeard lives in a castle, so there is an element of anachronism to the retelling: it contains gothic elements and still adheres to certain features of the fairytale. In reinventing the story Carter changes its ideological perspective in a number of ways. She also adds a depth and subtlety which is not present in the original: a heavily schematised story about good and evil, in which good inevitably wins.

Carter revisits the story in ways which sexualise it, and also turn it into a critique of patriarchy, wealth and class. In the fairytale the sexual element is totally suppressed, but in Carter's version Bluebeard is a lustful old man whose sexual desires are sadistic and pornographic. Female desire, and its contradictions, are also explored: the girl says 'I felt both a strange, impersonal arousal at the thought of love and at the same time a repugnance I could not stifle . . .' (Carter 1981, p. 15): her desires are eventually met by the blind, poor and powerless piano tuner. While the fairytale hinges on the triumph of good over evil, the rewriting questions the concept of innocence. In the fairytale the heroine is simply nosy, but Carter's reworking implies that corruption is integral to human behaviour. The heroine is not a conventional model of feminine virtue and innocence as she is in the fairytale. She says, 'I sensed in myself a potentiality for corruption which took my breath away' (Carter 1981, p. 11), and is seduced in the first place by Bluebeard's wealth and power. So Carter reconceives the story from a feminist point of view: it becomes a fiction about gender politics and a power struggle between the sexes which the wife eventually wins. It is salient that it is her mother who rescues the girl rather than her brothers (as in the original fairytale), therefore reinforcing the importance of female support systems.

Throughout, the rewriting is imbued with a psychological depth missing from the original. For example, when Bluebeard returns, the girl, instead of experiencing only fear, as she does in the fairytale, is filled with a mixture of fear and pity. Carter increases the story's capacity for psychoanalytic interpretation: the girl's ambivalent relationship with Bluebeard can be read as an Oedipal one, the locked room might be the unconscious or the womb. A plethora of further possible meanings are accentuated by the transmutation of the magical aspect of the fairytale into allegory and symbol. The husband smells of arum lilies which are symbols of death, and the girl constructs her own identity through the multiple mirrors in her husband's bedroom.

'The Bloody Chamber', then, alerts us to perspectives which are repressed in the fairytale, subverts many of its values and expands its psychoanalytic and political horizons. Carter sticks to the story form of the fairytale, and this helps to highlight other changes in the narrative. However, a rewriting can be in a completely different genre: for example a classic novel might be transformed into a long poem.

How can I rewrite?

For Exercise 3 the actual choice of text is important. Your rewriting is likely to work more effectively if you choose a well-known narrative: if you pick one that is not known to your audience they will not be able to appreciate what has been changed in the rewrite, unless you can somehow juxtapose the two.

Once you have chosen your source, there are also a number of issues which you will want to consider:

- Which elements are missing, suppressed or minimised in the original text?
- How can the story be politicised? Which moral, ethical or cultural assumptions can be challenged?
- Who is speaking/narrating and from what perspective? Can the hero/villain roles be reversed or problematised?
- Can the location and era be changed or modified?
- How much of the original content should be retained? How divergent is the rewriting going to be?
- What will be the style, form or genre of the rewritten text (e.g. a poem or a parody)?
- What will be the language style? If, for example, the original language is nineteenth century, part of modernising the piece could be to change it to a 21st-century idiom.
- Can you transmute features of the original text into metaphor and symbol in the rewritten one?

This exercise also makes demands on your narrative technique, and you may find it useful to return to it after you have done the exercises in Chapter 5.

The rewrite in Figure 4.1 of the Cinderella tale is a lively and unusual take on the fairytale by student Alice Coltheart (1998). Alice employs a variety of journalistic styles, from tabloid to more elite newspaper, and includes personal and employment ads to give the story a contemporary spin.

Figure 4.1: 'Untitled' (Coltheart 1998)

Prince Charming Charity Masquerade Ball: Social Event of the Year

Thousands of socialites are expected to attend this year's Prince Charming Charity Ball. The ball is to be held on Saturday August 22nd at the home of the renowned eligible bachelor, Mr. Prince Charming. Charming was somewhat eccentrically named by his parents, Crystal and Charles Charming, who made their fortune in computers. The ball is expected to attract a bevy of television and movie industry starlets, the cream of our fashion designers, and possibly even some surprise overseas guests, says a source close to Charming.

Monday, August 10th—*Who Weekly* p. 10

Fairy Godmother Wanted

By western suburbs female, young, impoverished, mistreated by step-sisters and neglected by frivolous father. Determined to move up in the world but needs help to do it. Previous experience in man trapping essential, plus ability to conjure up all necessary items for the job—very imited budget available. Non-paid job but guaranteed personal satisfaction and percentage of future wealth if successful. First project to be extremely challenging. Immediate start.

Ph: 3217823 and ask for Cindee.

Wednesday August 11th— *Daily Telegraph* Employment Section

Prince Charming Charity Ball A Hit; But Who is his Mystery Girl?

Last night's Masquerade Ball at the Vaucluse home of Prince Charming was the most successful yet: see the social pages for exclusive photos of the guests. Over $200,000 was raised for charity, however the question on most of the partygoers' lips concerned the identity of Charming's masked female companion, with whom he danced tirelessly all night. Unlike his previous parties, where Charming has been known to eschew female company to converse with business associates, last night Sydney's most eligible bachelor could not be prised from the company of the tall, slim, brown-haired girl. Phoning several high-profile model agencies revealed that she is not on any of their books, although most of them expressed interest in her after witnessing her statuesque beauty and the way it bewitched the terminally single Prince Charming. It is predicted that several hundred Sydney females will be gnashing their teeth this morning after last night's disappointment.

Sunday, August 23rd—*Sun Herald* p. 2

Desperately Seeking Cindee

We danced all through night,
I held you close, I held you tight,
You ran as it struck midnight,
I looked for you, you were nowhere in sight.

Then my personal bodyguard came to me,
On my front stair a shoe he did see,
I know it was yours cause it was so dainty,
So now I'm looking for a girl who fits a size three.

Your princey baby wants you back,
Without you, smoochy, I ain't got jack,
Come to my Vaucluse mansion before I crack,
I'll marry you, the moment you come back.

Monday August 24th—*Sydney Morning Herald* Personals Section

Charming House Stormed By Females: 10 Arrested

A dramatic scene occurred yesterday when hundreds of females descended on Villa Bonita, the Vaucluse residence of Mr. Prince Charming. Police were called to break up the crowd of women who overran Charming's property after a rather sentimental personal ad was placed in yesterday's Herald, apparently pleading for a woman named Cindee, who had a size three foot, to come forward. It is thought this woman is the masked beauty with whom Mr. Charming whiled away the hours at his Charity Masquerade Ball on Saturday Night. The ten women arrested are all being charged with trespassing.

Tuesday August 25th—*Sydney Morning Herald* p. 5

Sydney Socialites in Shock! Prince Charming's Belle revealed to be 22 year old Campbelltown cleaning lady!

The matrons will be talking about it over their tea and cucumber sandwiches for an eternity. After a month-long search by Mr. Charming, a woman has come forward who claims to be the one he danced the night away with at his Charity Ball last month. She is none other than Ms. Cindee Narelle Carruthers, a 22 year old woman from Sydney's west, who tends the house of her father and his two daughters from his second marriage, and is occasionally employed casually as a cleaner at the nearby McDonald's.

Since the discovery, Ms. Carruthers has not commented to the press, preferring to stay within the confines of the Charming residence, however a representative of Mr. Charming spoke to the media earlier today on behalf of both of them. He issued the following statement: "Mr. Charming wishes you to know that he is not the sort of man who would let issues of class stand in the way of such a thing as true love. He has asked Ms. Carruthers for her hand in marriage, and she has accepted. They are looking forward to a long and happy life together and hope that the media will allow them to live their lives together away from the glare of the spotlight."

It is not yet known how Ms. Carruthers managed to gain entry to the $250 per head event, however it is believed her two stepsisters were also present.

Sydney Morning Herald—Tuesday September 25th p. 4

Prince Charming Weds Western Suburbs Belle

Cindee Narelle Charming, née Carruthers, wed her Prince Charming in a beautiful seaside ceremony yesterday, three months to the night since they met at Charming's Masquerade Ball. The reception was held at the Regent, and the couple are to live in a new, sumptuous home in Point Piper.

The Wentworth Courier—
November 22nd p. 2

The truth revealed: "I was employed to help Cindee Charming trap her Prince"

Mary Godmother thought she had found the perfect job when she read a classified advertising for help in trapping a man; "I've been married to the man of my dreams for 45 years and I used more clever tricks to snag him than you can poke a stick at", says the 65 year old grandmother of 17. Little did she know that she would end up causing the biggest stir Sydney's social scene has felt in years. Her employer was none other than Mrs. Cindee Charming, who wrote in the advertisement of her "determination to move up in the world". The ad promised financial remuneration in the event of a successful outcome for Mrs. Charming, then known as Ms. Carruthers. However Mrs. Godmother says "After taking on the job, I gave Cindee encouragement, foolproof tips, I ran her up a beautiful dress for the ball on the Janome, and I even got my hubby, Fred, to drive her to the ball in our vintage Rolls. But I didn't even get a thank you card in return, let alone the money that was promised to me. I'm now writing a book on how to marry a rich man, and I am hoping this will bring in some extra money, but at the moment I am living on the pension and times are tight. I just want what is rightfully mine".

Woman's Day—December 1st p. 5

DISASTER STRIKES FOR CINDEE CHARMING

In what can only be described as a double whammy, the most talked about woman in Sydney, Mrs Cindee Charming, announced today she was being divorced by her husband of two months, the wealthy heir Prince Charming, after a damning interview was published in the latest edition of *Woman's Day* with a woman who says she was employed by Mrs. Charming to help her to find a wealthy husband. Following hot on the heels of this announcement came another, this time from Mrs. Godmother, Mrs. Charming's alleged employee, who announced she will be suing Mrs. Charming for $10 million. It is not known whether the Charmings signed a pre-nuptial agreement.

The Financial Review—December 20th p. 1

CONCLUSION

In this chapter we have explored various techniques for recycling texts, to make you more aware of the intertextual possibilities of writing. Once you have tried these techniques, you may decide they are going to be central to your future writing practice, or you may simply draw on them from time to time. You may want to use them in a very overt way (for example by including quotations in your work), or more obliquely as a method of triggering ideas for your own writing. We will be considering further approaches to recycling texts and intertextuality when we visit fictocriticism in Chapter 9. We will also be returning to the idea of recycling again in Chapter 7, through the postmodern concept of rewriting history.

REFERENCES

Brewster, A. and Smith, H. 2002, 'ProseThetic Memories', *Salt.v16. An International Journal of Poetry and Poetics: Memory Writing*, (ed). T.-A. White, Salt Publishing, Applecross, Western Australia, pp. 199–211.

Carter, A. 1981, *The Bloody Chamber and Other Stories*, Penguin, London.

Coltheart, A. 1998, 'Untitled', unpublished.

Costello, M. 1994, 'Covering Letters (A Found Story)', *Small Ecstasies*, University of Queensland Press, St Lucia, Queensland.

Duggan, L. 1987, *The Ash Range*, Pan Books, Sydney.

Eliot, T.S. 1963, *Collected Poems 1909–1962*, Faber & Faber, London.

Mac Low, J. 1985, *The Virginia Woolf Poems*, Burning Deck, Providence.

Matterson, S. 1990, 'Contemporary and Found', *World, Self, Poem: Essays on Contemporary Poetry from the 'Jubiliation of Poets'*, (ed.) L.M. Trawick, The Kent State University Press, Kent, Ohio, pp. 187–95.

Phillips, T. 1980, *A Humument: A Treated Victorian Novel*, Thames & Hudson, London.

Rhys, J. 1966, *Wide Sargasso Sea*, W.W. Norton & Company, New York.

Stewart, A. 1998, '.romance (1981)', *I/T: Selected Poems 1980–1996*, Here & There Books/Split Records, Sydney, Book and CD.

Williams, W.C. 1983, *Paterson*, Penguin, Harmondsworth, Middlesex. First published in 1963 in one volume by New Directions Books.

Wolfreys, J. 2004, *Critical Keywords in Literary and Cultural Theory*, Palgrave Macmillan, Basingstoke, Hampshire.

Young, I. 1972, 'Poem Found in a Dime Store Diary', *Contemporaries: Twenty-Eight New American Poets*, (eds) J. Malley and H. Tokay, Viking Press, New York.

CHAPTER FIVE
Narrative, narratology, power

Narratives are an immensely important part of our daily lives. They take the form of stories, and they are to be found in newspaper articles, historical reports, advertisements, soap operas, gossip and conversation. They are also an important aspect of creative writing: the stuff of novels and short fiction. In this chapter I'll be drawing on narratology, a particular theory of narrative, and I'll be looking at such matters as narration, focalisation (point of view), the manipulation of time and the concept of character.

Many books about writing help you to reproduce particular types of narrative form. My approach here will be slightly different, and will involve analysing the dynamics of narrative and applying them to creative practice. This chapter, therefore, will help you not only to understand narrative structure, but also to stretch and experiment with it. Much storytelling is rooted in realism and hinges on stabilising realist conventions. If you want to experiment, you sometimes have to twist, subvert or invert those conventions, and turn realism on its head.

Narrative is a genre, but it is also an important aspect of our social consciousness and interactions. The way in which fictional technique can influence the ideological and psychological aspects of the text—particularly with respect to power relationships, cultural identity and memory—is an important aspect of this chapter and is discussed further in Chapter 7.

exercises

1. Rewrite the same passage in a number of different ways using various types of narrators who are both inside and outside the story (these are known as homodiegetic and heterodiegetic narrators respectively). Experiment also with metafictional, overt and covert narrators. Consider the way in which different kinds of narration affect the dynamics of power, both within the narrative and between narrator and reader.
2. Write a piece which emphasises the relationship between the narrator (the person who is telling the story) and the narratee (the person to whom the story is being told).
3. Write two short narrative passages: one in which the grammatical position of the subject is fixed and one in which it is unsettled.
4. Write a short piece which illustrates narrative foreshadowing.
5. Create a text which includes non-narrated elements: i.e. incorporates passages in which the narrator is absent.
6. Build a point of view (focalisation) using the triggers sensing, feeling and thinking.
7. Create a point of view which alternates between exterior action and internal thought.
8. Write about the same incident from two or three completely different points of view or focalisations. Use this as a means to explore different forms of subjectivity and divergent cultural viewpoints.
9. Write a text which restructures the narrative and moves between different points in the past and the present. Consider, if relevant, how the structure of your piece relates to the operations of memory.

ENTER NARRATOLOGY, ENTER POWER

You can learn a great deal about shaping narratives from acquainting yourself with **narratology**. Narratology is a theory of narrative, and was an outgrowth of structuralism: it is an analytical system for understanding narrative structure. Narratologists break down the macrostructure of narrative form into its micro-elements. Narratology challenges traditional formulations of narrative as a plot with characters. Instead it breaks down narrative into its constitutive parts. Narratology takes some of the mystique out of storytelling, emphasises the construction of narratives, and alerts us to the distinction between what I call real life and text life. Narratology, then, is concerned with the nuts and bolts of narration, it does not focus primarily on the thematic aspects of fiction: for example, how characters behave, or how they live their lives, but on their function within the narrative. Narratology, therefore, provides certain indispensable tools and terms for thinking in detail about narrative technique.

Narratology has come under fire in recent years for a view of narrative which is too stripped of context. It is certainly true that narratology is somewhat reductive. It does not fully address the social and cultural discourses in which narratives are embedded, and the way these can reinforce or question the unequal power relationships between different social groups. Furthermore, it does not explore the power dynamics which are intrinsic to the process of narration itself, since who tells the story, and how, is itself an exercise in domination and control. For example, narration can be 'authoritarian' in reflecting only the point of view of the narrator, or 'democratic' in presenting several different perspectives. However, the limitations of narratology can be overcome if we can combine such analysis with a more thematic, discourse-related approach to writing, as I hope to do in this and later chapters: the two are not mutually exclusive. We need to combine implementing narratology with an awareness of post-structuralist theory, for example the influential work of Michel Foucault who argued that power relationships underlie all discourse. (For more about Foucault's ideas, see *Understanding Foucault* Danaher, Schirato & Webb, 2000.)

Because narratology is based on systematic analysis, rather than a humanist approach to narrative, it often employs terms rather different from those with which you may be familiar: for example, flashbacks are referred to as **analepses**. These terms are often more specific than the ones they replace, and I have used them, though sometimes in conjunction with more traditional terms.

Narratologists define narrative as a sequence of events. They distinguish between the *what* of the narrative, its content, and the *how* of the narrative, its form. Narratologist Seymour Chatman calls the what of the narrative **the story**, and the how of the narrative, **the discourse**. In these terms, it is the discourse with which narratologists are principally concerned (Chatman 1978) and which we will explore in this chapter.

A particularly good book to read on narratology is Rimmon-Kenan's *Narrative Fiction* (1983). Although this book is geared towards literary analysis rather than creative activity, it can be implemented (with imaginative adaptation) as a manual for narrative technique. It can be complemented with Mark Currie's *Postmodern Narrative Theory* (1998), which gives an account of more recent developments in narrative theory, and stresses the ascendancy of the cultural in narrative theory.

NARRATION, NARRATORS, IDEOLOGY

Narration determines the degree of involvement and ideological investment of the narrator: the distance or nearness to the material, and the degree of empathy and control. The following sections outline some of the considerations which go into setting up the narration, and rewrite the same passage demonstrating different aspects of narrative technique. This is so you acquire a sense of alternative ways in which you can nuance the narrative, create your own storyline, and mimic this process of rewriting.

Introducing the narrator

Exercise 1 suggests you rewrite the same passage using a number of different kinds of narrator. It also asks you to consider the way in which different kinds of narration affect the dynamics of power, both within the narrative and between narrator and reader. A narrator can be outside the story or within it. In narratology, a narrator who is outside the story is **heterodiegetic**, a narrator who is within the story is a **homodiegetic** ('Diegesis' means narration or telling). Being within or outside the story creates distance and partiality which are important factors in the dynamics of narratorial power.

There are also different types of heterodiegetic and homodiegetic narrators. Both can appear in the first person or third person, be intrusive or unobtrusive, reliable and unreliable—again this has subtle effects on the reader–narrator relationship. By rewriting the same passage several times, I hope to show you some of the ways in which heterodiegetic or homodiegetic narrators can be employed, so that you can try others yourself.

Let's first look at the heterodiegetic narrator:

Example 5.1: Heterodiegetic narrator (third person)
Sophie's position as director of the gallery was now in jeopardy. Nobody on the board was supporting her. Her desire to move the gallery in a more progressive direction, and to include much more contemporary art, was looked on with disdain by many of the board members. She was a good financial manager, the gallery had thrived under her leadership, but her primary agenda was creative development, not profit and loss. Her propensity to say this, and her

blunt style, annoyed the suits and ties who wanted to think of the gallery simply as a company with shareholders. There was also a great deal of in-fighting: the board wanted more power, but was divided amongst itself. And two of the artists who were sitting members—and who might have been expected to back Sophie—did not, because they felt she had not supported their work. There were also many unspoken prejudices about dealing with a woman.

This passage gives us ostensibly a bird's eye view of the situation, and the predicament that Sophie finds herself in. Note that it is written in the third person, that the narrator is fairly distant, and that this accentuates the *apparent* impartiality. It tells us something about Sophie's motives, but also gives us information about the board to which Sophie would not be privy. So the narrator is in possession of more information than any of the individual characters. However, it is important to note that the narrator is not entirely distant and impartial. To some extent she expresses her own bias, and her sympathies seem to lie with Sophie rather than the board (I am treating the narrator as female here though the gender is ambiguous). She refers to the board members as 'suits and ties' which is somewhat satirical because it suggests conformity, and she also says that the board has unspoken prejudices. Of course, the narrator could have suppressed this bias had she wanted to. She could have used the words 'board members' instead of 'suits and ties', and 'opinions' instead of 'prejudices'. We see here the power of the narrator, who can manipulate what the reader knows in relation to the characters. Particularly important is the way these linguistic nuances affect the ideological position of the text: to make the changes I have suggested would be to make the passage more conservative. As it stands it is somewhat disdainful of the world of business and the power structures which prop it up; the narrator is also sympathetic to the problems which Sophie experiences as a woman in a position of power. As such, we feel that she has more empathy with Sophie than the board.

Although in the preceding example we can feel the presence of this narrator, she is relatively unobtrusive. However, a narrator can be much more of a felt presence in the narrative. Let's look at an instance where the heterodiegetic narrator is obtrusive:

Example 5.2: Heterodiegetic narrator, intrusive and metafictional (first person)

Now I'm going to tell you Sophie's story so sit back readers, listen and don't interrupt. It's difficult to know where to start, but it's all a case of economic irrationalism. The big guys wanted her out because they couldn't agree amongst themselves. And quite frankly they didn't like being bossed around by a woman. But don't start assuming things, or pulling precipitously at the textual strings, because I hold them. Sophie wasn't a naive victim, she knew what she was about. She was as much of a game player as the rest of them.

The narrator here is still outside the story, but the passage is written in the first person, and his presence is much more intrusive (I am treating this narrator as male though again gender is ambiguous). The narrator is also identifying strongly with the author by making us very aware of the process of writing, and the fact that what we are reading is a construct or fiction. This narratorial obtrusiveness is a feature of postmodern fiction (though it is also present in eighteenth-century and nineteenth-century fiction). A narrator of this kind, sometimes known as the **metafictional** narrator, makes us aware of the writing process and reminds us that we are reading a fiction. This eruption of apparent authorial presence in the story has become quite commonplace in fiction. See, for example, narratorial intrusions in Cynthia Ozick's *The Puttermesser Papers*, 'Stop. Stop, stop! Puttermesser's biographer, stop! Disengage, please.' (1998, p. 16). Another example is J.M. Coetzee's *Elizabeth Costello* (2003, p. 16), where the narrator interrupts to say he will skip a scene, draws attention to the 'realist illusion', and distinguishes the writing of the text as a 'performance' which is distinct from the narrative itself.

Take note also of the difference in voice and language in Example 5.2: the language is colloquial in places ('the big guys', 'bossed around') but seems to be more aggressive. The narrator (who is much more critical of Sophie than the previous one) is asserting his power, and trying to control the power relationship between himself and the reader in a more direct way than in the previous example.

The homodiegetic narrator, by contrast, is a character in the story, and is likely to talk to us in the first person. The obvious choices for the homodiegetic narrator would be Sophie or one of the board members, because they are the people who are privy to the relevant information. Let's look at the way Sophie might talk about the situation:

Example 5.3: Homodiegetic narrator, central character (first person)

I began to panic, I felt helpless and as if everything was stacked against me. It seemed highly likely they would try to ditch me as director of the gallery. Nobody on the board was supporting me, and there was very little I could do. My success in running the gallery was actually loaded against me. My desire to move it in a more progressive direction, and to include much more contemporary art, was looked on with disdain by many of the board members. That I had the finances under control, and that the gallery was thriving, meant nothing to them. It was all power games I knew that, and Bob and Eric—the artists on the board—must be playing their own game because they certainly haven't been backing me.

This is a much more emotional and partial account of the situation. Notice how Sophie stresses her own powerlessness and casts herself as a victim. Note also the use of the past tense: I have couched it so that Sophie is telling the story partly retrospectively. She does switch to the present tense at the end, but the past tense gives her more opportunity to be thoughtful and introspective.

However, the homodiegetic narrator can also be a minor character in the narrative:

Example 5.4: Homodiegetic narrator, minor character (first person)

And what about Sophie? You may well ask! That woman's got too many new-fangled ideas for me, and I was delighted to see her trounced the other day at the board meeting. She is always trying to put herself forward and it would be all very well if all we had to do was hang up paintings and hope people would look at them, but that's not what it's all about. She's got her head in the clouds! I can't see anything in the pictures she's trying to promote, they don't mean anything to me, and I suspect they don't mean anything to anyone else. With taste like hers let loose, there will be nobody in the gallery by next year.

Here the narrator uses the first person to insert himself more directly into the narrative. He is probably one of the characters in the novel (again I am treating the narrator as male). He sounds like one of the board members who does not sympathise with Sophie, in which case he is a homodiegetic narrator. However, he could be a narrator outside the story who is taking it as read that he has special information: this is somewhat ambiguous in such a small extract.

Again the first person brings the narration much closer to home, and more sense of the character of the narrator is established. This narrator comes over as philistine and conservative. He is not someone who is going to spend too much time considering anybody else's point of view. This is important for how we view the story: when confronted with this narrator we are likely to sympathise heavily with Sophie's position. At issue here is also the reliability of the narrator. On the whole we expect narrators to be trustworthy, but they may seem less so when there is an obvious distance between their ethical stance and that of the author. In general, when the narration is in the third person we expect it to be soundly based, if biased. When it is in the first person there is a greater sense it could be false or exaggerated.

In fact, there are many experimental ways of playing with the reliability, status and overtness of the narrator. For example, in the story 'The Shape of the Sword', the Argentinian writer Jorge Luis Borges (1970) begins the story with third person narration, and then gives the narration over to an unnamed narrator who tells a story about himself and a character called Vincent Moon. It is only at the end of the story that the narrator shows his cards and reveals that he is in fact Vincent Moon, then we have to go back through the story and reassess what he's been telling us. So here Borges is playing a narratorial power game with us by withholding the identity of the narrator, and this gives a double motion to the story. Similarly, in the story 'Jan Godfrey' by New Zealand writer Janet Frame (1989), the narrator claims to be writing a story about Alison Hendry, and then declares she is Alison Hendry at the end, though her identity remains ambiguous. Sophie's story could possibly be told by her, without any revelation until the end that she is the director, though this would entail many adjustments to the narration.

All the above examples involve a realist scenario, but similar techniques could be used in less realist, more allegorical narratives. For example, the narrator could be a higher power who is directing the action, or an inanimate object that is viewing the action from its own perspective. Either way the same range of narrative techniques could be activated, and the same dynamics of power could apply.

Calling the narratee

In any narrative the narrator is actually speaking to someone who is known in narratology as the **narratee** (see Exercise 2). The narratee may be the reader, but the narrator can also address another of the characters in the book. Use of the second person form 'you' creates a particularly intimate (sometimes even intimidating) relationship between narrator and narratee. Let's try writing Sophie's story in the second person:

Example 5.5: Second person narration
You thought you could be idealistic and get away with it, you were always optimistic about how things would turn out. You were good

at running the gallery and thought that nobody could touch you
at it. You wondered whether your bluntness sometimes caused
offence, if you would be hijacked by your own honesty. But you
couldn't turn art into profit and loss, and that was that.

Here the narrator posits what she imagines to be Sophie's point of view by
confronting her as narratee with her ideas about it. The second person
form gives the narrator a certain power, even enabling her to take the
moral high ground (although I am treating the narrator as female, gender
again is ambiguous).

The second person can also be employed in narration to set up ambiguities about who is being addressed, and is used most often in
experimental fictions. By means of the pronoun 'you', the narrator can
speak partly to someone else in the narrative, and partly to the audience,
thereby implicating the reader in what is happening (this mode of address
is also often to be found in poetry). And the second person can be used
very effectively, on occasion, to imply a split subjectivity, so that one part
of the self seems to be looking to see what the other half is doing, so that
the self is both acting and acted upon. The short story 'Shopgirls', by
American writer Frederick Barthelme (1989), is a very good example of
second person narration.

We would normally expect the narratee, if apparent, to have a sustained
presence. However, in an experimental narrative the narratee might
appear and disappear from the narrative in a disconcerting and unsettling
way. By this means, it would be possible to call into question not only who
is telling the story, but to whom it is being told.

The subject positions

The question of the narratee leads us to the issue of subject position. We
have already seen how the narration can be written in the first and third
person, or less commonly, in the second person. Exercise 3 asks you to
write a passage in two ways, one that fixes the subject position and one
that unsettles it.

In many short stories and novels the grammatical position is kept the
same all the way through. In most narratives there is a tendency to stabilise
the grammatical position of the narration, but experimental narratives
might shift from one grammatical position to another: the quicker and
more frequent the move, the more disruptive it becomes. This unsettles
our sense of subject position, of who the subject is, the position that he or
she is adopting, and of his or her relationship to others in the story. Let's
transpose part of Sophie's story into an experimental mode in which—her

confidence shattered—she tries to come to terms with herself in the mirror, and her difficulties are reflected in a destabilised subject position:

Example 5.6: Destabilising the subject position
I cannot say who this is. Your eyes attract and resist. She is avoiding my look. I turn my head, look over my shoulder. If you move I will shift too. She drifts past the mirror, hesitates, pauses. You want to know more, part the waves and dart through. She backs away, needs to find words for what she has dreamed.

Obviously there is an ambiguity here about whether there are two people or one. But the fact that a mirror is involved makes us suspect that there is one person, and that we are exploring her divided subjectivity. This can be seen as another 'take' on the mirror exercise in Chapter 1; one which brings the idea of doubles and reflections into the writing not only thematically, but also at a technical and grammatical level.

What is the point of changing the subject position in this way? Most significantly it explodes, at a fundamental and grammatical level, the idea of an unproblematic, unified self. It emphasises that we all consist of split, or even splintered, selves. A good example of writing which moves between the first and third person, and creates this sense of a split self, is *The American Woman in the Chinese Hat* by American writer Carole Maso (1995). In the following passage the narrator both expresses herself in the first person, but also looks at herself in the third person:

Example 5.7: Destabilising the subject position
The next day in Vence I go to the municipal pool. La piscine municipale.

She hears the sound of water over rocks.

She watches the French swim. Notes their preference for the breaststroke. She watches a woman in a black bathing suit light a cigarette. She feels the pervasive and strange eroticism in these days. The slight breeze presses her toward men she doesn't know. Men whose language she can't speak.

She is wearing her Chinese hat. She is holding her open notebook.

Often these days she finds she refers to herself in the third person as if she were someone else. Watching from afar.

From *The American Woman in the Chinese Hat* (Maso 1995, p. 21)

Subtle changes of subject position are mainly found in experimental fictions. They are a fascinating feature of the novel *Waste* by Australian author Sabrina Achilles (1995), where transformation into the third person sometimes subverts the continuous flow of the first person, and vice versa.

The knowing narrator

The narrator can control not only our ethical attitudes towards the story but also our degree of knowledge and awareness of the progress of the narrative. In this sense, as well as many others, the narrator 'holds the cards'. The narrator can forewarn us of events or withhold information (see Exercise 4). Sometimes the reader knows more than the characters (or some of them), sometimes less. Sometimes the narrator drops hints about the outcome, note the end of this next example:

Example 5.8: Narratorial foreshadowing

Sophie's position as director of the gallery was now in jeopardy. Nobody on the board was supporting her. Her desire to move the gallery in a progressive direction, and to include much more contemporary art, was looked on with disdain by many of the board members. She was a good financial manager, the gallery had thrived under her, but her primary agenda was creative development, not profit and loss. Her propensity to say this, and her blunt style, annoyed the suits and ties who wanted to think of the gallery simply as a company with shareholders. There was also a lot of in-fighting: the board wanted more power, and two of the artists who were sitting members and might have been expected to back Sophie didn't, because they wanted a director who would support their work more readily. There were also a number of agendas held by the members of the board about dealing with a woman, which Sophie was later to discover had a profound impact on the outcome.

Such hints are usually just enough to make us want to read on and find out what happens.

In some instances the narrator knows more than the character. In such cases, the narrator gives the character's perspective, while hinting that there is more to the matter than meets the eye, and that this may prove critical in the outcome of the story:

Example 5.9: Narratorial foreshadowing

Sophie kept looking at the new board member and wondering where she had seen him before. He looked so familiar and yet she didn't know his name. Perhaps he just looked like someone else?

It was difficult to say. He looked through her as if he didn't know her, but his unawareness seemed rather studied, which made her uneasy and suspicious. It was to be several months before Sophie was to remember where she had seen him.

In Barbara Vine's popular novel *The Chimney Sweeper's Boy* (1998), each character and the reader are continuously at different stages of awareness about the full story: the revelation of unintended incest between two brothers. At the end there are only two characters, the author and the reader, who are in full possession of this story; all the other characters are in a state of partial awareness. This withholding, and gradual leaking, of information (not only with respect to the reader but also other characters in the novel) is most graphic in detective novels or other very plot-orientated fictions.

The absent narrator

Finally (see Exercise 5), you may want to introduce 'non-narrated' elements as part of your narrative: these could be entries from diaries, letters, newspaper entries or advertisements. In Sophie's story such a non-narrated element might be the boardroom minutes or a newspaper leak about her impending 'resignation'. Non-narrated elements can be useful in breaking up and creating variety in the narration. They can give different perspectives on an event, and can problematise the notion of an objective reality. So-called 'factual' evidence is never completely objective, and always has underlying ideological investments which may not be fully disclosed. For instance, a newspaper report always includes the journalist's bias.

In order to create non-narrated elements, you might find it helpful to refer back to the section on non-literary forms in Chapter 3.

FOCALISATION

Narration affects point of view, which is sometimes known in modern narrative theory as **focalisation** or orientation. A point of view is a particular perspective taken by a narrator or character on an event or situation. When Sophie was narrator she described the situation from her own point of view because she gave her own perspective on what was happening. However, narration is not identical to point of view: one narrator may relay the points of view of several contrasting characters. So the next question is, how does narration relate to focalisation? There are two obvious ways of projecting a point of view: one in which a third person narrator tells us what a particular character is thinking and feeling; the other in which the voice of the character actually takes over so that narrator and focaliser become almost inseparable. The advantage of the third person is that you can oscillate between a more distant perspective, which is an overview, and a particular character's point of view. You can look both with the character and at them. The advantage of the first person, however, is that you can capture that character's voice (or voices), and move more obviously close to their thought patterns.

In Example 5.3 the narrator was Sophie, and the point of view was obviously hers. However Sophie's point of view could also be projected through a third person narrator:

Example 5.10: Point of view, third person narration

Throughout that week Sophie began to realise that her position was weakening. It was hard to tell what people on the board were thinking: she could only guess. She did not know whether the position was becoming so extreme that she might be ousted. The board members had an outlook that was so fundamentally opposed to hers that it was impossible to persuade them of anything: they didn't understand art, and more to the point they didn't like it. All they were interested in, as far as she could see, was profit and loss. She suspected they disliked aspects of her manner, but she didn't know how far it would take them. Such matters were difficult to assess.

Any point of view is not only a matter of individual outlook, it will inevitably reflect the **cultural discourses** in which a character is caught or which she or he seeks to evade. A person's perspective depends on a whole array of factors, such as social situation, age, sex or ethnicity. For example, an Australian-born child's perspective will be radically different from her Polish grandmother's way of looking at the world, partly because of the generation gap, and partly because her grandmother was born into, and emigrated from, another culture. Sophie's point of view partly results from her identification with discourses about the significance of art, and partly from a certain disdain for commercial values (even though she may be a good financial manager).

Constructing a point of view

Sometimes when you approach point of view you may have a particular person (fictional or otherwise) in mind. Let's try now, however, to build up a point of view without any pre-existing idea in mind (see Exercise 6).

A point of view usually consists of three components:

- *sensing* (how an object/event/person looks, sounds, feels, smells)
- *feeling* (emotional/affective reaction to the object/event/person)
- *thinking* (conceptualising the event and accommodating it to a particular ideological position).

So if you want to build up a point of view you don't necessarily have to have an idea: you can just build it from those three words, sensing, feeling, thinking.

Let's see how these components can suggest a point of view, even without any preceding context. When you have set down these basic words, you can start building up a scenario:

Example 5.11: Constructing a point of view

- *sensing* (child overhears parents' conversation)
- *feeling* (finds the conversation threatening)
- *thinking* (reassesses his attitude towards his parents)

Once you have done this, it is easy to take it one stage further, refining and developing the narrative:

Example 5.12: Developing a point of view

sensing: A child from an affluent background overhears his mother and father quarrel. They speak in a way which suggests he is not his father's genetic son.

feeling: The child begins to reassess his feelings towards his father. He starts to let his colder feelings towards him predominate. He also feels betrayed, but still loves his father.

thinking: The child begins to worry about who his biological father might be and why he has been lied to. He begins to imagine that he has always felt somewhat alienated from the comfortable middle-class environment of which he is part.

Here we are projecting the way the child sees the situation. In fact we are arriving at a particular contemporary version of the Oedipal complex, where the child feels ambivalent towards the father who may or may not be his genetic parent. We also see the way he is dangerously caught up in conservative discourses about the value of 'blood' relationships which are largely at odds with his emotional position and adoptive status. Maybe he is misinterpreting the overheard conversation, and maybe his conclusion is totally erroneous, but we are building up how he is sensing, feeling and thinking about the event irrespective of its truth-value. We can also see here how, although the expression 'point of view' deceptively suggests singularity, any focalisation is itself comprised of difference. The boy's perspective hinges largely on contradictions and ambiguities in the way he thinks and feels about the incident. Many creative writing books stress the need for a consistent (and implicitly circumscribed) point of view. However, I believe that you are likely to obtain the most exciting results if you explore the contradictions and ambiguities which make up a point of view, even when—or perhaps because—they threaten to explode the coherence and continuity of it.

One aspect of point of view, which also accentuates difference, is the alternation between exterior action and interior thought (see Exercise 7). Let's see how this works in outline:

Example 5.13: External action and interior thought (outline)
external action: Showing a creative text to fellow students. Behaving in a cool, self-possessed way.
interior thought: Unsure whether they are going to like it.
external action: Explaining the text.
interior thought: Unsure whether they will understand what the objective is.

In prose this could be developed in two different ways:

Example 5.14: External action and interior thought (written as prose)
a) Jane handed round the photocopies to the other students in the class. She expected them to think the poem was awful, and felt as if she was turning red. She could hardly believe it when they all said it was the most interesting piece that week.
b) Jane stood up handed round the photocopies.
What are they thinking, will I be exposed?

The first example (5.14a) uses the third person all the way through. In the second (5.14b) Jane's voice is introduced to convey her thoughts, and the italics show where the change from exterior action to interior thought actually occurs. The first makes for a flowing narrative, but the more disjunctive use of the voice in the second example can be quite arresting.

Multiple focalisations

Exercise 8 at the beginning of this chapter asks you to show the same incident from different points of view or focalisations. It also suggests you use this as a means to explore different forms of subjectivity and divergent cultural viewpoints. For this exercise the incident stays the same, but the perspective on it changes.

In our scenario about Sophie, we saw how different narrators had conflicting perspectives on the situation: we were rewriting the same story in different ways which were alternatives to each other. However, a very stimulating way of structuring a fictional text can be to make it pivot on several perspectives.

Multiple focalisations are likely to occur where there are several narrators. In Jean Rhys's *Wide Sargasso Sea* (1966) the narration moves between Rochester's first wife and Rochester himself, so sections of the book are related by different people. Similarly, in William Faulkner's *As I Lay Dying* (1963), the story is told by several people, with their names at the top of the section they are narrating. And the same technique is used in Julian Barnes's *Love, etc,* (2001) where three characters give their perspectives on a love triangle in short alternating monologues. Multiple focalisations can result in complex texts in which narratorial control is loosened, and objective reality is difficult to ascertain: the story becomes competing versions of events which can never be verified. Multiple focalisations also present the possibility of producing hybrid texts in which opposing cultural viewpoints (for example, different ethnicities, sexualities and generations) can clash or complement each other. Sophie has problems because she is female, and tends to have a more bohemian/artistic outlook than the other board members. However, her problems are still the relatively minor ones of an affluent white, middle-class person (she has a well-paid job and although she might lose it can almost certainly replace it with another). Such problems might be thrown into sharp relief by the perspective of the indigenous artist whose work she has represented in the gallery, or the disabled assistant who works part-time for her during the week.

The easiest way to create multiple focalisations is to construct two or three different versions of the same incident which follow each other consecutively:

- point of view A
- point of view B
- point of view C.

Initially, don't chop and change between perspectives, which will complicate matters, but learn how to sustain one point of view without moving onto the next. You can entitle each section by the name of a character, such as Joan or Sally or Ross, or you might want to give each a more subtle, oblique title.

Let's look at this diagrammatically. I'm using a diagram with two points of view here, but it's probably most stimulating if you have three:

Example 5.15: Two different focalisations

	Point of view 1	Point of view 2	
	sensing	sensing	
incident	thinking	thinking	**differences/ similarities**
	feeling	feeling	

The two points of view focus on the same incident (at the left-hand side of the diagram), but there can be differences and similarities (at the right-hand side of the diagram) at the level of sensing, feeling or thinking about it. Sophie and the board member both perceive that there is a problem and that Sophie is likely to lose her job, but they conceptualise the event in opposing ways and have diverging emotional reactions to it. The board member has little understanding of—or interest in—contemporary art and therefore dismisses Sophie as having her 'head in the clouds', while Sophie thinks the board members are so conservative that they are unable to see that she has been quite successful in running the gallery. Sophie's emotional reaction is also more intense than the board member's because she has much more to lose. A good example of an incident narrated through multiple focalisations, which are simultaneously similar and different, is Margaret Atwood's *The Robber Bride* (1994). Here the apparent resurrection of Zenia from the dead is shown from the perspective of three friends, Tony, Roz and Charis, who are lunching together, and who have hated and feared her. These accounts all converge, but emphasise different perceptual, emotional and conceptual aspects of the situation.

When you are writing about an incident from two different points of view, you can use the third person for both but imply contrasting perspectives. If you do this, you will be using one overall narrator, but that narrator will be projecting two perspectives. That way you project into the characters' minds, but you also have the freedom to comment on their actions or thoughts, or to use words which are not entirely their own to express their point of view. For example, you can write from a child's point of view, but use some words which a child would not use. You can partly maintain the narrator's way of speaking and vocabulary while still projecting those of the child.

Alternatively, you can structure each of the three points of view in the first person. If you do that you need to think about voice, grammar and vocabulary. Voice is particularly important: one point of view might be a very flat account, another highly emotional (though remember that the concept of voice is an over-simplification and that any character may have several voices). If you use the first person you may find yourself writing a series of interior monologues which consists of each character's unspoken but internally verbalised thoughts.

Another possibility is to create one account in the first person, one in the third person, and one in the second person. This can produce an unusual and experimental effect.

Let's look now at a student response to this exercise, Bryoni Trezise's 'An All-time Favourite Motto'. Bryoni uses two points of view as a vehicle for wittily satirising gender relations:

Example 5.16

George has always admired Jeanette. He likes the way she slides from tile to tile. All hips and bottom, manoeuvred expertly to emit just the right amount of sway. Sway is very important to George. A supremely executed sway never goes astray. That's George's third favourite motto. On Sundays Jeanette wears her flaming turban of voracious orange. Jeanette's Sunday soufflé. That's what George calls it. He can't help noticing her licorice assets. Her smoothly sculpted leg, the sizzle in her step. She flickety-flicks her fingers with morsels of efficiency. She's a tasty morsel herself, you know. All *hips* and *bottommm*. George is reminded of sausages squirming in sweet mustard. A sideways glance from beneath a finely arched eyebrow. A sign! She wants me . . .

um. I was just
wondering how many
men can a girl
take at once 'cause
you know
I've always
just
wondered about the big ones what's
it like with
really big
ones do they fit you

must get all the guys you're
really pretty

(George sweats and, thankfully, doesn't speak his thoughts aloud.)

The man smiles at me and only has one tooth. In all my relationships I find that I am perpetually unamused yet perpetually trying to impress. One gives me a bunch of forget-me-nots with a card reading "don't forget-me-not". Kitsch. One gives me a porcelain pig ("It'll remind you of me," he says). One gives me a rubber dog ("It'll remind you of you.") This, he doesn't say, but he thinks it wholeheartedly.

On Mondays Jeanette wears her hair like a prowling lioness. George notices that next to all of the other gobbling chickens Jeanette's scent is far superior. He likes the way her neck arches upwards and slightly to the left, allowing just enough angle to sound a slow lioness's growl from underneath her collarbone. A growl a day never goes astray. That's George's second favourite motto. George enjoys plunging his eyes into Jeanette's soupy marshmallow neckline. His eyes taste her fairy-floss lips. He imagines them melting under the heat of his breath. He knows she's waiting. He thinks of the burning leather interior of his car and longs to have Jeanette's smooth billabong body spread along its surface . . .

it's uncomfortable in

                            your car and my back

                    hurts and I'm

squirming because I

                    know it shouldn't feel like this

fish face with your purple cold codfish caresses

                                    ruminating

                                    round and round

like some decrepit old cow chewing dead grass

I know you try

but

why must you thrust your

varicose tongue down my throat when it's

all in vein.   all feigned.

Jeanette sweats and, unfortunately, doesn't speak her thoughts aloud. A squirm in the hay never goes astray. That's George's all-time favourite motto. He ripples his tooth in an eager smile, and gets down to business.

'An All-time Favourite Motto' (Trezise 2000, pp. 37–9)

NARRATIVE RESTRUCTURING

In this section we will explore the structure of the narrative and the way that events are shaped and ordered. The major factor in this is the organisation of time.

The arrow of time

Time is a very important factor in a narrative, because both the past and the future have a bearing on the present. It is through the organisation of time in the narrative that we confront both history and memory, which are non-linear, and involve complex two-way interactions between the present and the past. When we remember, for example, we do not simply dig up buried memories: our current experiences are constantly affecting the way we conceptualise what has happened. In fact Freud used the term **Nachträglichkeit**, meaning 'afterwardness', to convey this idea that our impression of the past is constantly being transformed by the present (see King 2000; Middleton & Woods 2000). Again, then, the way the narrative is structured is not simply formal but ideological and political: for example Toni Morrison's *Beloved* (1988), in telling the story of Sethe, an ex-slave, keeps moving backwards and forwards in time in relation to the abolition of slavery. The complex structure is not simply a means of ordering the story, it is a way of showing the massive, continuing impact of slavery—and the suppression of the history of slavery—on those who were slaves, their descendants and American collective memory.

It is tempting to think that writing a good narrative simply consists of thinking up a good story and then letting it unfold for itself. But the creation of narrative involves a radical restructuring of the raw material of the story, particularly with respect to order: it means bending and breaking what

Stephen Hawking calls 'the arrow of time' (Hawking 1988). If you look closely at how any narrative is structured, it's very different from just telling it 'how it is'. In this section I'm going to talk you through some of the different aspects of organising a narrative. However, in doing this, I will not resort to well-known models for structuring the order (e.g. end before the beginning; story within story). That is not because there is anything wrong with these models: you may find yourself using them, or discover that your own schemes approximate to them, and that is fine. However, the systematic approach that I outline below may enable you to think of more intricate and original means of ordering your material and intimately relating it to the subject matter. That way, you do not rely on standard structures for storytelling, but are free to adjust the parameters to suit your own purposes.

The past, the present, the past, the present

In structuring a narrative you need to think about the time sequence: the relationship between the past and the present. This is the focus of Exercise 9 which asks you to write a piece which moves between different points in the past and the present (and to consider, if relevant, how the structure of your piece relates to the operations of memory). Strict chronology doesn't necessarily make for evocative storytelling, so in order to obtain the best effect you will probably have to shuffle the events, in other words real-time is very different from story-time. If you just start at the beginning and work through to the end of the story, it is likely to be rather boring; you need to think about the order in which the events will seem most effective. Structuring the material may mean radically altering the chronology, and it may mean cutting out a lot of events. When you organise the structure you decide what to put in, and what to leave out, you build or deflate expectation and control pace.

In common usage the idea of going back into the past has been known as a flashback, and going forwards into the future as flashforward. In narrative theory a flashback is known as an analepse, and a flashforward as a **prolepse** (analepse occurs much more frequently). Again these are more technical terms which emphasise the non-linear aspect of time in memory and history.

In a narrative of any complexity there is never just one past or one present. A story can go back to several different points in the past and, of course, it can progressively move forwards in the present. So the relationship between the past and present is a very fluid and complex one. When you sequence a narrative you have to think about how to interrelate these different points in time. It is also useful to think of the past as discontinuous and never as one homogenous block: there is a near-past, or a mid-past, or a far-past (or several near-, mid- or far-pasts). Consequently there are many questions you might ask yourself about the organisation of any narrative. For example, do you want to start in the present, and then go back to the far-past, and progressively move forwards to the present? Or do you want to start in the near-past, and move backwards to the far-past, and then shift into the present. We saw in Chapter 3 how important it was to think of a structure in terms of chunks of text which can be reordered. If you think of time as a series of infinite points, infinitely divisible into segments, and if you think of those segments as ones which could be endlessly rearrangeable, then you can see just how flexible the structure of the narration can be. Of course, these are not purely formal decisions but will depend on the subject matter.

'The Empty Lunch-Tin', by Australian author David Malouf (1986), begins with a woman who sights a young man on her lawn. The young man reminds her of her dead son, though he is quite different from him. But the incident also triggers memories about the Depression in Australia when she was a child, and of a school friend, Stevie Caine, who came from an economically deprived background. He used to come to school with an empty lunch-box, and died a young man during the war: she seems to have felt a love for him which she has never fully acknowledged. During the story the woman undergoes a process of rehabilitation (she makes her son's favourite biscuits which she has not done since he died), and takes down the pictures which have remained for years on the walls of his bedroom. She also realises that the young man on the lawn reminds her of Stevie Caine. There is an implication that he is a ghost whose return she welcomes, and who enables her to come to terms with her multiple losses.

The story is about the relationship between the past and the present, because it is about working through memories. But this negotiation between the past and present is also *structured* into the narrative. The action begins in the present and moves forwards in the present: it also shifts back to various different points in the past through the woman's consciousness. In fact, the story starts in the present, then goes to the near-past (the death of Greg seven years ago), then the far-past (the Depression), then back into the present as the woman does her housework, makes the biscuits and revisits her son's old room. Through these actions the story moves forwards in the present, but with references to the far-past (the woman's childhood) and the near-past (of Greg's death). After that we retreat into the far- to mid-past (the story of Stevie Caine), before moving into the present again, now further on in time.

This is a very schematic account of the story, which does not do justice to the way structure and content reinforce each other. In fact, Malouf shows us the bearing the past has on the present in a very subtle way, mainly by juxtaposing events and relationships from different points in the past with the present, and suggesting a complex interaction between them. Greg, Stevie Caine and the ghost-like figure on the lawn all exist at separate points in time, and are pulled from different social contexts, but are nevertheless interconnected in the psyche of the elderly woman and her experiences of loss and recovery. When we are reading this story, it's very easy for its structure to pass us by because we become absorbed in the events. But it is the narrative organisation which links past and present experience, personal and historical memory. This kind of structure should be the basis for your text in Exercise 9.

Time in Sophie's story (even accepting that this is really only a fragment of a narrative) could be structured in many alternative ways. For example, we could start (i) with Sophie's dismissal, and then move back into various points in the near-, far- and mid-past to events which had led to it. Or we could begin (ii) halfway through the story at the point at which Sophie's problems are starting to gather momentum, and the narrative could alternate between moving back to the near-, mid- and far-pasts, and forwards in the present to the climax of the story. Or the narrative could (iii) 'begin at the beginning' and tell Sophie's story from the time of her appointment to her dismissal. Each of these ways of structuring the narrative has certain advantages and effects: for example, starting with Sophie's dismissal means that we know what the denouement of the story is, we will then be able to interpret, as we read, how the preceding events have led to this. On the other hand, if we do not know the end when we start to read, there will be more opportunities for suspense and manipulation by the narrator of what we do and don't know.

Let's set out (ii) which starts halfway through the story:

Example 5.17

Present: A boardroom vote in which Sophie realises that people she regarded as allies want her removed from her position.

Near-past: Bob and Eric come to see her to complain about lack of representation of their work. They also hint that they will not support Sophie in the boardroom unless she does represent their work.

Mid-past: Sophie is appointed as director of the art gallery.

Far-past: Sophie looks back to the time she was an art student.

Further on in the present: The boardroom moves against Sophie and dismisses her.

Far-past further on: After graduating, Sophie lacks confidence about her own art work; decides to go into arts administration.

Further on still in the present: Sophie realises that she really wants to be an artist rather than a manager. Instead of going into another directorial position, she sells her house, goes to live in the country, lives on a small income and devotes herself to art, though she receives no public recognition and makes no sales from her artworks.

This structure (which begins and ends at different points in the present) maximises the impact of delving back into Sophie's past in the middle of the narrative. It enables us to gradually understand how her perception of the past can enable her to make a radical decision about her future. There are, however, many other possibilities.

It will also be up to you how much you 'spell out' the links between the past and present: that is, the degree to which you show how they inter-relate and what their causal relationship is. In experimental narrative the links between past and present may be less apparent than in a more conventional narrative. Or they may be radically subverted, as in *Time's Arrow or The Nature of the Offence*, by British novelist Martin Amis (2003), where the story is told backwards. This matter will be considered in more detail in Chapter 12, when we consider time–space compression.

CONCLUSION: THE OPEN AND THE CLOSED

All narratives lie at a point along the continuum between open and closed. A closed narrative is one which is largely resolved. Most detective stories are closed in the sense that they end in disclosing who did the murder (though there is an increasing tendency for detective-story writers to stretch the genre and leave some ambiguity in the matter, creating a more open narrative). The more resolved Sophie's situation is, the more closed the narrative will be. For example, if she obtains another job in a gallery, and finds out exactly why she was dismissed, then the narrative will be relatively closed. However, if the story is conveyed in such a way that we as readers start to have doubts about what has really happened, whether there have been problems in the boardroom and whether Sophie has been dismissed at all, then the narrative will be very open.

Many of the modes of writing we have been looking at in this chapter tend toward openness. For example, multiple focalisations create ambiguities about where the truth of the matter lies. Openness of this kind makes for very active reading because the reader has to either choose between alternatives or allow for all the different possibilities of meaning. Roland Barthes (1974) distinguished between **readerly** texts, where the author has tight control over the narrative and its interpretation, and **writerly** texts where readers are encouraged to exercise their interpretative powers to the full. Readerly texts are more closed, writerly texts more open. Most experimental narratives tend towards a greater degree of 'writerliness'.

Open narratives also tend to address history in a more multifaceted way, because they do not close off alternative possibilities. Closed narratives can tell powerful stories; but they can also—as postcolonial theorist Homi Bhabha (1994) has argued—marginalise and exclude. More open narrative strategies are sometimes required to address the complexities of history and subjectivity, because no single story can ever speak for all cultures and identities. In Chapter 7, Postmodern f(r)ictions, narrative openness, and the way it affects how we view history, identity and reality, will be explored further. We will also explore postmodern adaptations and rethinkings of character and plot.

REFERENCES

Achilles, S. 1995, *Waste*, Local Consumption Press, Sydney.

Amis, M. 2003, *Time's Arrow or The Nature of the Offence*, Vintage, London. First published in 1991 in Britain by Jonathan Cape.

Atwood, M. 1994, *The Robber Bride*, Virago, London.

Barnes, J. 2001, *Love, etc*, Picador, London. First published in 2000 by Jonathan Cape.

Barthelme, F. 1989, 'Shopgirls', *Enchanted Apartments, Sad Motels: Thirty Years of American Fiction*, (ed.) D. Anderson, McPhee Gribble Publishers, Melbourne, pp. 49–62.

Barthes, R. 1974, *S/Z*, (trans.) R. Miller, Hill & Wang, New York.

Bhabha, H. 1994, *The Location of Culture*, Routledge, London.

Borges, J.L. 1970, 'The Shape of the Sword', *Labyrinths: Selected Stories and Other Writings*, Penguin, Harmondsworth, Middlesex, pp. 96–101.

Chatman, S. 1978, *Story and Discourse: Narrative Structure in Fiction and Film*, Cornell University Press, Ithaca, New York.

Coetzee, J.M. 2003, *Elizabeth Costello: Eight Lessons*, Knopf, Random House Australia, Sydney.

Currie, M. 1998, *Postmodern Narrative Theory*, Macmillan Press, Basingstoke, Hampshire.

Danaher, G., Schirato, T. and Webb, J. 2000, *Understanding Foucault*, Allen & Unwin, Sydney.

Faulkner, W. 1963, *As I Lay Dying*, New York, Penguin London. First published in 1930 in the United States.

Frame, J. 1989, 'Jan Godfrey', *Goodbye to Romance: Stories by Australian and New Zealand Women 1930s–1980s*, (eds) E. Webby and L. Wevers, Allen & Unwin, Wellington, pp. 122–6.

Hawking, S.W. 1988, *A Brief History of Time: From the Big Bang to Black Holes*, Bantam Press, London.

King, N. 2000, *Memory, Narrative, Identity: Remembering the Self*, Edinburgh University Press, Edinburgh.

Malouf, D. 1986, 'The Empty Lunch-Tin', *Transgressions: Australian Writing Now*, (ed.) D. Anderson, Penguin, Ringwood, Victoria, pp. 97–103.

Maso, C. 1995, *The American Woman in the Chinese Hat*, Plume, New York.

Middleton, P. and Woods, T. 2000, *Literatures of Memory: History, Time and Space in Postwar Writing*, Manchester University Press, Manchester and New York.

Morrison, T. 1988, *Beloved*, Picador, London.

Ozick, C. 1998, *The Puttermesser Papers*, Vintage International, New York.

Rhys, J. 1966, *Wide Sargasso Sea*, W.W. Norton & Company, New York.

Rimmon-Kenan, S. 1983, *Narrative Fiction: Contemporary Poetics*, Methuen, London and New York.

Trezise, B. 2000, 'An All-time Favourite Motto', *Unsweetened*, (eds) S. O'Leary, A. Lucas and S. Yip, UNSW Union.

Vine, B. 1998, *The Chimney Sweeper's Boy*, Penguin, London.

CHAPTER SIX
Dialoguing

We usually understand by the term dialogue a conversation between two or more people. So the important feature of dialogue is that it involves an exchange, the nature of which I will be exploring in this chapter. The exchange can be of many different types, and can also change as the dialogue progresses.

Dialoguing is fundamental to the way that we use language: we are usually speaking to, or writing for, someone. Words and meanings are constantly modified by social interactions, which is why literary theorist Mikhail Bakhtin called language **dialogic** (Holquist 1981). Dialoguing is extremely important in all cultural and political contexts, and is fundamental to communication. The breakdown of dialoguing, the failure to be able to creatively exchange views and understand another point of view, can produce extreme tension in personal relationships. But it can also lead more widely to social prejudice and cultural divisiveness: to racism, sexism, and ultimately to violence and war. Literary dialogue can explore the ups and downs of communication, and the way power relationships can underlie even the most innocuous verbal exchanges.

Dialogue can be part of any type of writing, so whatever your particular interests you can include it in your work. Although it is most commonly found in novels or plays, it can form the basis for poems, or may feature in performance pieces which are not conventional plays. And writing can be construed as dialogue, even if it is not technically in dialogue form. For example, there can be internal as well as external dialogue, characters may talk to themselves as well as to other people. Or dialogue can occur between voices that are not involved in a conversation, in the normal sense of the word. For example, in a radio piece the voice might be multitracked so there are several different versions of it, and it dialogues with itself. Some of these modes of dialoguing will be explored further in Chapter 10.

There are conventions about how dialogue functions in any particular literary genre, and you can either follow or break these. In plays, for example, dialogue is usually not interspersed with any authorial comment: it stands on its own and everything has to be implied or stated through it. On the other hand, in novels or short stories it is usually interspersed with authorial comment. This is because dialogue in a play is acted out in front of us, while in a novel the action usually takes place on the page. This is the norm, and you may wish to follow it, but you can also overturn these same conventions as a way of rethinking the nature of dialogue and how we represent it. For instance, the convention of leaving the dialogue to itself is disrupted in the play *Pandering to the Masses: A Misrepresentation* by American playwright Richard Foreman (1977). In this play, Foreman's taped voice comments on the action, and even the construction of the play. On the other hand in the novel, *Paradise*, Donald Barthelme (1987) suddenly shifts from normal narrative writing into whole chapters of dialogue, without any authorial comment whatsoever.

Dialogue can be conceived either by writing directly on the page or aurally. You might want to improvise dialogue with a friend and record it, or you might want to use a multitrack recorder and dialogue with yourself. Most importantly, read what you write aloud, so you achieve a real sense of how it sounds. That way you will develop your ear for dialogue.

exercises

1. Devise a question and then create a range of responses to it. If you wish, develop one question and response into a more lengthy dialogue.
2. Create two short pieces of dialogue: one realist and one non-realist.
3. Create a dialogue which hinges on a power struggle between two people.
4. Create a dialogue which:
    a) progresses from low levels of communication through to high levels of communication or vice versa, or
    b) shows an unusual or unconventional form of communication.
5. Create a polylogue: that is, a text based on several voices rather than only two.

> 6. Create a text based on a contemporary form of dialoguing such as an email exchange or a TV chat show.
> 7. Create a dialogue in an unusual generic context.
> 8. Collaborate on a text and 'dialogue' with another person.

WHAT CAN DIALOGUE DO?

One function of dialogue in a narrative or play can be that it reveals character and furthers the action. Playwrights often use dialogue in this functional way. However, I am going to suggest that you think of dialogue, at least initially, in a less functional way, so that you are not simply making it fit in with a preconceived notion of character or plot. That way you can be more explorative. Think of it as an open-ended exchange with an infinite number of possibilities for development. Try and make the process of writing dialogue generative—make each exchange spark another one. You can build your dialogue as you go: write down an initial statement and take it in a number of different directions.

A good way of thinking about dialogue is to imagine alternative exchanges to any one question (see Exercise 1). So let's think about some of the possible alternatives to the innocuous question 'What time will you be home tonight?' Look at the various possibilities below—obviously these are only some of many alternatives:

Example 6.1: Different responses to a question
Q. What time will you be home tonight?
A. Six o'clock?
(direct answer)

Q. What time will you be home tonight?
A. I don't know.
(uncommunicative)

Q. What time will you be home tonight?
A. What do you think?
(challenging, throwing it back to the other person)

Q. What time will you be home tonight?
A. Why should I tell you? Why are you always trying to pin me down?
(aggressive)

Q. What time will you be home tonight?
A. As soon as I can.
(acquiescent)

Q. What time will you be home tonight?
A. Time is in your throat but you cannot swallow it.
(poetic: reflective, not totally functional)

Q. What time will you be home tonight?
A. What time will I be home tonight?
(repeating the question instead of giving an answer)

All these mini-dialogues represent different types of social interaction, alternative ways in which dialogue can be dialogic. If we try to imagine these as exchanges which might take place in the middle of a play, there are three important points to be made. First, there is the degree to which the exchange suggests a realist genre of writing. Most of them do. But the reply 'Time is in your throat but you cannot swallow it' is more poetic and less realist than the others. It is not the kind of reply you would expect to hear in everyday life, and implies a type of writing which focuses on inner rather than outer realities. Second, there may be emotional investments or power struggles embedded even in a very simple exchange. For example, when the answer to the question 'What time will you be home tonight?' is 'What do you think?' there is an attempt to evade the question and push it back on to the questioner in a bullying fashion. More seems to be implied here than a simple question and reply. There is a context beyond the question, to do with the relationship and balance of power between these two people, which is impacting on the exchange. Third, the exchange may demonstrate low or high levels of communication, or may fall anywhere between those two extremes. In other words, dialogue may not always be dialogic in the sense of enhancing social interaction: sometimes it may inhibit or displace it.

For Exercise 1 try doing this for yourself. Make up any question and then create a range of responses to it. Construct extra types of response from the ones I have created. If you feel inclined to do so, develop one of the exchanges into a more lengthy dialogue.

REALISM RETREATS

Exercise 2 asks you to create two pieces of dialogue, one which is realist and one which is non-realist: the second could be a rewrite of the first. In fact, all dialogue ranges from realist to non-realist. Realist dialogue is based on the conversation we are used to hearing around us, though sometimes in dramatically heightened situations. For example, there is a passage in Arthur Miller's *Death of a Salesman* (1985, pp. 10–11), near the beginning of the play, which is an excellent example of a realist dialogue. In this passage Willy Loman complains to his wife that he is no longer valued in his job, and also that Biff his son is not ambitious. The dialogue has a clear function in setting up Willy's character, and implying sources of conflict which will erupt later in the play. It characterises Willy as unable to come to terms realistically with life, and his diminishing job prospects, incapable of viewing his son as an independent being, blinded by material values, and supported by a wife who partially, if not completely, colludes with his attitudes. All these difficulties are shown to be more intense as the play progresses, and the plot hinges on the revelation of the sources of Willy's difficulties, and the effects of his failings on others. Such dialogue seems to mimic familiar modes of conversation, but there is a lot more patterning in the dialogue of a play or novel than in real life: it is highly edited even when based on observation. To see how this works, you might want to record a conversation and then edit it as a dialogue: you will see then how much you will need to reshape your material. You will have to cut out irrelevant and repetitive exchanges, and bring character and situation much more to the fore.

Death of a Salesman is largely about Willy's inability to face reality, but its basic dramatic mode is nevertheless realism. However, dialogue in contemporary drama is not necessarily realist. If you read the dialogue below from the play, *A Letter for Queen Victoria*, by American playwright Robert Wilson, you can see how it doesn't develop as we might expect, the sequence is often highly irrational.

Example 6.2: Non-realist dialogue

(CURTAIN UP)

1   (SCREAM SONG)
2   (SCREAM SONG)

1   SHE BROKE HER NECK
2   THAT'S NOT WHAT I DID

1   OH YOU WERE
2   THANK YOU

1   YEAH WELL THAT STUFF
2   WERE THEY WERE THEY A . . . YEAH I KNOW

1 HAVE YOU BEEN HERE BEFORE?
2 NO, THIS IS THE FIRST TIME . . . OK, THANK YOU VERY MUCH

1 HAVE YOU BEEN HERE BEFORE?
2 NO, THIS IS THE FIRST TIME . . . OK, THANK YOU VERY MUCH

1 NO, GRACE, YOU NEVER HAVE TOLD ME ABOUT IT BUT SOMEDAY YOU
   MUST
2 NO, I HAVE NEVER HANDLED A PROBATE CASE, I'VE TOLD YOU THAT

1 THANK YOU GRACE   I MEAN YOU'RE NOT A COOK . . . YOU
2 I MEAN I COME HOME FROM WORK AND EXPECT A MEAL ON THE TABLE
   I MEAN A MAN IS A WOMAN

1 SHE RESENTS IT
2 OH, THAT'S A PROBLEM

1 SO WHAT IF SHE DID
2 YOU MUST NOT TELL MANDA IT HER BIRTHDAY PLEASE DON'T TELL
   ADAM

1 MANDA SHE LOVE A GOOD JOKE YOU KNOW. SHE A LAWYER TOO.
2 LET'S WASH SOME DISHES.

From *A Letter for Queen Victoria* (Wilson 1977, pp. 55–6)

This is not functional dialogue of the type we find in *Death of a Salesman*, and interaction does not occur in the normal way. A response to a particular statement often seems (though to varying degrees) unconnected with the statement that precedes it. For example, 'that's not what I did' could conceivably be a response (if rather an odd one) to 'she broke her neck', but 'thank you' does not seem to follow on at all from 'oh you were'. At other times the response may seem to fit, 'have you been here before/no, this is the first time . . .', but such chunks of the dialogue are repeated over and over again in a mantric way which subverts dramatic conventions. The exchange doesn't establish a particular context and then develop it, as the dialogue of a substantively realist drama such as *Death of a Salesman* does. Rather it hints at a context, and then withdraws from it or slides into another one. So there seems to be a secret, 'no, Grace, you never have told me about it but someday you must', but it is followed by an allusion to a probate case with no tangible connection to the previous remark. Instead the dialogue turns into an apparent domestic dispute about cooking, though a reference to the law reappears later, 'she a lawyer too'. This reminds us of the probate case, and holds out a tentative, but not fully realised possibility of cohesion. The piece has a number of grammatical peculiarities too, which often makes it very difficult to tell whether the speakers are referring to themselves, each other, or other people. For example, although the 'she' in 'she broke her neck' appears to be a third party, speaker 2 seems to respond as if the remark concerns him/herself. The passage also lurches precipitously between registers: alternating between the poetic and the clichéd, the visionary and the banal.

In fact, this dialogue is not trying to reflect normal conversation, reveal character, or further plot. Rather it seems to include thought processes which are not usually revealed in conversation, and allows the irrelevant, the independent and the redundant to enter the exchange. In other words, it keeps elements which are edited out in other plays. Such dialogue might seem to highlight miscommunication, our inability to make our intentions and feelings transparent to others. But I would suggest that it may actually demonstrate the opposite: the possibility of freer forms of communication normally suppressed in social interactions. For it brings to the surface unconscious thoughts, insecurities and non-sequitors which are usually tightly controlled and partially hidden in daily conversation, but nevertheless have a strong bearing on it.

In order to try this, you might want to use the Wilson piece as a model, and/ or rewrite your realist dialogue in a way which subverts transparent revelation of character and situation.

Dialogue may also be non-realist in other ways. For example, in the novel *Time's Arrow or The Nature of the Offence*, by British novelist Martin Amis, the order of events is reversed and so is the dialogue. Example 6.3 is an extract from a doctor–patient dialogue which the narrator calls 'talk-down' (Tod, the doctor, is revealed later in the book to be a Nazi war criminal):

Example 6.3: Dialogue written backwards
Tod: 'It might start a panic.'
Patient: 'Shout *fire*.'
Tod: 'What would you do if you were in a theatre and you saw flames and smoke?'
Patient: 'Sir?'
Tod pauses. 'That's an abnormal response. The normal response would be: "Nobody's perfect, so don't criticize others."'
'They'll break the glass,' says the patient, frowning.
'What is meant by the saying: "People in glass houses shouldn't throw stones"?'

'Uh, seventy-six. Eighty-six.'
'What's ninety-three minus seven?'
'1914–1918.'
'What are the dates of the First World War?'
'Okay,' says the patient, sitting up straight.
'I'm now going to ask you some questions.'
'No.'
'Sleeping okay? Any digestive problems?'
'I'll be eighty-one in January.'
'And you're . . .what?'
'I don't feel myself.'
'Well, what seems to be the problem?'

From *Time's Arrow or The Nature of the Offence* (Amis 2003, p. 35)

The effect of this 'backwards' dialogue is quite strange. The patient seems to be giving more and more bizarre answers to Tod's questions, but they also fit with Tod's assertion 'That's an abnormal response'. In fact, we can read the dialogue both forwards and backwards, though the effect is different in each case. For conversation is not always linear or progressive in the way we might imagine, while cause and effect can sometimes be reversed with meaningful results. If we read the dialogue as it stands, the patient's responses are bizarre, but they are still recuperable as 'real' if we think of the patient as wayward or psychologically disturbed. On the other hand, if we read the dialogue backwards the patient's responses appear relatively normal. The doctor interprets them as abnormal, but we are likely to think they are not, and that the doctor is being overly controlling. Either way, it is the patient's mental faculties which are in doubt, and the power relationship between patient and doctor which is central. Turning dialogue upside down may reverse its political and psychological import, but not necessarily render it as nonsense.

POWERING UP YOUR DIALOGUE

Exercise 3 focuses on the way dialogue can express emotional investments and power relationships. The importance of power relationships in dialogue is very well made by Keith Johnstone in his book *Impro* (1981). *Impro* is about improvisational techniques in acting, and is therefore mainly relevant to the creation of dialogue in performance, but the book contains many insights which are significant for writing in general.

An important aspect of Johnstone's work is his emphasis on the inevitability of power relationships within dialogue. In this respect his work parallels, and gives practical realisation to, the view of cultural theorist Michel Foucault, mentioned in Chapter 5, that power relationships underlie all discourse. Johnstone suggests that any conversation involves each person adopting high or low status with regard to the other person. If somebody says something to you, you have the option of adopting high or low status in relation to it: that is, adopting a superior or inferior position. Working with actors in improvisation, Johnstone's advice is 'to get their status just a *little* above or below their partner's' (1981, p. 44). Johnstone argues that in any given encounter people are always adopting either low or high status. Power games operate continuously, not just between competitors, but also between friends.

Johnstone says:

> My belief . . . is that people have a preferred status; that they like to be low, or high, and that they try to manoeuvre themselves into the preferred positions. A person who plays high status is saying 'Don't come near me, I bite.' Someone who plays low status is saying 'Don't bite me, I'm not worth the trouble.'
>
> (1981, p. 43)

Johnstone also talks about the see-saw principle:

> Walk into a dressing room and say 'I got the part' and everyone will congratulate you, but will feel lowered. Say 'They said I was too old' and people commiserate, but cheer up perceptibly.
>
> (1981, p. 37)

Dialogue, then, can be structured around participants adopting high or low status with regard to each other. But it can also involve a struggle over, or a change of, status. A good example of such dialogue is to be found throughout Edward Albee's *Who's Afraid of Virginia Woolf?*. The play hinges on power struggles between wife Martha and husband George. They both try to dominate and gain advantage over the other, and who is 'winning' continuously oscillates. In the following example Martha taunts George, who then turns the tables by saying he doesn't want to 'bray' like her. But Martha has another card up her sleeve, because she has invited guests without telling him. There is some reversal of stereotypical gender roles here. George is the passive one who is 'tired' and wants to be left alone. Martha is assertive, demanding and aggressive:

Example 6.4: Dialogue as power struggle

GEORGE: I'm tired, dear ... it's late ... and besides ...

MARTHA: I don't know what you're so tired about ... you haven't *done* anything all day; you didn't have any classes, or anything ...

GEORGE: Well, I'm tired ... If your father didn't set up these goddamn Saturday night orgies all the time ...

MARTHA: Well, that's too bad about you, George ...

GEORGE [*grumbling*]: Well, that's how it is, anyway.

MARTHA: You didn't *do* anything; you never *do* anything; you never *mix*. You just sit around and *talk*.

GEORGE: What do you want me to do? Do you want me to act like you? Do you want me to go around all night *braying* at everybody, the way you do?

MARTHA [*braying*]: I DON'T BRAY!

GEORGE [*softly*]: All right ... you don't bray.

MARTHA [*hurt*]: I do not *bray*.

GEORGE: All right. I said you didn't bray.

MARTHA [*pouting*]: Make me a drink.

GEORGE: What?

MARTHA [*still softly*]: I said, make me a drink.

GEORGE [*moving to the portable bar*]: Well, I don't suppose a nightcap'd kill either one of us ...

MARTHA: A nightcap! Are you kidding? We've got guests.

GEORGE [*disbelieving*]: We've got what?

MARTHA: Guests. GUESTS.

GEORGE: GUESTS!

MARTHA: Yes ... guests ... people ... We've got guests coming over.

GEORGE: When?

From *Who's Afraid of Virginia Woolf?* (Albee 1965, p. 13)

For Exercise 3 think of a situation which involves a possible power struggle. Such a situation might be:

- between parent and child
- in the workplace
- between politicians of different persuasions
- between lecturer and student
- between school teacher and pupil
- between a migration officer and a migrant
- between a waiter and a customer
- between members of a rock group or a string quartet.

You may want to make one of the participants adopt low status initially, while the other adopts high status. Bear in mind that the balance of power in any such struggle can easily change, within a few exchanges.

THE RISE AND FALL OF COMMUNICATION

Exercise 4a asks you to create a dialogue which progresses from low levels of communication through to high levels of communication, or vice versa.

Most domestic and global problems are created by ineffective communication, whether deliberate or unconscious. Communication between friends, nations and different cultures, and within families and institutions, is often unsatisfactory, sometimes to a catastrophic extent. War signals the ultimate breakdown of communication: the substitution of weapons for words. With respect to smaller-scale social interactions, communication may be rather one-sided. One participant may dominate the conversation, for example, by pouring out personal revelations without leaving much room for similar confessions from the listener. On the other hand, when two participants are communicating well they are in 'call and response' mode. The dialogue is mutually interactive, genuinely dialogic, so both participants feed ideas to each other. Questions are asked to elicit significant information and increase understanding; answers are given which can then be the source of further questions. In this kind of dialogue there will normally be a progression, because each call will build upon the previous response. An important point here is the accumulative nature of the process, the progression towards mutual understanding. In Charlotte Bronte's *Jane Eyre* the proposal scene between Jane and Rochester starts with limited communication between the characters because both are hiding their true feelings (that they love each other). However, as Jane starts to show her emotions, Rochester is able to reveal his own, and there is a steep rise in understanding (Bronte 1985, pp. 279–85). This results in a consummation of communication as they each realise that they are loved by the other and can talk directly about their feelings. Important here is the way they respond more and more to each other's calls as the scene progresses, and also the high degree of emotional investment they both have in the outcome.

Some playwrights—most notably Harold Pinter—present dialogue as entirely non-communicating. In Pinter's short revue 'Last to Go' (1990), for example, the two participants (a barman and a newspaper seller) do not call and respond, rather they keep repeating each others' words so that the conversation stagnates. Questions are asked, and answers are given, but there is no attempt to elicit or give real information. In fact, as Deirdre

Burton points out, both characters are continually questioning and confirming matters that they both know, that they know they both know, and that the audience knows they know (1980, pp. 10–12). In Pinter's dialogues there tends to be no real movement towards engagement or understanding, though menace may lurk below the surface and suddenly explode. His plays satirise the way we often make conversation for the sake of it, in order to give an appearance of communication when there is not really any. But they also explore the dark, violent results of inadequate communication.

For Exercise 4a, you might want to create a situation between two people who have the potential to communicate, though they may not be able to consistently implement this. Show how high levels of communication dissipate into low levels and vice versa.

Other writers explore ways of communicating which are unusual or unconventional, and this is the focus of Exercise 4b. Unusual communication can highlight the circumscribed nature of most social exchange. Mark Haddon's novel, *The Curious Incident of the Dog in the Night-time*, for example, centres on the consciousness of a highly intelligent but autistic boy called Christopher and his interactions with others. The following is a short extract when Christopher is talking to a neighbour about the murder of the dog Wellington. Christopher is trying to find out who killed him:

Example 6.5: Unconventional communication

So I said, 'Do you know anything about Wellington being killed?'
And she said, 'I heard about it yesterday. Dreadful. Dreadful.'
I said, 'Do you know who killed him?'
And she said, 'No, I don't.'
I replied, 'Somebody must know because the person who killed Wellington knows that they killed Wellington. Unless they were a mad person and didn't know what they were doing. Or unless they had amnesia.'
And she said, 'Well, I suppose you're probably right.'
I said, 'Thank you for helping me with my investigation.'
And she said, 'You're Christopher, aren't you?'
I said, 'Yes, I live at number 36.'
And she said, 'We haven't talked before, have we?'
I said, 'No. I don't like talking to strangers. But I'm doing detective work.'
And she said, 'I see you every day, going to school.'
I didn't reply to this.
And she said, 'It's very nice of you to come and say hello.'
I didn't reply to this either because Mrs Alexander was doing what

is called chatting where people says things to each other which aren't questions and answers and aren't connected.
Then she said, 'Even if it's only because you are doing detective work.'
And I said, 'Thank you,' again.
And I was about to turn and walk away when she said, 'I have a grandson your age.'
I tried to do chatting by saying, 'My age is 15 years and 3 months and 3 days.'
And she said, 'Well, almost your age.'

From *The Curious Incident of the Dog in the Night-time* (Haddon 2003, pp. 50–1)

This is a very good example of dialogue which can occur when someone either cannot, or will not, participate in the accepted conventions for conversation. Christopher does not respond in the 'normal' way to Mrs Alexander's overtures, and does not trot out what might be considered to be suitable replies. For example, his explanations of why someone might not know they had killed Wellington (because they were mad or had amnesia) are beyond what is required by the conversation. He also says things, such as 'I don't like talking to strangers', which are so frank that social etiquette would normally require them to be suppressed. And he is unable to engage in small talk which he calls 'chatting'. Such dialogue points to the ways in which Christopher cannot fulfil the conventional social requirements of conversation. But it also highlights the advantages of his mode of dialoguing. He transmits an honesty and capacity for logical thinking often missing from conversation. In fact, most daily conversation adheres to conventions which limit rather than extend communication, and which can be a barrier to genuine understanding.

Communication in dialogue, however, is not only between participants: there is also the question of how the reader or audience is positioned. In Pinter's plays characters do not really make contact with each other when they speak. In Henry James's novels and stories the characters often seem to understand each other, but it is difficult for us as readers to catch the full significance of the exchange. James uses dialogue as a way of perpetually deferring meaning, of keeping the reader in a state of partial awareness. Such dialogue points to complex situations and emotions which readers cannot fully grasp because they do not have all the information required. Here the game of communication is being played with the reader as much as between the participants.

POLYLOGUING

Although dialogue technically involves two people talking to each other, it may include several people and many different voices. In this case it is called a **polylogue** (see Exercise 5). If you think in terms of several interchanges at different levels of communication, the whole notion of what it means to dialogue can become more and more complex.

Both polylogues and dialogues can be made up of overlapping voices— they do not necessarily have to consist of one person speaking and stopping, and another one speaking and stopping. Also people can dialogue with themselves: a polylogue may be a monologue in which the speaker adopts many different voices.

CHATTING AND CHAT SHOWS

Dialoguing takes a variety of social forms in contemporary society, from a private chat between friends to public debate (see Exercise 6). New technologies have also extended the range of ways we talk to each other. Mobile phones are used for everything from planning social events to terrorist attacks—governments sometimes send out alerts of such attacks based on raised levels of telephone 'chatter'. Chat is now a common social phenomenon from TV chat shows to web-based chat rooms. To extend your notion of dialoguing, create a dialogue or polylogue based on one of the following exchanges:

- a telephone conversation
- an email exchange
- a radio or television interview
- a television chat show
- a talkback radio show
- a political television debate
- a classroom tutorial
- an Internet chat room.

In composing such a dialogue try to capture the social conventions which characterise it: for example, the language used in email and chat-room exchanges is part of a developing code of electronic communication and net etiquette. Try also to draw attention to the power relationships and hidden agendas which often characterise such communications. The chat show interview, for example, may not be so much an even-handed dialogue as a process of manipulation by the interviewer. Likewise, in a political debate, the opinions of both sides may merely reflect the party-line, though their own individual biases may sometimes show through the cracks. Your dialogue might parody such interactions by subverting expectations of how they are normally conducted. For example, you might want to reverse the roles of television interviewer and interviewee so that the interviewee gains the upper hand, or make the political debate descend into an embarrassing litany of personal confession.

DIALOGUING ACROSS GENRES

Dialogue can also appear in less likely contexts, and in genres other than drama or fiction (see Exercise 7). The prose poem, 'The Sound', by American poet Maxine Chernoff, takes the form of a dialogue. Instead of incorporating it into a short story or play, Chernoff uses the decontextualised dialogue form (which focuses on the exchange rather than the characters behind the voices) to humorously depict the need to communicate about a difficult topic:

Example 6.6: The prose poem as a dialogue
—I hate it when we have sex and you make that sound.
—What sound?
—The sound you make when you're about to have orgasm.
—What sound do you mean?
—I can't describe it. It sounds like no other sound you ever make.
—But why do you hate it?
—It scares me.
—Why would it scare you?
—I guess it's because we're at an intimate moment, and you
   make an unfamiliar sound.
—It must be my intimate-moment sound.
—But it doesn't sound intimate. It sounds . . . well . . . brutal.
—I make a brutal sound?
—Yes, I think that's how I'd describe it.
—Make the sound for me.
—I can't.
—Of course you can. You remember it, don't you?
—I'm embarrassed to make it.
—You're not embarrassed to tell me, but you're embarrassed
   to make it?
—Right.
—Just try.

—All right. It's something like 'Yowwwww-oh-woe-woe.'
—And that sounds brutal to you?
—It does.
—It sounds to me like I'm very happy.
—It doesn't sound happy to me.
—What sound would you like me to make?
—I don't have an alternative in mind. I just thought I'd tell you
   that the sound you make, well, it brings me out of the moment.
   Sex ends for me when I hear that sound.
—That's good, isn't it?
—Why is it good?
—Because you know I've had an orgasm when you hear it.
—But what if I want to do something more to you?
—More? We've both finished by then. What more would we do?
—What if I still want to kiss you and you're making that sound?
—Well, I guess you could try and see.
—Should I try now?
—Why do you think I want you to kiss me when you can't
   stand the sound I make at my most vulnerable moment?
—I didn't mean I couldn't stand it. I just meant it's distracting.
—Maybe you should gag me.
—Then you'd make the sound but it would be even worse.
—Why would it be worse?
—It would sound all muffled and sad, like the voice of
   someone locked inside of a trunk.
—So, you'd rather I sound brutal than all muffled and sad?
—I guess so.
—You must really love me then.

'The Sound' (Chernoff 2000)

THE COLLABORATIVE DIALOGUE

So far we have been talking about dialoguing within a text. But now I want
to talk about dialoguing as a way of working: that is, dialoguing in collaboration (see Exercise 8). We tend to think of creative writing as an
individual activity, but very imaginative work can arise out of joint effort.
Collaboration is one of the main practical ways in which we can rebut the
claustrophobic myth of the individual writer, and make our artistic practices less egocentric, more outward looking and more collective.

A collaboration between two writers can happen in many different ways. Two writers can sit together in a room and work together, for example, by alternately writing a line or a section each. But collaboration does not have to depend on the two writers being in the same space, and usually doesn't. Collaborations can take place through email, for example, or could result from chat-room conversations, or MOO encounters over the Internet. Collaboration can be with someone you know very well or a complete stranger. However, when collaboration occurs, it will demand a very high level of response to each other's work.

Collaboration can be very stimulating because your own ideas are constantly being triggered and moulded by the other person. You will frequently find that responding to your collaborator's contribution results in a text which you would not have written otherwise. The other person's interests and style may help you to broaden your horizons and take you into unchartered territory. Another advantage and delight of collaboration is that you have a ready-made audience of one. Knowing that someone will immediately read and respond to your work may motivate you to write faster and better. Merging your writing with that of another person—while retaining an awareness that their work is different from your own—is a fascinating experience.

There are no good or bad ways to collaborate. It may be best to decide on a topic, though this can be quite broad. Nor is it a necessity since ideas and topics may emerge as you write. You may want to write a section each: this is very productive because it gives you a chance to still partly retain your own writing direction while inevitably also losing it. Whatever mode of working you choose you will need to be very flexible in how you respond to the other person's work. You may, for example, at one point in the collaboration extend one of your collaborator's ideas; at another point you might turn a quotation they have introduced into a narrative or poem; at another decide to completely change the topic, and so on.

When you collaborate:

- Do not struggle to maintain your own identity, try to take as much, or more, interest in the other person's writing as in your own.
- Be explorative with the structure of the piece. It can, for example, be in sections and each can be different from the one before and after. Do not feel you must stick to any particular genre: a poem can be followed by a short narrative, and so on.
- Do not feel that you necessarily have to stick to the order in which the collaboration was originally written. Sections written in response to each other might be more effective if prised apart in the final text. On the other hand, sections which were not written consecutively might be placed side by side because they seem to resonate together.

When I collaborated with Anne Brewster we usually wrote a section each, though occasionally one of us would write two or three passages consecutively. We often responded quite directly to each other, and I rarely felt that I would have written a particular piece in the same way if I hadn't been collaborating. Nor do I feel that individual sections completely stand on their own: they seem most effective in the context of the whole text. In the following extract, the first section was initially written by Anne, the second by me. However, we commented on and edited each others' work in ways which merged our endeavours.

Example 6.7
Lost in Thought

Today, at last, I had some time for reading. I sifted through all sorts of bits and pieces, everything from Levinas to de Certeau.

In the mid-afternoon I forced myself to take a break and do the shopping. Driving to the supermarket and wandering among the aisles I didn't feel quite adequate to the task at hand. I wasn't thinking of anything in particular; I was simply suspended, lost in thought.

De Certeau says: *like those birds that lay their eggs only in other species' nests, memory produces in a place that does not belong to it ... It derives its interventionary force from its very capacity to be altered—unmoored, mobile, lacking any fixed position.*

∽

what I know now must change
what I lost then. what you have
never owned you recreate.

<blockquote>the present coughs into the faces of the past
knocks pictures sideways on the wall.</blockquote>

so memory digs up birds have flown away
are laying eggs in foreign beds

From 'ProseThetic Memories' (Brewster & Smith 2002, p. 199)

This example shows how collaboration consists of 'dialoguing' and is an interactive process. As you can see, I have taken up the de Certeau quotation in the first section with the metaphor of the birds, and the sense of movement is also projected in the second stanza through a different series of metaphors. My passage is in a quite different genre and style to Anne's passage, but it is strongly dependent on ideas generated in hers (which in turn 'dialogue' with de Certeau). In this case the order of the sections reflects the sequence in which they were written. However, in many other places we reordered the sections.

Collaboration is an area in which it is sometimes difficult to find good models and examples. Although there were some early surrealist experiments in collaborative writing near the beginning of the twentieth century, and despite the fact that collaboration has grown in popularity, it is still relatively rare amongst writers. However, *Zoo* by John Kinsella and Coral Hull (2000), *Sight* by Lyn Hejinian and Leslie Scalapino (2000), and Frances Presley and Elizabeth James's *Neither the One nor the Other* (1999) are three good examples of the collaborative form.

So far I have only talked about collaborating with writers, but collaboration can also involve work with artists and musicians, where there is the excitement of working across different media. These kinds of collaboration will be addressed as part of Chapters 10 and 11.

CONCLUSION

In this chapter we have seen how dialogue is fundamental to language as social interaction and have explored ways in which it relates to issues of power. We have also seen how dialogue is not genre-specific: it can be part of poems as well as plays and fictions. But dialoguing is a broad concept useful for thinking about writing in general. A challenging text would tend to converse with itself, to open up ambiguities and contradictions in the form of different stances, registers or points of view. You may find dialoguing to be a creative stance which you want to adopt in a more general way, and this may encourage you to write beyond the confines of your own individual point of view. Collaborating with another person may also help to make you more aware of how you can dialogue with yourself.

This chapter relates to the fictional strategies outlined in Chapters 5 and 7, but it has also taken us into the area of performance which will be explored more fully in Chapter 10. And it has prepared us for cross-genre forms (discussed in Chapter 9), in particular fictocriticism, which dialogues between critical and creative work.

REFERENCES

Albee, E. 1965, *Who's Afraid of Virginia Woolf?*, Penguin, London.
Amis, M. 2003, *Time's Arrow or The Nature of the Offence*, Vintage, London. First published in 1991 in Britain by Jonathan Cape.
Barthelme, D. 1987, *Paradise*, Penguin, New York.
Brewster, A. and Smith, H. 2002, 'ProseThetic Memories', *Salt.v16. An International Journal of Poetry and Poetics: Memory Writing*, (ed.) T.-A. White, Salt Publishing, Applecross, Western Australia, pp. 199–211.
Bronte, C. 1985, *Jane Eyre*, Penguin, London. First published in 1847.
Burton, D. 1980, *Dialogue and Discourse: A Sociolinguistic Approach to Modern Drama Dialogue and Naturally Occurring Conversation*, Routledge & Kegan Paul, London.
Chernoff, M. 2000, 'The Sound', *The Prose Poem: An International Journal*, vol. Web Issue 5, http://www.webdelsol.com/tpp/tpp5/tpp5_chernoff.html.
Danaher, G., Schirato, T. and Webb, J. 2000, *Understanding Foucault*, Allen & Unwin, Sydney.
Foreman, R. 1977, 'Pandering to the Masses: A Misrepresentation', *The Theatre of Images*, (ed.) B. Marranca, Drama Book Specialists, New York, pp. 1–36.
Haddon, M. 2003, *The Curious Incident of the Dog in the Night-time*, David Fickling Books, Oxford.
Hejinian, L. and Scalapino, L. 2000, *Sight*, Aerial/Edge, Washington.
Holquist, M.J., (ed.), 1981, *The Dialogic Imagination: Four Essays by M.M. Bakhtin*, (trans.) by Caryl Emerson and Michael Holquist, University of Texas Press, Austin.
Johnstone, K. 1981, *Impro: Improvisation and the Theatre*, Methuen, London and Boston.
Kinsella, J. and Hull, C. 2000, *Zoo*, Paper Bark Press, Sydney.
Miller, A. 1985, *Death of a Salesman*, Penguin, Harmondsworth, Middlesex.
Pinter, H. 1990, 'Last to Go', *Complete Works: Two*, Grove Press, New York, pp. 245–8.
Presley, F. and James, E. 1999, *Neither the One nor the Other*, Form Books, London.
Wilson, R. 1977, 'A Letter For Queen Victoria', *Theatre of Images*, (ed.) B. Marranca, Drama Book Specialists, pp. 37–110.

PART II
Advanced strategies

CHAPTER SEVEN
Postmodern f(r)ictions

This chapter introduces and elucidates the concept of postmodernism, showing how contemporary fictional strategies relate to a broader context of contemporary thinking and culture. We will build on the fictional strategies we learnt in Chapter 5, but in ways which question the norms of narrative structure. We will also address aspects of fiction, such as character, which were not fully addressed in Chapter 5.

The chapter explores the fruitful **frictions** which postmodern fiction creates. There is friction, for example, between sustaining narrative momentum and breaking it up, between projecting character and rethinking it in less realist ways. Such frictions are also cultural: postmodernist fiction sometimes explores versions of history which are in conflict with official accounts or constructs new worlds which exist in a state of tension with our own.

A sense of postmodernist writing as friction is not new and was conceptualised in the volume *Frictions: An Anthology of Fiction by Women* (Gibbs & Tilson 1983) which was very innovative for its time. However, here we re-introduce the idea of frictions as a writing strategy. This chapter invites you to explore these f(r)ictions for yourself both at a formal and thematic level.

exercises

1. Create a postmodern fiction which engages with plot but subverts it. You can create a whole text or simply an outline.

133

2. Create a postmodern character who:
   a) is loosely differentiated (that is, not clearly differentiated from others in the narrative)
   b) has one all-pervasive trait
   c) is non-human.
   Or create:
   d) a character who has been marginalised by society.
3. Create a postmodern fiction which rewrites a historical incident.
4. Create a postmodern fiction which constructs a new world.

WHAT IS POSTMODERNISM?

Postmodernism has been the focus of many conflicting and complementary definitions, but the term is usually applied to certain social and cultural trends since 1945. (Although whether certain trends or cultural artefacts before 1945 can be considered postmodern is also an issue.) Most theories about postmodernism, however, include certain common assumptions, which are also intertwined with the insights of post-structuralist theory. These are:

- There is no single or objective truth, only multiple versions of, or perspectives on, the truth.
- History is discontinuous, and full of gaps and silences. Official histories repress the stories of those who are marginalised through ethnicity, sexuality and disability.
- The subject is not unified, but divided and multiple; we all have many different 'selves'.
- Concepts of space and time have radically changed within postmodern culture, and have become more relative. Time is seen as non-linear and compressed, and there is more awareness of different types of time (social, subjective, scientific). Space is also seen as unbounded, dynamic and socially produced. Globalisation, new information technologies, ease of travel and multinational companies compress distances between spaces.
- Representation is somewhat illusory: language is not a transparent window on the world (even a very 'lifelike' text is a construct of words).
- Postmodern society is increasingly post-industrial and technological: we are becoming an 'information-based' society. Postmodern culture also involves the greater incorporation of technology into artworks.
- Gender and race are social constructions rather than simply biological states. Human beings are caught up in social discourses, and power

relationships: these constrain and dictate their actions, rather than allowing them to act entirely as free individuals.

POSTMODERN FICTIONS

Postmodern novelists have tended to critique the conventions of the traditional realist novel and the assumptions behind it. As broad generalisations from which to work outwards, we could say that postmodern fictions tend to subvert conventional narrative in the following ways:

- They call into question the concept of plot. Postmodern fictions do not necessarily have a plot, or they have plots which do not resolve, or they consist of several plots whose superimposition undermines their resolvability. It is often through the subversion of plot that postmodern fictions play with, and question, the notion of objective truth.
- They subvert the notion of three-dimensional, unified and realistic characters: e.g. characters may be 'types', or may only demonstrate extreme or unlikely behaviours.
- They are not necessarily realist. Rather they use allegory, fantasy and the construction of new worlds, to escape from—or enlarge on—realist writing and the straightjacket of representation. This is a way of opening new psychological and social dimensions.
- They are intertextual, and often involve rewriting, quotation or pastiche (e.g. rewriting of classic texts, myths or fairytales). The author's personality and interests are not omniscient, and texts are partly made of other texts, hence the idea of 'the death of the author' (see Chapter 4).
- They play with space and time. Sometimes they compress events in different times and places so they occur simultaneously. Sometimes they jump disjunctively between different times and places.
- They subvert or expand genre—sometimes through parody. They often employ formal hybridity and variety.
- They suggest there is no one historical truth. We learn of history through narratives which are themselves constructions: these often favour those in power and marginalise others. Postmodern fictions play with the relationship of fact and fiction, and question the objectivity and validity of conventional history.

For more about postmodern fiction, read: *Postmodernist Fiction* (McHale 1989) and *A Poetics of Postmodernism* (Hutcheon 1988).

We will now look at some of the ways in which engaging with postmodernist fictions can impact on how we write.

TO PLOT OR NOT TO PLOT?

The traditional idea of a plot is that it hinges on rising and falling action. According to the Freytag Pyramid (devised in 1863 by critic Gustav Freytag), a plot is deemed to have an exposition, a complication, a climax, a reversal and a catastrophe. Explication and complication make up one side of the triangle, and reversal and catastrophe the other side, with climax at the top (Olsen 1999, p. 89). This can only be a skeleton model since, for example, the climax and catastrophe may be simultaneous, or there may be several climaxes. For the narratologist the definition of plot is somewhat looser: it consists of a sequence of events, causal links, and the arousal of expectations with various alternative outcomes. Stories usually consist of events which open alternatives (known as kernels) and those that 'expand, amplify, maintain or delay' actions (known as catalysts) (Rimmon-Kenan 1983, p. 16).

Many important novels are heavily plot-based. The advantage of a plot is that it drives the action forwards, shapes the material, and holds the attention of the reader: such advantages are not to be underestimated and are the basis for many fine novels. On the other hand, the subordination of material to a strong plotline can have disadvantages. A plot can be a straightjacket, an artificial construction into which everything in the narrative has to be pushed. It may force the writer to make causal links between disparate events, and produce pressure towards closure and the elimination of alternatives. Used too tightly, it can stifle digression, open-endedness, philosophical rumination, symbolic significance and generic variety. It may also result in an unnecessary emphasis towards catastrophic events, rather than significant, small-scale ones.

Postmodern writers have often questioned the significance of plot. They have not totally jettisoned it, nor, even if desired, is it very easy to do so entirely, since any sequence of events can start to acquire some of the features of a plot. However, they have certainly loosed, broadened or subverted it, and their work often creates friction between building up narrative expectations and thwarting them. Many postmodern fictions do not have a plot in the sense of a cataclysmic event to which all events lead, and from which they fall away. A postmodern fiction might instead circle round a particular idea, project the thoughts of a person throughout a short period of time, or focus on a number of minor ups and downs. Some postmodern novelists, such as Paul Auster, strongly retain some aspects of plot while jettisoning others. The plotline may be one that never fully resolves, or consists of competing plotlines, or has several alternative resolutions. Such subversions of plot, while they loosen the storyline, often strengthen the metaphorical and allegorical possibilities of the narrative.

In the novel *The Unconsoled* (Ishiguro 1996), by British-Japanese author Kazuo Ishiguro, the action moves towards a performance by the internationally renowned concert pianist Ryder which never actually happens. Intersecting storylines unfold throughout, and seem to point towards a particular end, but come to rest, not in what does happen, but in what does not. In Paul Auster's 'City of Glass' in *The New York Trilogy* (1988), the central character Quinn assumes a false identity as a detective, Paul Auster. He is employed by Peter Stillman Jnr, and his wife Virginia, to chase Peter Stillman Snr, who Stillman Jnr believes wants to murder him. But the chase eventually dissipates. Stillman Snr disappears, and it is never really clear whether he was a real threat or not. At the very end, the story fades out, the narrator claims not to know anything about Quinn's whereabouts, and Quinn could be alive or dead. A number of possibilities present themselves, but what has occurred is very uncertain. Stillman Snr may have killed Virginia and Peter Stillman, or they may have murdered him. Or the whole scenario may have been made up from the beginning by the Stillmans. No outcome is necessarily more likely than another. In both cases the novels are extremely allegorical and metaphorical.

Broadening the concept of plot does not mean losing interest in structure or shaping the story. In fact, a relatively plotless fiction will probably require a stronger structure to keep the reader's interest alive. There are two main sets of possibilities here, though each has many different manifestations. Firstly, a plot structure can be employed but subverted, so the story may hold our interest by seeming to work towards closure which never actually occurs. Alternatively, other kinds of structure can be substituted for narrative structures (either partly or entirely) while still retaining a story element if desired. The first category of strategies is the focus of the next section, the second category is explored throughout this book and also within Chapter 9.

PLOTTING THE PLOTLESS

In order to subvert a plotline (Exercise 1) we may need to undo some of the normal grids of the plot, for example the causality between events and the resolution of the outcomes. Begin by imagining a situation in which the readers' expectations and interest are raised but never fulfilled:

Example 7.1: Raising but not fulfilling expectations

A father receives a letter from a daughter he has never met who was adopted as a baby. The story seems to pivot on our curiosity about the meeting, and our expectation is that the story will end with the meeting. We think that there may be some unexpected twists in the meeting itself. However, instead the story revolves around reminiscences, and imaginings about the daughter, and the meeting itself never materialises.

This certainly subverts plot expectations but it is still recognisably plot-orientated. However, you could take the whole process one step further:

Example 7.2: Raising non-specific expectations

X receives a letter from Y which alludes to a meeting. But we are never told what the contents of the letter are, or why the meeting is required. X then reminisces about the past, and we are continually guessing about what is in the letter.

In this example plot is still present in the sense of raising expectations. But it becomes much vaguer, and causality is loosened.

Another way in which plot can be subverted is when it is over-determined. In many postmodern novels, events double up, repeat themselves, and reflect back on each other, and there are multiple coincidences as in the following example:

Example 7.3: Over-determined plot (outline)

X discovers the murder of a teacher in the school in which he works. The next day he discovers a murder of another member of staff and then another. All the events happen at the same time, on the same day, in successive weeks, with different murder weapons which nevertheless look alike. He develops an obsessive interest in the victims and tries to trace their lives outside the school. He finds that they all worked simultaneously and secretly in other schools.

As you can see from this, there is an abundance of plot, but to some extent the different elements double up and collapse into each other, and do not retain their individual places in the fictional scheme.

This process can be taken even further by devising a plot in which the same story develops in different ways which conflict with each other:

Example 7.4: Conflicting storylines (outline)

Scenario One: X receives a letter from a previously unknown daughter and decides to meet her. Scenario Two: X receives a letter from someone who claims to be his daughter, he is unsure whether this claim is true, talks to the putative mother, and decides that the girl is not his. Scenario Three: X goes out to look for his adopted daughter, finds her, sees her from a distance in the street, and then decides that he will not meet her after all.

Here we see how there are multiple versions of the plot, but one version seems to call into question the validity of the others. Alternative storylines often make us more aware of psychological and political resonances which would not have been there otherwise. They make us see 'the other side of the story'. They have become quite common in postmodern fiction, for example, in Doctorow's *The Book of Daniel* (1982) and John Fowles's *The French Lieutenant's Woman* (1987). They have also recently infiltrated popular culture in films such as *Run Lola Run* and *Sliding Doors*.

In Robert Coover's postmodern story 'The Elevator' in *Pricksongs and Descants*, one narrator tells us different versions of the story about Martin riding up and down in the elevator (Coover 1989, pp. 100–9). The story is told in the third person, not by Martin himself, so we might initially expect some objectivity. But the ride in the elevator keeps appearing in different forms. On one occasion Martin is the object of derision by people in the elevator who make fun of him, but on another occasion he is locked in an amorous embrace with the operator girl who he fancies. Are we being told the story of what did happen in the elevator on different occasions; what could happen, or what Martin fantasised about; or is it a mixture? There is no one version which seems to be the 'real' one. There are so many incompatible versions of the story that we lose any sense of where the truth lies. It makes us think about how subjective reality is, and how stories are always fictions: constructs, rather than facts. This story, and Coover's 'The Babysitter' (1989) also in *Pricksongs and Descants*, are excellent models for writing in this way. I urge you to read them and use them for that purpose.

CHARACTER REBORN, POSTMODERN IDENTITIES

The traditional view of characters is that they should be 'well-rounded': that is, behave like flesh-and-blood human beings. This view is based on **mimesis:** the idea that literature is an imitation of life, and that characters should be as lifelike as possible. In realist novels, authors generally suggest how characters come to be the people they are, and give us some access to their inner lives: there are implied causes and effects, even though these may be subtle, complex and incomplete. A character is seen as an individual who is clearly differentiated from others: even when that character has conflicts they are contained within a recognisable and knowable personality.

Narratologists, on the other hand, remind us that characters are constructs, even if they often seem to be like real people. They refer to characters as **actants**, or **existents**, neutralising the human element. Narratologists see characters as agents in the story, as much as people in their own right: characters make things happen and set the story in motion. Characters for narratologists are made up of different **traits**. The more complex the depiction and inter-relationship of these traits, the more psychological depth the character will seem to have.

Post-structuralist and postmodern theories have transformed even further the way we think about character (see Exercise 2). Traditional ideas of character are implicitly based on notions of a unified self that both postmodern theory and psychoanalytic theory tend to explode. As we have seen, postmodern theory sees the subject not as unified, but as split or splintered. In postmodern fictions a splintered subjectivity is everywhere to be seen. In fact in literary studies, the concept of character has been largely replaced by the notion of postmodern identity, which centres on a fluid and multiple subjectivity. It plays down individuality, since we are all caught up in social discourses of gender, ethnicity and economics. Postmodern conceptions of subjectivity stress *difference.* This has been paralleled in postmodern fictions by a more open approach to character. Again this approach is frictional: creating a tension between realist and less realist conceptions of character.

The reaction against the well-developed character has taken a number of different forms, some of which will be explored in the following section.

Loosely differentiated characters

In postmodern fictions a character may be looser, less consistent and more incomplete than a realist character. In addition, characters are not always clearly differentiated in the narrative, since they may be transformations of each other (see Exercise 2a). This projects, on the one hand, the plurality of identity, and on the other, how people's personalities, roles, backgrounds, experiences and ways of viewing the world overlap. At a more general level it suggests that events, ideas and identities are always many-faceted and interconnected.

In Paul Auster's 'City of Glass' (1988), for example, the central character, Quinn, is constantly identifying with, and even being absorbed into, other characters. He has a pen name, William Wilson, and identifies with one of the characters in his novel, Max Work. At the beginning of the story Quinn takes on the identity of Paul Auster, a private detective whose name shadows that of the author. But Quinn can also be identified with Peter Stillman Snr and Peter Stillman Jnr: the people he is working for and investigating (while his own dead son is also called Peter). Through these kinds of doublings, 'City of Glass' plays with a lack of differentiation between authors, readers, writers and characters.

In Kazuo Ishiguro's *The Unconsoled* (1996) there is also a merging of characters. Some of the characters appear first in one role and then another. For example, Gustav, the hotel porter, also seems to be the father-in-law of Ryder the central character. The characters exist in their own right, but are also projections of Ryder's consciousness and memory: they deliver lengthy monologues distinct from most day-to-day conversational interactions. Characters and events in the novel double up: for example, the young pianist Stephan's anxieties about his parents' attitude towards him seem to mirror Ryder's own. Again this suggests character identification and overlap rather than differentiation.

In order to create a set of loosely differentiated characters, devise a character whose identity transforms into two other characters. You could, for example, try to create a trio of characters who are reader, author, character; daughter, mother, grandmother; or murderer, victim, detective. If you like, you can make their names line up with each other (perhaps they all have names which begin with the same letter and seem related). My text 'Secret Places' which can found in Chapter 12 (Figure 12.1, p. 272), is an example of such an approach. Here the 'characters' have the names Cass, Cathy and Casuarina, and can be conceived of as both the same and different people. In another piece called 'Viola's Quilt', (Smith 2000b, pp. 14–17), I used the names Viola, Violet and Varvara for a similar triumvirate.

You can make the characters seem similar through physical or mental characteristics, through their professions or interests, or through their habits. They might be earlier or later versions of the same person, projected into different geographical spaces or historical eras. Whichever way you approach this, you will need to find a way of linking them through similarities as well as differences. In each case you will want to create some ambiguity about whether this is a similar or a different person, the degree of ambiguity (small or large) is up to you.

You can undertake Exercise 2a on a very simple level initially, and then build it up in a more complex way. You can introduce larger numbers of characters if you wish. Or lack of differentiation can be extended to objects and events as well as characters, so that it infiltrates all aspects of the narrative.

One-trait characters

A postmodern character may be one-dimensional, and characterised by a particular, all-pervasive trait, rather than (like the rounded character) a mixture of traits (see Exercise 2b). In the context of realist fiction such characters have sometimes been regarded as 'flat', lacking in the mixture of behavioural traits which brings the character to life. The trait may give us a particular insight into certain types of obsessive behaviour, but it does not necessarily give us a balanced picture of that person. Such pieces usually have satirical intent, and highlight not only that character's idiosyncracies, but flaws in the make-up of contemporary society. The character does not have to be lifelike, and in general there is a trend away from straight realism. The anorexic woman I created as a person-in-action in Chapter 2 was a one-trait character, because all we learnt about her was her relationship to food.

Characters of this type are sometimes known as 'surface' characters. This term is used to distinguish them from 'in depth', three-dimensional depictions of characters in realist fiction. The anti-hero of the novel *American Psycho*, by American writer Bret Easton Ellis, is in some respects a surface character, because he is completely obsessed with himself and the impression he is presenting. The ultimate end-product of a consumer society, everything in his life is subservient to commodification, image and appearance. Rather than telling us how he feels, or observing the world around him, he talks about the designer labels he is wearing:

Example 7.5
There's a black-tie party at the Puck Building tonight for a new brand of computerized professional rowing machine, and after playing squash with Frederick Dibble I have drinks at Harry's with Jamie Conway, Kevin Wynn and Jason Gladwin, and we hop into the limousine Kevin rented for the night and take it uptown. I'm wearing a wing-collar jacquard waistcoat by Kilgour, French & Stanbury from Barney's, a silk bow tie from Saks, patent-leather slip-ons by Baker-Benjes, antique diamond studs from Kentshire Galleries and a gray wool silk-lined coat with drop sleeves and a button-down collar by Luciano Soprani. An ostrich wallet from Bosca carries four hundred dollars cash in the back pocket of my black wool trousers. Instead of my Rolex I'm wearing a fourteen-karat gold watch from H. Stern.

From *American Psycho* (Ellis 1991, p. 126)

To create a surface character, write a short piece which focuses on a particular trait (Exercise 2b). That person might be predominantly indecisive, greedy or optimistic. To allow yourself to gain maximum benefit from the exercise, do not allow your piece to stray into a well-rounded characterisation. You will see how this will open up a different set of opportunities from realist fiction in allowing you to focus sharply, and in detail, on a particular type of behaviour, and to highlight the obsessions, blindspots, energies and neuroses which are a familiar part of contemporary society.

Non-human characters

Postmodern fictions are sometimes based on characters who are not fully human (Exercise 2c), such as the half-goat, half-man at the centre of John Barth's *Giles Goat-Boy or, The Revised New Syllabus* (1987). Other examples of the animal point of view would be that of the stowaway woodworm in Julian Barnes's *A History of the World in 10½ Chapters* (1990), and the dinosaur in Calvino's *Cosmi-Comics* (1993, pp. 97–112). Such non-human characters project a different perspective on human behaviour and history, one which sees it in a conceptually defamiliarised (and sometimes satirical) light. The animal point of view is often used to critique the hierarchy the human world imposes, and the way we place animals at the bottom of it by highlighting the blindness and prejudice of anthropocentricity.

In order to meet this challenge, write a piece (Exercise 3c) from the point of view of an object or animal. What does this say about the merits and limits of a human way of viewing the world?

Marginalised characters

Postmodern novels often concentrate on characters who are at the periphery of society, or have been marginalised because of their gender, sexuality, ethnicity, class, age or physical disability. A good example of this is Sethe in *Beloved* (Morrison 1988) who has been the victim of slavery: she symbolises the whole American predicament of silence and suffering surrounding slavery. Concentrating on such characters is a way of reacting against the comfortable, white, middle-class world which has preoccupied some fiction writers.

The question of point of view here is hazardous. *Beloved* is written by an African-American, Toni Morrison, but it would raise a plethora of different issues about cultural identification, and the right to speak for others, if it were not. In a sense, fiction writers have always projected into situations, perspectives and cultural backgrounds that were not their own. But there are political sensitivities surrounding this, and the degree to which anyone from one social or ethnic background has the right to adopt the perspective of a person from another. It is important to remember that however strong your fictional writing, you can never totally escape from your own cultural experience and its bias. You are always implicated in your own cultural context: if you are a westerner trying to write from a non-western perspective, it may be impossible for you to totally bridge the gap.

In order to confront this you need, first and foremost, to be aware of the political issues involved. If you decide to cross cultural barriers, the armory of technical equipment you have acquired while you have been working with this book should be of assistance. It should help you achieve the right degree of proximity and distance in relation to your material. For example, you may need to project a marginalised character through the eyes of someone who is privileged in that society; rather than assuming that you can, without any problem, assume that marginalised person's perspective.

For Exercise 2d, create a character who has been largely shunned or marginalised by society. Your person might be a poor person, a prisoner, a refugee, a disabled person or a woman. You will need to conceive of this character within their own cultural background, and this may require detailed research.

F(R)ICTIONAL HISTORIES

Rewriting the past

Another important trend in postmodern fiction has been rethinking the representation of the past. Postmodern fictions have often revamped history, but in ways which subvert official accounts. These fictions are what Linda Hutcheon (1988) calls 'historiographic metafiction'. They tend to rub together fact and fiction: their object is not only to research the past, and then imaginatively reinvent it, but also to question the notion of historical truth. Such fictions often suggest that historical events can be viewed in very different ways from the official versions of them. They penetrate the vested interests at the origin of historical accounts, and show how they were designed to suit those who were in political power at the time. They create friction between the history we have been told, and the history which might have been.

Postmodern fictions sometimes rewrite history from the perspective of a person whose point of view has been suppressed in the official documentation of the event. A rewriting may give voice to someone who has been silenced or excluded because, for example, they are part of an ethnic minority, female or disabled. There have been many postcolonial and feminist rewritings of history of this type.

As already mentioned, the fallibility of historical truth is also a central issue in postmodern/post-structuralist theories. The works of de Certeau, Hayden White, Foucault and others emphasise that history is discontinuous, non-linear and multilayered. However, historical accounts tend to homogenise history into a unified and official version which pretends to the status of fact, and suppresses events which might perturb the status quo.

The novel *Libra* (DeLillo 1989) is a rewriting of the assassination of US President John F. Kennedy in 1963. The death of JFK is, in some respects, a special case. It is one of the most well-known events in media history: most people who read the book will have seen the media replays, and may have their own personal theories about what actually happened. There have also always been alternative theories about the assassination which have competed with the official version of Lee Harvey Oswald as a lone assassin and an isolated madman in search of celebrity status. However, DeLillo's rewrite is an imaginative reconstruction of the events that led to the killing, suggesting that Oswald was manipulated by both left- and right-wing forces, and pro and anti-Castro factions. These forces played on his delusions of grandeur, his socialist ideals, and his hope that the killing would lead to a better life for him in Cuba. The book psychologises Oswald, revealing both his sympathetic and darker sides, humanising but not glorifying him. Oswald is shown to be a product of a capitalist, imperialist society which ignores its poor and mercilessly punishes non-conformists. DeLillo steers a convincing 'frictional' course between the official version of events, and some of the more extreme conspiracy theories that surrounded it.

In British writer Julian Barnes's *A History of the World in 10½ Chapters* (1990), the first chapter rewrites the story of Noah's flood from the point of view of a woodworm who was a stowaway on the boat (though the worm's identity is not revealed until the last page). It exposes the story of the ark as a myth built up to bolster the reputations of both God and Noah, and disputes the bible's claims on truth and morality. This rewrite is highly politicised: power struggles abide between Noah and the animals. Noah himself is shown to be extremely exploitative, an unprepossessing bully. According to the woodworm, he is the dictator of a repressive, undemocratic regime: in the ark there were 'punishments and isolation cells'. But God is also shown to be extremely divisive, since there were much less favourable conditions for those animals categorised as 'unclean' rather than 'clean'. The woodworm's point of view inverts many socially accepted ethical hierarchies: he sees animals as superior to humans. For him the animal kingdom, unlike the human kingdom, is built on ideals of equality and decency. Humans are treacherous towards animals, and continually use them as scapegoats.

Like many rewrites, the story superimposes a contemporary perspective on a historical scenario: the woodworm refers to smear campaigns and isolation cells. It brings aspects of the story up to date, while retaining some vestiges of a historical setting.

Rewriting a historical event

To create a postmodern fiction which rewrites a historical incident (Exercise 3), you need to decide with which period of history you want to engage. The effect of rewriting an event in living memory will be distinct from revisiting one from a previous era. The main difference will be that most recent events have been recorded by—and filtered through—the media, inevitably in a biased way.

You may need to research the period you are writing about. There is a range of materials, such as academic articles on the period, newspapers articles, biographies, and library and museum archives, which you can use as the basis for this. However, the purpose behind rewriting will not be that you faithfully replicate the facts, but that you imaginatively interact with them. It is very easy to become so immersed in historical research that the writing becomes wooden and bogged down in data. One way of avoiding this is to use historical information as a resource, but only refer to it intermittently while you are writing. Or use the material as a solid base, but then make sure you transform it effectively.

There are a number of strategies you can use for rewriting a historical episode:

- Rewrite a well-known historical event from the perspective of someone who is on the margin of that event. This approach gives you the opportunity to bring out elements of the story suppressed in the official historical accounts of it.
- Choose a historical period or incident about which very little is known, and use it as the basis for a creative text. The advantage here is that you have a lot of imaginative flexibility in the way you portray the scenario.
- Take a contemporary figure (such as a politician who is in power at the moment), or a set of contemporary figures, and place them in a completely different historical context where they would have to face new difficulties. There will be room here for satire and humour.
- Portray a historical event through conflicting versions of that event. You may wish to use different genres and modes of reporting, such as newspaper reports and letters. Alternatively, or in addition, filter different versions of the story through a number of narrators and focalisations.
- Create a text which is based on the history of an imagined region. You might want to produce an overlapping of real and unreal histories as Salman Rushdie does in his novel *Shame* (1995) or Graham Swift in *Waterland* (1992).
- Choose a recent event which has been shown repeatedly on the TV. Create a version which challenges the media rendition(s) of it.
- Create a scenario which allows you to question the way we record and

hand down historical accounts. For example, imagine a museum or library in which all the alternative histories and memories of the past are hidden. Write about the experience of entering and spending time in this museum.

F(R)ICTION AS FANTASY

Making new worlds

Postmodernist novels have often portrayed 'other worlds' which do not exist in reality. These worlds are in a f(r)ictional relationship to our own: they arise partly out of our criticisms of, and hopes for, the world we live in. Exercise 4 asks you to create a postmodern fiction which constructs a new world.

Brian McHale, in his book *Postmodernist Fiction*, makes a very interesting distinction between modernist and postmodernist writing (1989, p. 9). He argues that modernist fiction is characterised by an **epistemological** dominant (that is, problems of knowing), while postmodernist fiction is characterised by an **ontological** dominant (problems of being). Modernist fictions, then, are characterised by problems of knowing the world. They raise questions such as:

> How can I interpret this world of which I am a part? And what am I in it? . . . What is there to be known?; Who knows it?; How do they know it, and with what degree of certainty?; How is knowledge transmitted from one knower to another, and with what degree of reliability?; How does the object of knowledge change as it passes from knower to knower?; What are the limits of the knowable?
>
> (1989, p. 9)

But postmodernist writing, McHale points out, raise problems such as:

> What is a world?; What kinds of world are there, how are they constituted, and how do they differ?; What happens when different kinds of world are placed in confrontation, or when boundaries between worlds are violated?; What is the mode of existence of a text, and what is the mode of existence of the world (or worlds) it projects?; How is a projected world structured?
>
> (1989, p. 10)

Because postmodernist fiction has been so preoccupied with this idea of what constitutes the world, it has also often constructed new or alternate worlds. McHale points out that science fiction, like postmodernist fiction, is governed by the ontological dominant. McHale suggests that science fiction has a special relation to postmodernism, it is what he calls postmodernism's 'low art' double, its 'sister-genre in the same sense that the popular detective thriller is modernist fiction's sister-genre' (1989, p. 59). However, the creation of another world can take a lot of forms other than science fiction. There are many different types of world that you might create:

- a world in the future
- a world on another planet
- our world after a major change such as a nuclear war
- our world as it might have been if history had been different
- a world after death
- a utopia or dystopia
- a mixture of some of the above.

You might ask, what is the purpose of constructing another world when there is so much to say about this one? First, conceiving another world can be a way of commenting on the actual world we live in. In other words, it can produce social criticism about our world, it can have a satirical edge, and in consequence it can be highly political. Creating new worlds defamiliarises our own, making us see it afresh. Consequently, it can be a way of generating new ideas about our world, and how it could be constructed in an entirely different way, and with different values.

Second, creating another world can also be a way of exploring the unconscious, so that the new world consists of a hidden psychological reality in which forbidden things happen, or in which unrelated events are brought together. In this way it can be a surreal, or Freudian, landscape: one which reflects inner realities that are normally repressed.

Finally, some authors use the creation of a new world to talk about, and question, metaphysical beliefs. In other words they use it as a way of illuminating philosophical problems about the nature and purpose of existence. So to create another world is to pose the question of what the purpose of our own existence is.

Building your world

A number of issues about the physical construction of the world will need to be addressed:

- *Is the world going to be very close in time to our world or very distant from it?* Will it be in the future, the near future or the far future? I usually find pieces of this type more interesting when they are further removed from our world. But if you want to make the piece a critique of our society, it can be beneficial to forge a more explicit link between the world you are creating and the one we live in. Writers, in order to create new worlds, often draw on elements of traditional or past societies. American novelist Ursula LeGuin does this in *The Left Hand of Darkness* (1981). The world on the planet Winter, for example, has some quite medieval aspects to it: the merchants and processions, the royal court and the dress have medieval resonances. But there are also motor cars on the planet, so there is a time warp, a mixture of past, present and future.

- *Is your world going to have the same physical composition as our world?* Is the world going to be inhabited by human beings who need a supply of oxygen and have cells, blood and bones as we do? If the world is to be our world in the future, it will probably be similar in physical composition to our own, but if it is on another planet it may be radically different. For example, in LeGuin's novel, the beings she describes are androgynous, and they only engage in sexual activities at certain times in their cycles, a bit like animals who are in heat. Also, the conditions these people exist in are unlike our own—they live on a planet called Winter which is extremely cold all the year round, and their bodies are physically adapted to this climate.

Other physical laws we take for granted might be different in your new world: for example there might be a completely different concept of time. Perhaps time might move backwards: a concept discussed by physicist Stephen Hawking in his book *A Brief History of Time* (1988). Alternatively, you might ask yourself the question, what would be the consequence if people had more than five senses, or if people came back from the dead, or if there was no death?

If we are projecting into a future world, the impact of technology would be massive. You might want to consider some of the technological breakthroughs which could occur in the future, for example, in terms of transport, housing, reproduction or education. The novel *Neuromancer* by William Gibson (1984) creates a future world in the grip of technology: it was Gibson who invented the term cyberspace, and who spawned the genre of writing known as 'cyberpunk'. You need to weigh up the benefits and downsides of technology, if you are to construct a digitised world of the future. And you also might want to consider a post-technological society in which we return to simpler forms of communication.

Social organisation

Technology is, of course, related not only to physical organisation, but also to social organisation, which is one of the most stimulating aspects of considering a new world. Aspects of this you might think about could be:

- *Will there be a religion, or an activity, or a set of beliefs, approximating to a religion?* Almost every society originally had a religious base. Human societies have felt a need for religion as a way of organising their spiritual needs in a formalised way, but religions have also led to wars, conflict and repression. Religion is losing its centrality in contemporary western society, and many people seek transcendence through alternatives such as drugs or art. Will your world have a religion, an anti-religion or a substitute religion?

- *What will be the political and economic organisation?* The form of political organisation will determine the power structures in your world, which may be democratic, totalitarian or somewhere in between. You may want to consider economic alternatives to capitalism (or its most dire consequences), and also matters such as censorship, the legal system and the role of the media.

- *How will gender roles be organised?* There is the obvious issue here of career paths and domestic duties taken up by men and women, and the way that gender stereotypes might be inverted. But you might also want to consider the forms that sexuality will take, and what is considered socially acceptable. Will your society be organised into groups such as families, or into other forms of grouping? Will it invert heterosexual norms, or will there be more than two genders?

- *What will be the ethical basis of the society?* Ethics are largely socially constructed; what is acceptable in one society or era may not be in another. In medieval Britain a woman could be hanged for adultery, while the massacre and colonisation of indigenous people was considered acceptable by the majority of people all over the world in the eighteenth century. In his film, *The Ballad of Narayama* (1983), Japanese director Shohei Imamura envisages a completely different ethical basis to society from the one he and his audience are used to. In this poverty-stricken society, old people are taken up a mountain when they are 70 and left there to die, thereby leaving more provisions for the needy: this is considered honourable behaviour, whereas prolonging the life of parents and protecting them from death is considered dishonourable. Technological developments, such as genetic engineering, also raise new ethical issues for the future.

Language

When you construct a new world, language is a fundamental issue. Another world would not be likely to speak any of the same languages that we speak in this one, various though those languages are. If you write the whole text in a completely new language, it may be problematic because nobody will understand it. But you can invent some new words, and it may be necessary to do this anyway to allude to concepts which only exist in this new world. Alternatively, a small number of passages may be written in a new language, allowing most of the narrative to occur in standard language.

Some of the ways in which you might form a new language are:

- *Make up new words to create or allude to new concepts.* In *The Left Hand of Darkness*, Ursula LeGuin (1981) constructs the word 'shifgrethor' for a concept which is very important on the planet Winter and seems to be closely related to the idea of honour. Similarly, the novel *The Wanderground* (Gearhart 1979) uses new words, such as 'listenspread', to describe objects which do not exist in our world (the listenspread is a device for communicating).
- *Use words from different or early forms of English or from other languages.* *Riddley Walker* is set in a post-nuclear holocaust England which has regressed to the iron age. British novelist, Russell Hoban, partly uses words and spellings which suggest England's Anglo-Saxon heritage, and have become lost from the language. But he also constructs words which create a rich sense of a bygone language and era. The language is a mix of the oral and written: sometimes words are spelt the way they sound. Here is a sample:

Example 7.6
On my naming day when I come 12 I gone front spear and kilt a wyld boar he parbly ben the las wyld pig on the Bundel Downs any how there hadnt ben none for a long time befor him nor I aint looking to see non agen. He dint make the groun shake nor nothing like that when he come on to my spear he wernt all that big plus he lookit poorly. He done the reqwyrt he ternt and stood and clattert his teef and made his rush and there we wer then. Him on I end of the spear kicking his life out and me on the other end watching him dy. I said, 'Your tern now my tern later.' The other spears gone in then and he wer dead and the steam coming up off him in the rain and we all yelt, 'Offert!'

From *Riddley Walker* (Hoban 1982, p. 1)

You can create a futuristic language by:

- creating a language which is a hybrid of different languages and varying kinds of language use
- adding a prefix or a suffix to a pre-existent word
- slightly changing pre-existent words or putting them to a different usage.

In fact, this is happening all the time in language use: the rise of computerisation, for example, has produced considerable linguistic change. Look at the way we talk about *accessing* files—it's a new usage which has arisen with the widespread impact of computers.

Other ways of making up your own language can be found in Chapter 8.

Topography and location

You might want to think about the topography of this new world, its layout and its geography. Does it have roads or routes, volcanoes, craters, buildings and so on? How would you map it? It may help to build up a sense of how things look, smell, feel and sound in the world.

How detailed your descriptions of the place are, and what form they take, will depend on your objectives. You may want to create a concrete impression of a place, or alternatively construct a more dreamlike atmosphere for it. Or you may want to mediate between the two possibilities as the Italian writer Italo Calvino does. In his *Invisible Cities*, locations are created which are allegories for desire and memory.

The section 'Cities and Memories' is about a fictitious place called Isidora:

Example 7.7

When a man rides a long time through the wild regions he feels the desire for a city. Finally he comes to Isidora, a city where the buildings have spiral staircases encrusted with spiral seashells, where perfect telescopes and violins are made, where the foreigner hesitating between two women always encounters a third, where cockfights degenerate into bloody brawls among the bettors. He was thinking of all these things when he desired a city. Isidora, therefore, is the city of his dreams: with one difference. The dreamed-of city contained him as a young man; he arrives at Isidora in his old age. In the square there is the wall where the old men sit and watch the young go by; he is seated in a row with them. Desires are already memories.

From *Invisible Cities* (Calvino 1978, p. 8)

Isidora is not a 'real' place: it is a city which is an allegory for desire. It suggests that fulfilment lags behind desire itself. The descriptions of the staircases, telescopes and violins are visual and sensory, but do not give us an integrated, detailed or normalised impression of a place. The description therefore has a double effect: it seems both a physical reality, and also 'the city of his dreams'.

Narration and focalisation

An important aspect of how this new world is projected will be determined by narration and focalisation. Obviously you can use a more distant heterodiegetic narrator. But it can also be fruitful to make the narrator a person who is part of that world, and therefore has a perspective moulded by it. In fact, a defamiliarising exercise in point of view is when a person from one world looks at another through his or her own eyes. A good example of this is the poem 'A Martian Sends a Postcard Home' by British poet Craig Raine (1982, p. 169), where a Martian views our world through assumptions conceived in his own.

Techniques and triggers

By now you will probably have acquired numerous ideas for constructing a new world. However, if ideas don't easily come to you on this topic, you might like to use a few triggers. Even if you have plenty of ideas, you may be able, by using these techniques, to arrive at a more unusual conception. Most writers who construct a new world are negotiating some of these techniques, though perhaps quite unconsciously.

The techniques are:

- **Inversion**—One way of creating a new world is inverting what goes on in this one. So try inverting gender roles or ethical values (so that, for example, it is considered morally good to steal).
- **Extension**—Take an object or concept and see how much you can extend it. Begin with an aeroplane and then try to imagine other means of transport that could be developed, for example, supersonic airlines that could fly from Sydney to London in half an hour, or interplanetary travel machines, and so on.
- **Juxtaposition and recombination**—Juxtapose ideas, or events, which would be unexpected or even impossible in reality. For example, at the moment, in our world, power is largely associated with money and position, but perhaps in another world power could be associated with understanding of the environment. Try putting words/concepts on a piece of paper:
  blood   power   money   sex   writing   mathematics
  illness   study   light   darkness   travel
  Now try combining these words in unexpected ways. Imagine if sexual activity took the form of mixing blood, or illness was caused by study, or power was acquired through illness. It's a matter of developing novel ways of thinking about the physical and social world we live in.

CONCLUSION

Postmodernist fictional strategies question our comfortable assumptions about the past and contemporary society. They employ f(r)ictional techniques to suggest alternative narratives about the world and its histories. Building on the narrative strategies of Chapter 5, we have devised ways of rethinking character and plot. We have also explored the way in which postmodern strategies help us to reinvent our past and construct other worlds. This chapter has mainly focused on longer fictions, which work with narrative even if they partly dismantle it. Chapter 9 will explore subversions of genres which are shorter, but are also postmodern fictions.

REFERENCES

Auster, P. 1988, 'City of Glass', *The New York Trilogy*, Faber & Faber, London, pp. 3–132.

Barnes, J. 1990, *A History of the World in 10½ Chapters*, Picador, Oxford.

Barth, J. 1987, *Giles Goat-Boy or, The Revised New Syllabus*, Doubleday, New York.

Calvino, I. 1978, *Invisible Cities*, Harcourt Brace & Company, New York and London.

—— 1993, *Cosmi-Comics*, Picador, London.

Coover, R. 1989, 'The Elevator', *Pricksongs and Descants*, Minerva, London.

DeLillo, D. 1989, *Libra*, Penguin, New York and London.

Doctorow, E. 1982, *The Book of Daniel*, Picador, London.

Ellis, B.E. 1991, *American Psycho*, Picador, London.

Fowles, J. 1987, *The French Lieutenant's Woman*, Pan, London. First published in 1969 in Great Britain by Jonathan Cape.

Gearhart, S.M. 1979, *The Wanderground: Stories of the Hill Women*, Persephone Press, Watertown, Massachusetts.

Gibbs, A. and Tilson, A. (eds), 1983, *Frictions: An Anthology of Fiction by Women*, 2nd edn, Sybylla Cooperative Press and Publications, Melbourne.

Gibson, W. 1984, *Neuromancer*, Ace Books, New York.

Hawking, S.W. 1988, *A Brief History of Time: From the Big Bang to Black Holes*, Bantam Press, London.

Hoban, R. 1982, *Riddley Walker*, Picador, London. First published in 1980 by Jonathan Cape.

Hutcheon, L. 1988, *A Poetics of Postmodernism: History, Theory, Fiction*, Routledge, London.

Imamura, S. 1983, *The Ballad of Narayama*, Home Vision.

Ishiguro, K. 1996, *The Unconsoled*, Faber & Faber, London.

LeGuin, U. 1981, *The Left Hand of Darkness*, Futura, London. First published in 1969 in Great Britain by Macdonald and Co.

McHale, B. 1989, *Postmodernist Fiction*, Routledge, London and New York.

Morrison, T. 1988, *Beloved*, Picador, London.

Olsen, L. 1999, *Rebel Yell*, 2nd edn, Cambrian Publications, San Jose, California.

Raine, C. 1982, 'A Martian Sends a Postcard Home', *The Penguin Book of Contemporary British Poetry*, (eds), B. Morrison and A. Motion, Penguin, Harmondsworth, Middlesex.

Rimmon-Kenan, S. 1983, *Narrative Fiction: Contemporary Poetics*, Methuen, London and New York.

Rushdie, S. 1995, *Shame*, Vintage, London. First published in 1983 in Great Britain by Jonathan Cape.

Smith, H. 2000a, *Hyperscapes in the Poetry of Frank O'Hara: Difference, Homosexuality, Topography*, Liverpool University Press, Liverpool.

—— 2000b, 'Viola's Quilt', *Keys Round Her Tongue: Short Prose, Poems and Performance Texts*, Soma Publications, Sydney.

Swift, G. 1992, *Waterland*, Picador, London. Revised edn.

CHAPTER EIGHT
Postmodern poetry, avant-garde poetics

In this chapter we broaden some of the possibilities for writing poetry. In the first half we look at strategies for writing a contemporary or postmodern lyric. Traditionally the lyric was a short poem which expressed the writer's emotions, for example, about love or death. The lyric had musical qualities—usually rhythm and rhyme—and it would also in general address serious topics. As we will see the postmodern lyric may still be a short poem which addresses some of these topics, but it inverts many of the characteristics of the traditional lyric. The term postmodern lyric is therefore somewhat tongue-in-cheek, since such a poem overturns many of the assumptions on which the lyric was historically grounded.

In the second half we will pursue some of the possibilities for experimenting with different aspects of language, such as extending or resisting metaphor; games and systems; discontinuity; lexical experimentation; the poem as visual object; and prose poetry and 'the new sentence'. We also look briefly at the avant-garde poetics which accompany these strategies: that is, ideas and theories about formal experimentation in poetry and the political impact this generates.

These two parts of the chapter are in fact interconnected: the poems by Denise Riley and Emma Lew are good examples of postmodern lyrics which also employ some aspects of linguistic experimentation (particularly discontinuity).

exercises

1. Write a series of postmodern lyrics which engage with each of the following:
   a) the split self
   b) the subversion of voice
   c) political dissidence
   d) contemporaneous imagery or a taboo subject.
   Alternatively:
   e) write one postmodern lyric which engages with more than one of the above.
2. Create a series of linguistically experimental poems which engage with each of the following:
   a) the extension of metaphor
   b) homonyms and other games and systems
   c) syntax and grammar
   d) discontinuity
   e) lexical experimentation
   f) the poem as visual object
   g) prose poetry and 'the new sentence'.
   Alternatively:
   h) write one poem which experiments with more than one of the above.

THE POSTMODERN LYRIC

The split self

Writing a postmodern lyric does not mean giving up everything we know about the history of the lyric, but it does mean making it contemporary. Creating a contemporary lyric, therefore, almost inevitably means engaging with postmodern ideas of subjectivity. Whereas the traditional lyric was based on the concept of direct personal expression, postmodern theory and practice have alerted us to the problem that the self can never directly express itself, because self-expression is always mediated by language. That is, once we start to use words, language inevitably takes on a life of its own which is not identical with the feelings we are expressing, and there will always be a tension between the language and those feelings. Second, postmodern theory has alerted us to the notion that subjectivity is decentred, fragmented and multiple: it deconstructs the idea of a unified, expressive self. According to psychoanalytic theory, for example, the human subject who emerges from the Oedipal process is a *split* subject, torn precariously between the claims of the conscious and unconscious. Central to contemporary psychoanalytic theory is the Lacanian mirror stage, in which the infant feels the joy of recognition at seeing and recognising him or her self in the mirror, but also the despair of misrecognition, the knowledge that he or she can never be totally at one with the image. This sense of a radical split is particularly acute in language, where I can talk of myself but never fully represent, explain or communicate myself.

Poems have always borne witness to the split self. In the poetry of Thomas Wyatt, John Donne and many others, the self emerges as ambivalent, fractured or multiple. But in a postmodern lyric this sense of a split self is particularly acute, and is usually seen as a *modus vivendi* rather than as something which can be, or needs to be, 'cured'.

One way to write a 'split self' postmodern lyric (see Exercise 1a) is to think about personal experience—either your own or that of a fictional person—in terms of contradiction, antithesis and division. The concept of the split self is actually quite central to our experience; we often feel, for example, as if we are both acting and watching ourselves. However, the split self also arises out of the conflict between personal desire and the demands of society.

The poem 'Poem: i.m. John Forbes', by former creative writing student James Lucas—now a published poet—exemplifies the split self because it hinges on the tension between the necessities of domestic existence (making a home, running a car) and our ambitions and aspirations (writing poems):

Example 8.1
While peaking lungs slap shut
as thin air wallets
& kitchen floors resound
to confessions & to noisy fucks
you're out, reconnoitring
the package deal fringes
of paradise where dented
aspirations come to light
at carboot sales
of hawked and haggled
kits for D.I.Y. Parnassian binges
& the self-assembly funhouse
mirrors *quid pro quo* irony,
the acme of tough love,

requires, in other words
you kept your sense of humour
honest, even when you said
that poems are less important
than a mortgage & a kid.

'Poem: i.m. John Forbes' (Lucas 1999, p. 25)

Notice the way this tension is tightly written into the language in such phrases as 'dented aspirations' or 'the package deal fringes of paradise'. The subtle use of the second person 'you' also emphasises the split self: the poet (who is always a *fictional* construct within the poem) seems both to be talking to someone else and about himself. This distances the conflict and yet makes it concrete.

Another way of writing the split self is to dramatise it through narrative and situation. In Australian poet Steve Evans's 'Left', the divided self becomes a split life. The lyric in this poem stretches into a more narrative mode:

Example 8.2
one morning the body chooses
a different outfit
leaves the suit on the hanger
leaves the front door open
turns left rather than right
at the usual corner
and never returns to the old job
old house old family
who told it to do this?
what words were used?
what spell?

there it goes
into the next suburb
by nightfall it will be
almost beyond the city
blind to all previous logic
or finally seeing through it
who's responsible?
not me says the mind
I'm just along for the ride
any steps past this one

haven't been invented yet
the body makes it up as it goes along
it can happen to anyone

it is 1965
my father steps out
into a sunny August morning
his body hasn't told him yet
that today is a left turn day
that we'll never see him again
his suit already dead in the wardrobe
his kids asleep
his wife in the shower
and everything behind him
as he approaches the corner

'Left' (Evans 2004, p. 63)

Here the father seems to have been adopting a role in his daily life which
is at odds with other hidden desires and aspirations. The poem is drama-
tised in terms of a split between mind and body, though we can see that
this clear-cut distinction (or binary opposition as it is sometimes called)
does not really hold up. It is not simply that there is an opposition between
body and mind, but that there is a split which engulfs both mind and body.

Although we talk about a split self, in fact the self may be multifold. It
is usually *splintered* rather than split, as it is in 'I Am Told' by British/Dutch
poet Johan de Wit:

Example 8.3

I am a liar, I am lazy, I am a nut, I am a fascist, I am a stranger, I am
nice, I am unbelievable, I am beautiful, I am mad, I am deaf, I am a
schizophrenic, I am stupid, I am weak, I am meek, I am a perfectionist,
I am handsome, I am naive, I am mean, I am irresponsible, I am
intelligent, I am a craftsman, I am nervous, I am divorced, I am for-
getful, I am a homosexual, I am a crook, I am an elitist, I am spiteful,
I am an unbeliever, I am a European, I am an artist, I am a poet, I am
a writer, I am a typesetter, I am a labourer, I am a student, I am a
soloist, I am a soldier, I am a sergeant, I am a husband, I am a lover, I
am an ex-lover, I am a bad-lover, I am a sex-lover, I am a good-lover,
I am a body, I am a sex-maniac, I am a political animal, I am a wreck,
I am shy, I am tired, I am critical, I am sceptical, I am old, I am young-
looking, I am sincere, I am a dreamer, I am a wanker, I am depressive,

I am manic, I am sad, I am aggressive, I am violent, I am straight, I am dirty, I am thirty-seven, I am a loner, I am a walker, I am a street-walker-to-be, I am indulgent, I am an anarchist, I am a joker, I am authoritarian, I am a zombie, I am frightened, I am frightening, I am frantic, I am an early-riser, I am a drunkard, I am a bastard, I am ordinary, I am a-social, I am anti-social, I am non-sociable, I am incomprehensible, I am here, I am there, I am now, I am gone, I am a loser, I am a winner-to-be, I am careless, I am problematic, I am irresistible, I am unacceptable, I am innocent, I am guilty, I am far-sighted, I am strong, I am greedy, I am retarded, I am a talker, I am a friend, I am a masseur, I am a sociologist, I am a listener, I am a speaker, I am silent, I am quiet, I am restless, I am uprooted, I am lonely, I am unbalanced, I am balancing, I am a breadwinner, I am a hypocrite, I am a hypochondriac, I am precise, I am hostile, I am a purist, I am intense, I am sensitive.

So I am told, and I believe it, I do, I have to, I do, honestly, naturally, without asking questions, without wanting to know why I am.

'I Am Told' (de Wit 1986, p. 11)

Despite the fact that the poet uses the first person persistently here, he does not talk about himself in a way which attempts to describe the specifics of his own personality and individual situation. Instead he lists many different selves which are contradictory (the list veers towards self-criticism but is by no means entirely self-deprecatory). In fact, the list is so wide-ranging that it emerges as the possible description of almost anyone, rather than one particular person.

To create a split-self poem (Exercise 1a), you might want to write down sets of contradictions next to each other and see if you can transform them into a poem, for example:

- I feel tearful/I'm full of joy
- I like my work/my daily routine is drudgery
- I need to write/my words don't say anything.

Notice how the phrases do not cancel each other out but reverberate with each other to express ambivalence.

Or find a narrative or situation (or narratives and situations) which help to accentuate the idea of the split self.

Or create a list poem which evokes the split or splintered self using the de Wit poem as a model.

The subversion of voice

One of the challenges of writing a postmodern lyric is to avoid it becoming overly confessional, self-indulgent or self-aggrandising. A way out of this problem is to create a poem which does not take the concept of voice entirely at face value. For example, it might debunk the authenticity of personal experience, or adopt a register which seems at odds with the subject matter. Denise Riley is a British experimental poet whose 'Shantung' is starkly anti-romantic, 'in your face', depersonalised and improvisatory:

Example 8.4
It's true that anyone can fall
in love with anyone at all.
Later, they can't. Ouf, ouf.

How much mascara washes away each day
and internationally, making the blue one black.
Come on everybody. Especially you girls.

Each day I think of something about dying.
Does everybody? do they think too, I mean.
My friends! some answers. Gently
unstrap my wristwatch. Lay it face down.

'Shantung' (Riley 1998, p. 296)

Here, although the themes are love and death, the stance is satirical (anyone can fall in love with anyone else; tears make mascara dissolve). The poem is also provoking in the way it turns the tables with a subtle feminist jibe, 'Come on everybody. Especially you girls'. It suggests the poet thinks her primary concern is to shake the audience from its complacency, rather than communicate her own personal problems.

Another way of calling into question the authenticity of voice is by adopting an extreme or alien one. In 'Holes and Stars', by Australian poet Emma Lew, the narrator seems seriously disorientated:

Example 8.5
I just got my memory back.
Few loons and I would live
in a corner at the airport,
not for the sequence
but the agony we had to be in,

running off with the money
and faking our own deaths.
Will technology make me remote?
I don't know where I am,
I never know what's going to happen.

Everything is quiet,
stunned yet animated,
evolving yet wilting.
If I want to read a newspaper,
I reach out for it with my hand.
Funny how you've taken my theory
and decided to call it your own.
They will be making snow tonight;
it will be beautiful and we can afford it.
Come quickly,
by yourself,
bring the negatives.

'Holes and Stars' (Lew 1997, p. 5)

The disorientation is most potent in the lines, 'I don't know where I am, I never know what's going to happen'. But a set of disorientated scenarios and unanswered questions stalk the poem: is this someone recovering from an attack of amnesia; how does this relate to the faked deaths; who is making snow?

However, the postmodern lyric may also move sharply between different voices and registers. In 'The Klupzy Girl', by American poet Charles Bernstein, a number of alternative voices are adopted which convey different positions in the power hierarchy, as in the following extract:

Example 8.6

If we are
not to be phrasemongers, we must
sit down and take the steps that will
give these policies life. I fumbled clumsily
with the others—the evocations, explanations,
glossings of "reality" seemed like stretching
it to cover ground rather than make
or name or push something through.
"But the most beautiful
of all doubts is when the downtrodden

and despairing raise their heads and
stop believing in the strength of their oppressors."
To be slayed by such sighs: a noble figure
in a removed entranceway.
"This is just a little note
to say that it was nice working with
all of you. It has been a rewarding
experience in many ways. Although I
am looking forward to my new position with
great anticipation, I shall never forget
the days I spent here. It was like
a home-away-from-home, everyone was
just so warm and friendly. I shall ever
remember you in my prayers, and I
wish you the best for the future."

From 'The Klupzy Girl' (Bernstein 1983, pp. 47–8)

Here the poet is not only a mimic, he also shows how all talking is a form of mimicry. When people speak, they often repeat what they have heard others say in similar situations. These are words they think are appropriate for the occasion, and which situate them in a particular place in the social hierarchy. Implicit in the poem is the idea, also prevalent in post-structuralist/postmodern theories, that we cannot move out of language or out of discourse. We are always moving between discourses, and these inevitably speak for positions of power. The Bernstein poem is, in part, a collage of these different social discourses and their histories and failures. The first sentence, 'If we are not to be phrasemongers', for example, draws our attention to the potential vacuousness of language—and the gap between words and actions—while inevitably succumbing to it. The first voice in quotation marks which begins 'But the most beautiful of all doubts' attempts to situate itself as 'high status', the second 'This is just a little note . . .' as 'low status'. The first uses elevated, even pretentious language. The second is heavily reliant on clichés, and while trying to please gives a rather artificial impression: in fact the words may even seek to conceal problems in the workplace, which are the reason the speaker is leaving. Throughout the whole passage, different verbal registers are adopted sequentially, whether quotation marks are used or not. No particular register can be assumed to be the poet's own 'voice'.

For Exercise 1b create a poem which problematises the notion of voice. For example, focus on a voice which seems somewhat at odds with its subject matter, that refuses to take itself seriously, or that is alien or disorientated. Alternatively, write a poem which incorporates, and moves between, several voices.

The dissident lyric

One of the most influential insights of critical theory, originating in Marxist theory, has been that all texts are ideological. Texts which purport to be apolitical still inscribe a political view, even if a naturalised one. A dissident lyric (see Exercise 1c) overtly fuses the personal and the political. Your dissident lyric might be a poem about environmental damage, or consumerism, or gay politics. Such a poem would contextualise personal experience in terms of social attitudes.

The poet John Wieners said that he liked to make the audience feel as uncomfortable as possible. You don't necessarily have to make this a prime aim of your writing, but you might want to raise the consciousness of your audience about a particular social issue, and in some cases this might involve discomfort.

Wanda Coleman's poem 'the ISM' is a postmodern lyric which has a strong political edge. She is African American, and the poem seems to be about racism. The interweaving of the personal and political makes the poem particularly strong. Racism is seen to be central to the poet's life, and to affect everything she does: it is an unwelcome companion she would rather not have at her side. At the same time race is not addressed directly by name in the poem but somewhat obliquely (and all the more powerfully for that):

Example 8.7
tired i count the ways in which it determines my life
permeates everything. it's in the air
lives next door to me in stares of neighbors
meets me each day in the office. its music comes out the radio
drives beside me in my car. strolls along with me
down supermarket aisles
it's on television
and in the streets even when my work is casual/undefined
it's overhead flashing lights
i find it in my mouth
when i would speak of other things

'the ISM' (Coleman 1994, pp. 474–5)

Student Sophie Clarke writes movingly about social attitudes towards disabled people. This poem, which manages to be strong and gentle at the same time, deals with some difficult topics, such as the way disabled people are named (and denigrated) as 'spastic' or 'cripple', and the way they are vulnerable to sexual exploitation. In this sense the poem also has a subtle feminist aspect:

Example 8.8
little cripple spastic bent
over so I could slap her soft
butt that would not be appropriate
        treatment of such children has
        always been to keep them away from society
        is changing, just a little
        bit different from other girls
        are told that a nice boy will come
but she's not a girl anymore
not a girl
not a cripple
a woman who knows the nice boy
will not come except for
in one kinky moment where she bent
over his knee and he forgave her
spasms and held the little body
before closing the door
between her and society and leaves her
for a woman who is straight.

'Bent' (Clarke 2002, p. 82)

Writing a politically dissident lyric is a complex matter, since dissidence is as much a matter of form as content, a point raised by Charles Bernstein. Bernstein has said that what he cares most for is 'poetry as dissent, including formal dissent' (1992b, p. 2). You may want to combine your politically dissenting lyric with some of the linguistic experimentation which is the focus of the second half of this chapter.

The contemporary image, the taboo subject

A very important aspect of creating a postmodern lyric is ensuring that the imagery is highly contemporary (Exercise 1d). Inexperienced writers often arrive at imagery which is anachronistic. Instead of having relevance to the world around them, it mimics imagery to be found in romantic poetry: a world of fountains and clouds and mirages! In this exercise I am inviting you, instead, to use contemporary imagery: it may, for example, be urban, technological or media-based, and/or involve some icons of popular culture. You might want to write a poem about the media or about using the computer. Or you might want to write about contemporary problems, such as heroin addiction, which inevitably bring with them their own kind of imagery.

The poem might also deal with a taboo subject. When it was written 'P.M.T.' by Dorothy Porter (1991, p. 429) dealt with such a topic: premenstrual tension. This isn't a taboo subject anymore, partly because people have been writing poems about it! But there are other areas of experience, which are still surrounded with disgust, secrecy or fear, that you might want to address.

POETIC ACROBATICS, AVANT-GARDE POETICS

Experimentation has always been an important part of writing, and some writers in all eras have pushed at the boundaries of language and genre. However, the word experimental has been used more specifically in the twentieth and 21st centuries to describe certain movements which have been particularly directed towards experimentation with genre and language.

The experimental poetry movements of the twentieth century started with the work of the dadaists, surrealists, futurists and cubists. Although they were part of the movement known as modernism, these movements were labelled avant-garde. Avant-garde is a military term which was originally used to describe the military vanguard. It was adapted to describe revolutionary art movements which were ahead of their time and leaders in their field. The activities of these avant-garde movements began in the early 1900s, and spanned art, music and literature. Particularly important was the work of Gertrude Stein which had some connections with the cubist painters, and André Breton who was a leader of the surrealist movement. Experimentation continued throughout the century (for example, in the United States, in the work of The New York School of Poets, the Beats, the Black Mountain Poets, and the Objectivists, in the 1950s and 60s).

But throughout the 1980s and 90s, a number of experimental poetry movements arose in America, England, Australia and Canada which involved a massive reconsideration of the expressive, linguistic and political use of language in poetry, and these continue to be extremely influential on experimental poetry worldwide today. In America this movement was known as 'Language Poetry'. The Language Poets were a collective of left-wing, intellectual poets who formed what is sometimes called a 'postmodern avant-garde' (the avant-garde was originally identified with modernism, but has had continuing effects on experimental work during the postmodern era). They promoted experimental work through their poetry and theoretical essays. These outlined their poetics: that is, their theories about textuality and its political import and context. The Language Poets included Charles Bernstein, Ron Silliman, Lyn Hejinian, Bob Perelman, Carla Harryman, Barrett Watten, Leslie Scalapino and Rae Armantrout. These poets were part of an alternative tradition in American poetry, and tended to identify with the heritage of poets such as Gertrude Stein, John Ashbery, Charles Olson or Louis Zukofsky, rather than T.S. Eliot, Robert Lowell or Sylvia Plath.

In England a similar movement (though with its own distinctive characteristics) has come to be known as 'linguistically innovative poetries'. Poets who have been active in this field include Ken Edwards, Allen Fisher, Eric Mottram, Adrian Clarke, Frances Presley, Maggie O'Sullivan, Denise Riley, Robert Sheppard, Geraldine Monk, Caroline Bergvall, Bill Griffiths and cris cheek. They see their work as substantially differentiated from that of well-known British poets such as Craig Raine, Philip Larkin, Carole Ann Duffy, Simon Armitage or Andrew Motion. In Australia the poetry of John Forbes, joanne burns, Anna Couani, John Tranter, Pam Brown and Gig Ryan (amongst others) contained linguistically or formally experimental elements. But there is also a new wave of poets, such as John Kinsella, Peter Minter, Amanda Stewart, Kate Fagan, Michael Farrell, Emma Lew, Geraldine McKenzie and myself, who have taken various kinds of experimentation on board.

These language, and linguistically innovative, poets argued that language had been fetishised, commodified and consequently devalued, and that in order to change the world we have to radically change the way we use words. In other words, when we use language we are normally hardly aware of the words themselves and the forms they take. We think mainly about the content of what we are saying or writing, and the words simply become containers for meaning. These poets believed it was necessary to defamiliarise language, so that we meet language as if for the first time. In order to do this, they often subverted the conventions of grammar, syntax, spelling, punctuation and vocabulary. Their handling of language was acrobatic, often including linguistic handstands, cartwheels or splits. However, any particular mode of defamiliarisation can in time become familiar, and itself a convention. The subversion of linguistic norms, which the Language Poetry movement emphasised, has now become a familiar and recognisable mode of writing, though an extremely varied, flexible and evolving one.

The Language Poets were partly reacting against certain aspects of the free-verse tradition, and the way language in such poems did not usually stress the materiality of language itself. The characteristics of such free-verse poems—and the different poetic priorities of Language Poetry and linguistically innovative poetry—are very well delineated by Marjorie Perloff in her excellent essay 'After Free Verse: The New Nonlinear Poetries' in *Poetry On & Off The Page* (1998, pp. 141–67). According to Perloff, free-verse poems tend to consist of a speaking voice emanating from a feeling, perceptive subject, are image-based, and usually syntactically regular. The sound and visual aspect of the poems are also unobtrusive, and the poem flows and is non-linear. In contrast, what she calls the new 'postlinear' or 'multimentional' poem tends to be more discontinuous, less linear, less image- and line-based (there is likely to be more emphasis on overall visual design). It contains emotions, but these are not necessarily linked to a single perceiving subject, and it emphasises semantic multiplicity rather than a single meaning.

Central to the focus of these poets was the political aspect of poetry: they were interested in the social mediation of language, and the way in which language is a determining factor in power relationships. The Language Poets, for example, saw their work as a political struggle against what Charles Bernstein has called 'official verse culture' (1992b, p. 2). Bernstein believed that '*Poetry is aversion of conformity* in the pursuit of new forms, or can be' (1992b, p. 1). He has said that 'What interests me is a poetry and a poetics that do not edit out so much as edit in: that include multiple conflicting perspectives and types of languages and styles in the same poetic work' (1992b, p. 2). For Bernstein cultural diversity must manifest itself in ways which do not simply succumb to 'the model of representation assumed by the dominant culture in the first place' (1992b, p. 6).

Linguistic experimentation is also an important aspect of multicultural and indigenous writing, where poets mediate between their non-English cultural heritage and the English language. The Australian-Greek poet, PiO, is a good example of a poet who subverts standard English and the whole English-based poetry tradition. PiO might not identify as a 'linguistically innovative' poet, but we can still see his work partly in that light.

Similarly, linguistic innovation has also provided an opportunity for women to challenge language, and the way historically it has been made by men so that it expresses male rather than female values. Obviously women can write poems which challenge male constructions of the female, and can write about any topic from a feminist perspective. But this does not necessarily fundamentally affect how they use language, or the way poetic discourse inscribes the female. French feminist and psychoanalytic theorist, Julia Kristeva, in her essay 'Revolution in Poetic Language'

(Kristeva 1986, pp. 89–136), suggests that linguistic experimentation is a way that writing recaptures what she terms as the semiotic, the pre-linguistic realm, in which the child completely identifies with the mother. This precedes the symbolic order, 'the law of the father', which brings with it not only societal regulation and patriarchal domination but also the conventions of language. Although Kristeva is not completely successful in applying these ideas (the main example she gives of such writing is by James Joyce, a man!) she suggests important ways that we can theorise the idea of linguistically experimental feminist writing.

Finally, although linguistic innovation is particularly the province of poetry, much linguistically innovative work occurs in prose, or in genres which are a hybrid of poetry and prose, demonstrating how fragile the boundaries between different genres are. The later work of James Joyce, to take a classic example, is extremely linguistically innovative. Linguistic experimentation is also a relative concept, and there is no absolute dividing line between poets who are linguistically innovative, and those who are not. Rather there is a continuum of approaches from the mainstream to the experimental, with most poets situated somewhere between the polar extremes, and possibly even at different points on the continuum for different poems.

There are now many anthologies which include experimental poetry, or even make it their primary focus. These include *In the American Tree* (Silliman 1986b), *The New British Poetry: 1968–88* (Allnutt, D'Aguiar et al. 1988), *Postmodern American Poetry* (Hoover 1994), *From the Other Side of the Century* (Messerli 1994), *Out of Everywhere* (O'Sullivan 1996b), *Calyx* (Brennan and Minter 2000) and *Poems For The Millennium* (Rothenberg and Joris 1998). There are also a number of well-written critical books which illuminate this practice, including *A Poetics* (Bernstein 1992a), *My Way* (Bernstein 1999b), *The New Sentence* (Silliman 1987), *The Marginalization of Poetry* (Perelman 1996), *New British Poetries* (Hampson and Barry 1993) and *Leaving Lines of Gender* (Vickery 2000). You will also find Marjorie Perloff's books, for example *Radical Artifice* (1991) and *Poetry On & Off the Page* (1998), extremely helpful.

LINGUISTIC EXPERIMENTATION

We have already looked, in the first two chapters of this book, at various ways of experimenting with language: the following strategies will help you to respond to Exercise 2. They will widen your range and deepen your appreciation of the possibilities. The first strategy we will look at concerns the extension of metaphor.

Metaphor meets metonymy

Linguistically experimental poetry tends to react against the hegemony of metaphor in mainstream poetry, and the romantic idea of the poem as an organic whole of which all the parts are tightly interrelated. Most well-known poetry is metaphor- and symbol-driven. The lifeblood of a poem by Sylvia Plath or Ted Hughes is metaphor: when Sylvia Plath, in her poem 'Stillborn' (1981, p. 142) talks about stillborn embryos, you know that she is really talking about the difficulty of writing, and is using stillbirth as a metaphor for this. But as David Murray (1989) points out, metaphor works on the principle of seeing one thing through another by screening out the differences. In other words metaphor is actually intrinsically unstable, because it is always suppressing differences in order to point out similarities.

Even in a poem which is metaphor-driven we are aware of the instability of metaphor, of differences emerging rather than similarities. Experimental poems sometimes focus on these differences. As a result such poems are often more **metonymical** than metaphorical. A metonymical poem works by association and contiguity not similarity. A metonymy occurs when a part is substituted for a whole (crown for king, for example); where two or more words are closely associated, for example, by their physical proximity (eye, eyebrow and forehead); or where words belong to the same class of objects (pen, pencil, paintbrush). In addition much experimental work explores the idea of what I call 'new metonymies', that is, words which would not normally be associated but become so in the poetic sequence. An example of this would be the string of words desk, pencil, poem, cloud, secret, impetus, where the initially tightly controlled association (desk, pencil, poem) becomes progressively looser to include words which do not have a strictly metonymic basis. We began to experiment with this kind of loose associative sequence in the word association exercise in Chapter 1.

The prose poem 'wonderful' by Ania Walwicz, of which there was an extract in Chapter 1 (Example 1.9), is a good example of a metonymical approach to writing. It is radically different from the Rhyll McMaster poem in the same chapter, which uses the mirror as a metaphor. The metonymical poem is **centrifugal**, it sprawls outwards; the metaphorical poem is **centripetal** and pulls its elements inwards. However, many poems combine both strategies, and because language is inherently metaphorical (words speak of things other than themselves) metaphor is never completely absent from a poem. The relationship between metaphor and metonymy is well discussed by Jonathan Culler in *Structuralist Poetics* (1975) and *The Pursuit of Signs* (1981). The way in which metaphor and metonymy exist in, and are dependent on each other, is also discussed at length in *Hyperscapes in the Poetry of Frank O'Hara: Difference, Homosexuality, Topography* (Smith 2000a, pp. 80–101).

Morphing metaphors

As writers we can confront the differences that metaphor suppresses and turn them into a creative source. If the normal objective of a metaphor is to make a one-to-one comparison, then we can open it up by introducing multiple comparisons, or comparisons in which difference outweighs similarity. In this way we can create 'open' rather than 'closed' metaphors. The orthodox approach to metaphor is that it must be based on a one-to-one comparison, and that metaphors should never be 'mixed'. According to this view, a metaphor such as 'my anger gathered pace, then shut its eyes' is 'bad' because it is inconsistent: the two parts of the metaphor do not refer to the same ground of comparison. But, in fact, stimulating metaphors often involve comparisons which are wild, extravagant, incongruous, multiple or mixed. They may be more energising because they continuously refocus our attention, as one metaphor morphs into the next. Let's look at an example:

Example 8.9
Like musical instruments
Abandoned in a field
The parts of your feelings

Are starting to know a quiet

From '"Like Musical Instruments . . ."' (Clark 1994, p. 395)

The breathtaking simile, by American poet Tom Clark, which opens his poem '"Like Musical Instruments . . ."' consists of a number of components. There is the comparison between the feelings and abandoned musical instruments, but each part of the comparison is also a very powerful image in itself. The musical instruments abandoned in a field are silent because no one is playing them. The feelings are in parts, presumably because they are conflicting. Brought together the two images suggest that the feelings are calming down, that is, 'starting to know a quiet'. So there are several metaphors within an overall simile.

Similarly, in the opening of the poem 'Crossing the Bar', by American poet Susan Schultz, one comparison falls quickly on the heels of the one before, as it does in many of her dizzy and dazzling poems:

Example 8.10

Amid ships, workmen sprawl
like functions on a still graph,
absorbing late morning like time-
lapse prescriptions . . .

From 'Crossing the Bar' (Schultz 2000, p. 96)

Write a poem (Exercise 2a) which extends metaphor and uses open rather than closed metaphor. What happens to the focus of the poem when you write in this way?

Games and systems

In Chapter 1 you experimented with language through word association and phrase permutation, but there are many other forms of linguistic play. One of these can be to focus on a particular feature of language, and milk it for everything it is worth. For example, in Charles Bernstein's 'Of Time and the Line' the poet plays on meanings of the word 'line'. This strategy points the poem in numerous directions in quick succession:

Example 8.11

George Burns likes to insist that he always
takes the straight lines; the cigar in his mouth
is a way of leaving space between the
lines for a laugh. He weaves lines together
by means of a picaresque narrative;
not so Hennie Youngman, whose lines are strictly paratactic. My father pushed a
line of ladies' dresses—not down the street
in a pushcart but upstairs in a fact'ry
office. My mother has been more concerned
with her hemline. Chairman Mao put forward
Maoist lines, but that's been abandoned (mostly) for the East-West line of malarkey
so popular in these parts. The prestige
of the iambic line has recently
suffered decline, since it's no longer so
clear who "I" am, much less who *you* are. When
making a line, better be double sure
what you're lining in & what you're lining
out & which side of the line you're on; the

world is made up so (Adam didn't so much
name as delineate). Every poem's got
a prosodic lining, some of which will
unzip for summer wear. The lines of an
imaginary are inscribed on the
social flesh by the knifepoint of history.
Nowadays, you can often spot a work
of poetry by whether it's in lines
or no; if it's in prose, there's a good chance
it's a poem. While there is no lesson in
the line more useful than that of the pick-
et line, the line that has caused the most ad-
versity is the bloodline. In Russia
everyone is worried about long lines;
back in the USA, it's strictly soup-
lines. "Take a chisel to write," but for an
actor a line's got to be cued. Or, as
they say in math, it takes two lines to make
an angle but only one lime to make
a Margarita.

'Of Time and the Line' (Bernstein 1991, pp. 42–3)

The word 'line' is what we call a homonym: that is, it is a word which has many different meanings. Homonyms are commonplace in all kinds of poetry and are often used by poets to pivot from one meaning to another. But Bernstein pushes the homonym to an extreme where it becomes the focal point of the poem.

Bernstein's poem sets itself a task or limit: every sentence has to exploit the meaning of the word 'line'. We have already seen in Chapter 3, with regard to numerical structures, how setting limits can be very liberating and reap creative results. Try and think of other linguistic games of this kind that you can play, and other limits that you can set.

The members of the French group Oulipo (Ouvroir de Littérature Potentielle, or Workshop for Potential Literature), founded in 1960, set many such rules for themselves (Motte 1986; Mathews & Brotchie 1998). Members of Oulipo included George Perec, Raymond Queneau, Harry Mathews and Italo Calvino and their experiments were wide-ranging. For example, George Perec reinvented the lipogram, in which the author leaves out one particular letter throughout the text (Perec himself wrote a whole novel without the letter e). Members of Oulipo used countless other procedures such as the palindrome (a text which can be read backwards) or antonymy (replacing elements of a text with their grammatical or semantic opposites). Other systems they produced were highly mathematical, and members of Oulipo sometimes used them to produce lengthy novels such as George Perec in *Life a User's Manual* (1996) and Italo Calvino in *If on a Winter's Night a Traveller* (1992). These experiments have also been taken up more recently by some younger poets, such as Canadian Christian Bok, whose *Eunoia* (2001) uses only one vowel in each section, and was also written under a number of other self-imposed constraints.

Working with a constraint can be very productive because it pushes your work outwards in new directions. Because you cannot use language freely, you have to think of other less obvious alternatives: this may bring freshness and originality to your writing.

Using the Bernstein poem as a model, write a poem (Exercise 2b) which is based on one (or several) homonyms, such as the words 'lie' or 'die/dye'. Then write a poem based on another type of system: this might be the exclusion of a letter throughout a text or including a particular word in each sentence. However, it need not be any of these: think up your own system. What effect does this have upon your writing?

Syntax and grammar

Some poetry—including much free verse—sticks closely to normal sentence structure and grammar. However, much poetry written throughout the last few hundred years has not been grammatical in the sense that a piece of prose would be. In some experimental poetry a departure from normal grammar is particularly pronounced: the grammatical function that words have, and their place and position in the sentence, is seriously disrupted.

Grammar can be constraining because it is hierarchical. The sentences we use are hypotactic, that is, they contain a main clause usually with other subordinate clauses. This has the effect of making one idea in the sentence seem more important than others, or at least of making one central idea the focus of the sentence. Grammar also fixes meaning, and makes it as unambiguous as possible. For many social uses grammar is essential because we need to communicate with other human beings with as little ambiguity as possible, and prioritise some aspects of our communications over others. But in poetry we sometimes want to exploit the polysemic aspect of language: its capacity to generate many different meanings. We want to juxtapose ideas, and celebrate their co-existence, without locking them into a structure where one is subordinate to another. More generally, grammar is the product of a particular social context, and can be identified with the hegemonic culture: in many cases western imperialism. Non-Anglo-Celtic writers often mediate between English grammar and their own version of it: this kind of grammatical freedom can be seen in the poetry of Australian indigenous poet Lionel Fogarty.

In experimental poetries, words sometimes take on a different grammatical function from normal (for example, verbs become nouns); essential elements of grammar are left out (for example, a verb from the sentence); or the grammatical functions of particular words are not clearly differentiated, sometimes giving the appearance of word strings. The word association exercise in Chapter 1 is a good example of a text which does not function with regard to normal grammatical principles.

In the following short extract, 'I am Marion Delgado', by Ron Silliman, grammar is extremely abnormal:

Example 8.12
How do we recognize the presence of a
new season.
Field is the common sky.
Spring language.
What if blow-fly believe the sky is
the room.
A first time, not glow, of common is
the enemy.
Blow-fly objectify the expression.
A believe as stasis and casual as the
perfect.
Lion I'd bites.
A specific lion, mane, bites for the
peach-headed.
Realism is a swamp, not a gas.
How do you geometry light and dew.
Across a visits with a milky omitted.
Haze with a glow made of lights is the
sign.

From 'I am Marion Delgado' (Silliman 1986a, p. 69)

Here the word 'field' would normally be preceded by an article 'the', so would 'blow-fly', and the verb 'believe' would then usually be singular. 'Geometry' is grammatically a noun, but appears in this extract as a verb. In addition the sentence, 'A first time, not glow, of common is the enemy' is not grammatically congruent: in 'normal' prose we might expect it to read as 'a first time, a glow, a common enemy', in which each item would be equivalent to the next one. Words that do not seem to belong to each other are nevertheless grouped together, as, for example, in the sentence 'Blow-fly objectify the expression'. Important here is the lack of hierarchy in the sentence which does not have a clear object or subject, or subordinate one idea to another.

What is to be gained by writing like this? For a start, such an approach defamiliarises grammar. It focuses our attention on how language normally works, and how it can be stretched. And although it may seem that such a piece is very 'difficult' and obscures meaning, in fact it liberates it. For example, the sentence 'How do you geometry light and dew' is a very expressive way of talking about the perception of physical relationships and shapes in nature. Writing like this produces semantic flexibility: each sentence can be interpreted in several ways, producing more meaning rather than less. Such a passage also makes us think about the limits of language and the fact that conventional language cannot express the inexpressible. There are many things which are difficult to say within grammatical language structures.

This is a very extreme instance of grammatical subversion; however, much experimental poetry does not go this far, but rather takes some licence with grammar. Many poets flatten out the sentence, minimising grammatical pointers and connectives. The following poem, 'Make-Up' by Geraldine Monk, is a good example of that:

Example 8.13
ran cranberry over logan
Japanese ginger orchid
spice glow mandarines
              frost light clearly

stacked moonsmoke robe on aubergine
          snow
peppered sweet on two metallic
          lupins
frost laid oon aub mois.   Tang rang
                 ruby
                   apple

mixed snow fizz pink shantung
laid ginger rum on maple
got fizz tung rum ba plum
              or was it victoria

'Make-Up' (Monk 1988, p. 318)

The first line of the poem seems to suggest that cranberries overran logan-berries. But the syntax (the word order and the way the words are connected) is different from normal: the verb is at the beginning of the line and the word loganberry is truncated. The next two lines suggest flowers, fruits and aromas, but do not use a main verb, and are not struc-tured with regard to subject, verb and object. There is a density and compression here which is extremely sensory: the way in which words are piled onto each other, and not submitted to grammatical subordination, means that a number of stimuli are operating at once. This is a radically different approach to the more conventional nature poem where the poet's relationship to, and feelings about, nature might be more directly expressed. Such a nature poem requires grammar to express subject–object relations.

To experiment with grammar and syntax (see Exercise 2c) try two approaches:

- Create a series of phrases in which you turn nouns into verbs or verbs into nouns. An example would be 'the day lemons and dilates' where the noun 'lemon' becomes a verb. You will find that some words have more than one grammatical function anyway, but try to find some that do not. Begin by producing a list of unconnected phrases. Then, if you like, go one step further and turn the phrases into a poem, but this is not the primary objective.
- Write a short poem in which words are piled up without grammatical joiners. See what effect this has on the meaning.

Discontinuity

One of the main characteristics shared by most of the poems in this chapter is discontinuity. The poem may keep abruptly changing direction, or there may be unexpected shifts in voice or register. Discontinuity is as true, or more true, to the way we perceive the world as continuity, and within poetry it allows thoughts to develop freely and in several directions at once. Discontinuity and fragmentation are also often effective ways of addressing the gaps and fractures within memory and history.

These poems are sometimes a challenge to read because they move from one idea to another without a smooth transition, but they also lend them-selves to multiple interpretations and an active 'writerly' approach to reading which is very rewarding. If you find that your writing always seems to be very continuous, and that you always make everything in the poem fit tidily together, try writing a more discontinuous poem (Exercise 2d). Some ways you might do this would be to:

- Take three different poems you are writing and intercut between them to produce discontinuities.
- Write down twenty independent phrases or sentences, and then arrange them so as to produce some continuities and some discontinuities.
- Allow your mind to drift as you write, and include thoughts which do not follow on from each other.
- Write a continuous narrative, and then cut it up and rearrange it in such a way as to create discontinuities.
- Write a sentence and then follow it with another one which takes up the initial idea only tangentially. Continue this process. You will find that a mixture of continuities and discontinuities are produced by this approach.
- Go back to some of the previous exercises, such as collage and word association, which encourage a more discontinuous approach.

Discontinuity always goes hand in hand with continuity. Such poems also usually include numerous continuities, in the sense of recurring ideas which bind the poem together. Also, one of the advantages of using a discontinuous approach may be that it forces the reader to discover new links between disconnected ideas.

Lexical experimentation

Lexical experimentation is concerned with choice of words, what is traditionally known as vocabulary, but in linguistics is referred to as the lexicon. This can range from using very unusual words and making them a central part of the poem, to hyphenating words to recombine them, to making up words. Here are some examples of poets who have experimented with the lexicon. The following poem 'A Lesson from the Cockerel' is by Maggie O'Sullivan:

Example 8.14
POPPY THANE. PENDLE DUST. BOLDO SACHET GAUDLES
GIVE GINGER. GIVE INK. SMUDGE JEEDELA LEAVINGS,
TWITCH **JULCE**. WORSEN. WRIST DRIP. SKINDA. JANDLE.
                UDDER DIADEMS INTERLUCE.
                ICYCLE OPALINE RONDA.
CRIMINAL   CRAB RATTLES ON THE LUTE.
CONSTITUENTS   BLINDINGLY RAZOR-GUT.
                SHOOKER—GREENY CRIMSON
                NEAPTIDE COMMON PEAKS IN THE

SWIFT PULLERY.TWAIL,
HOYA METHODS: SAXA ANGLAISE
SKEWERED **SKULL** INULA.

'A Lesson from the Cockerel' (O'Sullivan 1996a, p. 74)

This poem evokes nature, but it is very different from a conventional nature poem. Words such as 'gaudles' and 'julce' will not be found in a dictionary, they are constructed words which nevertheless bear the traces of standard vocabulary ('julce' for example suggests juice), or transmit echoes of a largely lost early Anglo-Celtic linguistic tradition. Obviously there are other linguistic strategies at work here: the use of short staccato phrases and sentences and the accumulation of phrase upon phrase. But the creation of constructed words is central, and the overall effect is to evoke nature, and yet defamiliarise our perception of it.

Charles Bernstein's poem 'A Defence of Poetry' is a treatise on the relationship of sense and nonsense which encodes its own debate. The following is a short extract:

Example 8.15
Nin-sene.sense is too binary
andoppostioin, too much oall or nithing
account with ninesense seeming by its
very meaing to equl no sense at all. We
have preshpas a blurrig of sense, whih
means not relying on convnetionally
methods of *conveying* sense but whih may
aloow for dar greater sense-smakinh than
specisi9usforms of doinat disoucrse that
makes no sense at all by irute of thier
hyperconventionality (Bush's speeches,
calssically).

From 'A Defence of Poetry' (Bernstein 1999a, pp. 1–2)

In this poem–essay Bernstein challenges the way society conceptualises sense and nonsense. He implies that what might appear to be nonsense (certain types of off-beat writing) may in reality be a lot more 'sensible' than discourses, such as political speeches, which claim to convey public truths. To do this Bernstein plays with the lexicon. Most of the words here are recognisably from the English language, but they are certainly defamiliarised. At times the poem has a quasi-dyslexic feel to it which is almost childlike: words appear with the letters jumbled in a different order, like typos in a hurriedly written email. Letters are added to or sub-tracted from words, sometimes implying additional meanings. This seems strangely at odds with the intellectual content, and Bernstein challenges our ideas of what is, and is not, communicative.

In my own piece 'The Riting of the Runda', there is a short passage which consists of a constructed language:

Example 8.16
ICHBROHOB TISH EDRONE. RURUNS RO. EOB BROVICT WARSHAWE. WARSHAWASHAD. DOWIF-BRON SESH OBEXOBE XOBE. ICHBROHOB NUR PERWARWAN CHEBROCHA.

NUR LIHCOFLIH DROPSE RURUNS. TINSCREDIL XOB. EDRONE WOSHANS WARSHAWASHAD. OBDAH DOWIFBRON HOSHBOT DILCRETONS PEDWASDEP. ICHBROHOB ICHBROHOB ISS.

AD TISH XOOO DOWIFBRON. DROPSE TILCOFPER HOSTIM PROVICT. DROPSE TILCOFPER VOHICTCAV DARUN. XOB TISH UNUN UNUN DURMUGEDUM. RURUNS WARSHAWASHAD.

From 'The Riting of the Runda' (Smith & Dean 1996; Smith 2000b, pp. 6–10)

This language arose by breaking up words into syllables, and then gluing them back together again into different 'words'. In the context of the piece, it has an ambiguous status as the language of the Runda—a clan from which the woman who speaks the words is fleeing—or as a new language to which the woman aspires.

Strategies for creating languages usually have psychological or political purposes: otherwise constructing the language would simply be a game. Making a new language may be a way of tapping into the unconscious, a realm of thinking and feeling which is normally obscured. Or it may be a way of showing deficiencies or limitations in the language: it can demon-strate how the words we use are geared towards certain privileged social groups and exclude others. In particular, it may be a way of formulating a new feminist language.

Lexical experimentation does not have to use completely new words. Poets sometimes write in dialect or introduce words from other languages.

In order to create your own language (Exercise 2e), try some of the following strategies:

- Break up words and put the syllables back together in a different way.
- Add prefixes and suffixes to the word.
- Slightly change words by adding or subtracting letters, or systematically substitute one letter for another.
- Mediate between standard English and other languages. Employ a dialect or pidgin, or intersperse words from another language into your text.

The visual poem

Linguistically innovative poets often play with the visual layout on the page. We tend to think of lineation, the arrangement of the poem into lines, as a very important part of writing poetry. But there is a great deal else that you can do with a poem in terms of spatial arrangement: you can place the words anywhere and in any order. You may, in fact, want to challenge our normal reading strategy (reading from left to right), for this is culturally entrained—in some languages, you read from right to left. If writers use the layout on the page creatively, they can encourage readers to assemble the poem vertically or diagonally as well as horizontally, and/or in a different order each time. The white space on the page can also be used to create gaps, that is, as a means of punctuation.

Visual poetry has had a strong presence in the twentieth century, and was particularly prominent in the concrete poetry movement in the 1960s and 1970s. In concrete poetry the words visually presented their meanings. The poems often consisted of visual puns, sometimes only using single words. A concrete poem tended to look like the word it was referring to: the signifier and signified became identical. The experiments of the concrete poets stemmed from the dadaist, surrealist and futurist movements at the beginning of the century. Concrete poetry could be more readily international than other poetry, and thrived on contact between poets of different cultural traditions because translation was usually not a problem. Consequently concrete poetry anthologies featured poets from all over the world. For published examples of concrete poems see, *Anthology of Concretism* (Wildman 1970) and *Missing Forms: Concrete, Visual and Experimental Poems* (Murphy and PiO 1981), amongst others.

Visual poems range from texts with unusual and visually dynamic layouts, to ones with strong pictorial elements. Cyberwriting has also given a whole new dimension to visual poetry, as we will see in Chapter 11. For two examples of visual poetry see Examples 8.17 and 8.18 (pp. 187–8): 'In Parallel' by Yuriya Kumagai (1995a, p. 20) and 'Tofu Your Life' by Yunte Huang (1996, p. 29). (We have already seen Kumagai's work in a previous chapter. Yunte Huang is a Chinese poet now living in the United States.)

See also Example 8.19 (p. 188) 'Jouissance' by student Ben Garcia, which combines visual experiments with syntactical experimentation: it also alludes to the Australian poet Michael Dransfield. In addition it includes some phrase permutation (from Chapter 1), and a simultaneous structure (from Chapter 3), to make a comment on the uncertainties of postmodernism (Garcia 2000).

In order to make your writing more visual (Exercise 2f), try some of the following strategies:

- Avoid keeping exclusively to the left-hand margin. A line can start at many different positions on the page.
- Don't always think of the page in terms of the horizontal and vertical. Words can fill the space in any way and can be diagonal. Use a computer program which allows you to manipulate words visually on the page.
- Think of how the poem looks, and the impression its visual structure creates.
- Write a poem in which the visual structure (at least in part) mimics or counterpoints the meaning of the poem.
- Consider the visual appearance of words on the page in other languages. For instance, Japanese is a much more pictorial language than English, and the words tend to visually represent the meanings. Are there ways we can apply this kind of approach to writing in English?

Prose poetry, the new sentence

Prose poetry (see Exercise 2g) is an exciting and inherently innovative medium to work in because, by its very nature, it questions the division between poetry and prose. A prose poem usually combines some of the syntactic and metaphorical/metonymical characteristics of poetry, but also exploits the intellectual, narrative and logical possibilities of the sentence. In some cases the dividing line between poem and prose may be rather slight, and it may seem as if the poem could be organised either in sentences or lines. Prose poetry is a diverse and loose category, sometimes including short meditations or poetic narratives.

A particular type of prose poetry was central to the work of the American Language Poets. Ron Silliman, in a groundbreaking essay, formulated this as 'the new sentence' (1987). In prose poetry of this type, sentences do not usually follow on continuously or logically. Rather each one is a world in itself, containing its own narrative, aphorism or image. Every sentence is equal in weight to the preceding and following one, but the sentences do not combine to form an overall narrative or exposition. Nevertheless, the sentences in any particular paragraph (or in the whole text) may resonate with each other, through recurring ideas, contexts or images. This creates continuities which pull the poem together, while the discontinuities push it apart.

The new sentence can have many different manifestations. Ron Silliman's work explores many varied manifestations of the new sentence and his 'Sunset Debris' shows one imaginative use of it. This prose poem is a tour de force which lasts for 29 pages, of which I quote only the beginning. Each sentence is a question which does not necessarily follow on logically from the one before. Nevertheless it resonates with the other questions around it:

Example 8.20

Can you feel it? Does it hurt? Is it too soft? Do you like it? Do you like this? Is this how you like it? Is it alright? Is he there? Is he breathing? Is it him? Is it near? Is it hard? Is it cold? Does it weigh much? Is it heavy? Do you have to carry it far? Are those hills? Is this where we get off? Which one are you? Are we there yet? Do we need to bring sweaters? Where is the border between blue and green? Has the mail come? Have you come yet? Is it perfect bound? Do you prefer ballpoints? Do you know which insect you most resemble? Is it the red one? Is that your hand? Want to go out? What about dinner? What does it cost? Do you speak English? Has he found his voice yet? Is this anise or is it fennel? Are you high yet?

From 'Sunset Debris' (Silliman 1986c, p. 11)

Notice here how the sentences do retain normal syntax: poems which use the new sentence sometimes retain this syntax, sometimes jettison it.

Such prose poems also sometimes play with the relationship between narrative and anti-narrative and with the conventions of representation. Lyn Hejinian's prose poem, *My Life*, is a kind of anti-narrative: it poeticises and breaks up narrative continuity and replaces it with a more poetic cohesion. In the following passage there is no absolute narrative, chronology or overriding idea which holds the whole passage together, though there are many glimpses of multiple narratives, chronologies and ideas:

Example 8.21

A pause, a rose,
something on paper

A moment yellow, just as four years later, when my father returned home from the war, the moment of greeting him, as he stood at the bottom of the stairs, younger, thinner than when he had left, was purple—though moments are no longer so colored. Somewhere, in the background, rooms share a pattern of small roses. Pretty is as pretty does. In certain families, the meaning of necessity is at one with the sentiment of pre-necessity. The better things were gathered in a pen. The windows were narowed by white gauze curtains which were never loosened. Here I refer to irrelevance, that rigidity which never intrudes. Hence, repetitions, free from all ambition. The shadow of the redwood trees, she said, was oppressive. The plush must be worn away. On her walks she stepped into people's gardens to pinch off cuttings from their geraniums and succulents. An occasional sunset is reflected on the windows. A little puddle is overcast. If only you could touch, or, even, catch those gray great creatures. I was afraid of my uncle with the wart on his nose, or of his jokes at our expense which were beyond me, and I was shy of my aunt's deafness who was his sister-in-law and who had years earlier fallen into the habit of nodding, agreeably. Wool station. See lightning, wait for thunder. Quite mistakenly, as it happened. Long time lines trail behind every idea, object, person, pet, vehicle, and event. The afternoon happens, crowded and therefore endless. Thicker, she agreed.

From *My Life* (Hejinian 1987, p. 7)

This passage begins with the father's removal to, and return from, war. But the father's absence and return is not developed in a cohesive way in the sentences that follow, which have an ambiguous and oblique relationship with this first sentence. In fact the sentences are not ordered so that each follows on from the one before, or so they add up to a recognisable whole. Rather, the passage is a generic hybrid: it contains elements of narrative ('she stepped into people's gardens to pinch off cuttings from their geraniums and succulents') and description ('An occasional sunset is reflected on the windows'), but never coheres into overall narration or description. It intersperses image ('A little puddle is overcast'); impressions ('An occasional sunset is reflected on the windows'); philosophical ruminations ('Here I refer to irrelevance, that rigidity that never intrudes'); and well-known sayings ('Pretty is as pretty does'). It also mentions places and times without firmly locating or linking them. This raises questions about their relationship to each other: are the windows with the 'white gauze curtains' inside the rooms which 'share a pattern of small roses'; is the afternoon in the penultimate sentence, the afternoon of the day the father reappears? The subject position also continually changes, from she, to I, to you, so that there is no unified subject or agent of the passage, and no stable narrative position from which to view events. So the 'she' who takes the cuttings may be the child's mother, but this is not spelt out clearly. The passage consists of a cluster of impressions that are both independent from each other, and yet resonate together. It conveys the impressions, perceptions and emotions that make up a life rather than its chronological, spatial or logical ordering. As such it captures extremely well the disordered process of remembering, and the way that memories are always being reinvented in the present.

Write a poem, or series of poems, using the new sentence (Exercise 2g). If you find this difficult to do, you might want to use some of the techniques mentioned in the discontinuity section. For more about the new sentence see *The New Sentence* (Silliman 1987), and *The Marginalization of Poetry* (Perelman 1996, pp. 59–78).

CONCLUSION

Poetry and prose, then, are always intimately linked in experimental writing, which seeks to break up the norms of both poetry and narrative. In fact Lyn Hejinian's *My Life* draws us back again to the issue of representation first raised in Chapter 2, and reiterated time and again in different forms in this book. *My Life* is a more radical challenge to realist representation than the surreal and satirical rewritings in Chapter 2, because it challenges normal time–space relations, a cohesive subject position, and narrative linearity all at once.

More generally, this chapter has explored the varied terrain of postmodern poetry, and avant-garde poetics, to challenge both the lyric and free-verse traditions. We have built on the strategies for playing with language we encountered in the first two chapters, extended their range, and given them a political and literary context within contemporary experimental poetry movements. These strategies can be incorporated by you to varying degrees: a very small amount of linguistic experimentation goes a long way and may have far-reaching effects in your work. Such linguistic strategies can also be combined with performance and digital writing (see Chapters 10 and 11) to produce other contemporary forms of textuality.

Example 8.17

In Parallel

Will	They
He	Will
Walk	Walk
Down	Along
The	Parallel
Parallel	Lines
Path	So
That	That
Never	They
Crosses	Might
Hers	Always
Nor	Feel
Drifts	Each
Apart	Other's
Not	Absence
Too	So
Far	Strongly
Never	That
Too	Her
Close	Absence
So	Becomes
That	A
She	Synonym
Can	Of
Act	Her
Out	Presence
Her	To
Own	Him
Story	But
She	After
No	A
Longer	Lapse
Believes	Of
That	Several
The	Years
Quality	He
Of	Notices
A	His
Man	Life
Can	Has
Be	Become
Measured	An
By	Antonym
How	Of
He	Her
Directs	Life
And	And
That	He
Of	Is
A	Left
Woman	In
By	His-tory
How	While
She Acts Along His-story Line	She Is Living Her-story

'In Parallel' (Kumagai 1995a, p. 20)

Example 8.18

frame de frame
rule de rule

> your   life
> a   small
> square tofu

unnegotiable shape
soft to chopstick

'Tofu Your Life' (Huang 1996, p. 29)

Example 8.19

Jouissance

That I said you could not
Imperative of first Principles
Narratological sequence of plethora

You didn't know the big bear
You didn't know the texture of woven fibre
You didn't sand b/w your toes
It didn't start there

of events a sequence

mona
mona

mona mona   mona mona
mona mona mona   mona mona mona

mona
mona

monamonamona

Andy where are I?
That's the condition
Post-

```
sol          man
rush         die
mid          night
child        ran
```

Dransfield didn't like the re-write-
editors didn't like the dransfield-
the Dransfield can just do another one-

framed and baked derridans
Image-Music-Text
and back and back
all histories court.

'Jouissance' (Garcia 2000)

REFERENCES

Allnutt, G., D'Aguiar, F., Edwards, K. and Mottram, E. (eds), 1988, *The New British Poetry: 1968–88*, Paladin, London.

Bernstein, C. 1983, 'The Klupzy Girl', *Islets/Irritations*, Roof Books, New York, pp. 47–51.

—— 1991, 'Of Time and the Line', *Rough Trades*, Sun & Moon Press, New York.

—— 1992a, *A Poetics*, Harvard University Press, Cambridge, Massachusetts.

—— 1992b, 'State of the Art', *A Poetics*, Harvard University Press, Cambridge, Massachusetts, pp. 1–8.

—— 1999a, 'A Defence of Poetry', *My Way: Speeches and Poems*, University of Chicago Press, Chicago.

—— 1999b, *My Way: Speeches and Poems*, University of Chicago Press, Chicago.

Bok, C. 2001, *Eunoia*, Coach House Books, Toronto.

Brennan, M. and Minter, P. 2000, *Calyx: 30 Contemporary Australian Poets*, Paper Bark Press, Sydney.

Calvino, I. 1992, *If on a Winter's Night a Traveller*, (trans.) W. Weaver, Minerva, London. First published in 1981 in Great Britain.

Clark, T. 1994, '"Like Musical Instruments . . ."', *Postmodern American Poetry: A Norton Anthology*, (ed.) P. Hoover, W.W. Norton & Company, New York.

Clarke, S. 2002, 'Bent', *Unsweetened*, (eds) M. Armour, S. Scroope and S. Shamraka, UNSW Union, Sydney.

Coleman, W. 1994, 'the ISM', *Postmodern American Poetry: A Norton Anthology*, (ed.) P. Hoover, W.W. Norton & Company, New York.

Culler, J. 1975, *Structuralist Poetics: Structuralism, Linguistics and the Study of Literature*, Routledge & Kegan Paul, London.

—— 1981, *The Pursuit of Signs: Semiotics, Literature, Deconstruction*, Cornell University Press, New York.

de Wit, J. 1986, 'I Am Told', *Rose Poems*, Actual Size, Colchester, Essex.

Evans, S. 2004, 'Left', *Taking Shape*, Five Islands Press, Wollongong.

Garcia, B. 2000, 'Jouissance', unpublished.

Hampson, R. and Barry, P. 1993, *New British Poetries: The Scope of the Possible*, Manchester University Press, Manchester.

Hejinian, L. 1987, *My Life*, Sun & Moon Press, Los Angeles.

Hoover, P. (ed.) 1994, *Postmodern American Poetry: A Norton Anthology*, W.W. Norton & Company, New York.

Huang, Y. 1996, 'Tofu Your Life', *Tinfish*, vol. 4.

Kristeva, J. 1986, 'Revolution in Poetic Language', *The Kristeva Reader*, (ed.) T. Moi, Basil Blackwell, Oxford.

Kumagai, Y.J. 1995a, 'In Parallel', *Her Space-Time Continuum*, University Editions, Huntingdon, West Virginia.

—— 1995b, 'Untitled', *Her Space-Time Continuum*, University Editions, Huntingdon, West Virginia.

Lew, E. 1997, 'Holes and Stars', *The Wild Reply*, Black Pepper, North Fitzroy, Victoria.

Lucas, J. 1999, 'Poem: i.m. John Forbes', *Cordite*, vols 6 and 7.

Mathews, H. and Brotchie, A. 1998, *Oulipo Compendium*, Atlas Press, London.

Messerli, D. (ed.) 1994, *From The Other Side of the Century: A New American Poetry 1960–1990*, Sun & Moon Press, Los Angeles.

Monk, G. 1988, 'Make-Up', *The New British Poetry: 1968–88*, (eds) G. Allnutt, F. D'Aguiar, K. Edwards and E. Mottram, Paladin, London.

Motte, W.F. Jr. (ed.) 1986, *Oulipo: A Primer of Potential Literature*, University of Nebraska Press, Lincoln and London.

Murphy, P. and PiO (eds.) 1981, *Missing Forms: Concrete, Visual and Experimental Poems*, Collective Effort, Melbourne.

Murray, D. 1989, 'Unity and Difference: Poetry and Criticism', *Literary Theory and Poetry: Extending the Canon*, (ed.) D. Murray, Batsford, London, pp. 4–22.

O'Sullivan, M. 1996a, 'A Lesson from the Cockerel', *Out of Everywhere: Linguistically Innovative Poetry by Women in North America & the UK*, (ed.) M. O'Sullivan, Reality Street Editions, London.

—— 1996b, (ed.) *Out of Everywhere: Linguistically Innovative Poetry by Women in North America & the UK*, Reality Street Editions, London.

Perec, G. 1996, *Life A User's Manual*, (trans.), D. Bellos, The Harvill Press, London.

Perelman, B. 1996, *The Marginalization of Poetry: Language Writing and Literary History*, Princeton University Press, Princeton.

Perloff, M. 1991, *Radical Artifice: Writing Poetry in the Age of Media*, University of Chicago Press, Chicago.

—— 1998, *Poetry On & Off the Page: Essays for Emergent Occasions*, Northwestern University Press, Evanston, Illinois.

Plath, S. 1981, 'Stillborn', *Collected Poems*, Faber & Faber, London.

Porter, D. 1991, 'P.M.T.', *The Penguin Book of Modern Australian Poetry*, (eds) J. Tranter and P. Mead, Penguin, Ringwood, Victoria.

Riley, D. 1998, 'Shantung', *The Penguin Book of Poetry from Britain and Ireland since 1945*, (eds.) S. Armitage and R. Crawford, Viking, London.

Rothenberg, J. and Joris, P. 1998, *Poems for the Millennium: The University of California Book of Modern & Postmodern Poetry. Volume Two: From Postwar to Millennium*, Berkeley, University of California Press.

Schultz, S.M. 2000, 'Crossing the Bar', *Aleatory Allegories*, Salt Publishing, Cambridge, UK.

Silliman, R. 1986a, 'I am Marion Delgado', *The Age of Huts*, Roof Books, New York, pp. 69–75.

—— 1986b, *In the American Tree*, National Poetry Foundation, Orono, Maine.

—— 1986c, 'Sunset Debris', *The Age of Huts*, Roof Books, New York, pp. 11–40.

—— 1987, *The New Sentence*, Roof Books, New York.

Smith, H. 2000a, *Hyperscapes in the Poetry of Frank O'Hara: Difference, Homosexuality, Topography*, Liverpool University Press, Liverpool.

—— and Dean, R. 1996, 'Nuraghic Echoes', Rufus, CD, RF025, Sydney.

Smith, H. 2000b, 'The Riting of the Runda' *Keys Round Her Tongue: Short Prose, Poems and Performance Texts*, Soma Publications, Sydney.

Vickery, A. 2000, *Leaving Lines of Gender: A Feminist Genealogy of Language Writing*, Wesleyan University Press, Hanover and London.

Wildman, E. (ed.) 1970, *Anthology of Concretism*, 2nd edn, The Swallow Press, Chicago.

CHAPTER NINE
The invert, the cross-dresser, the fictocritic

In Chapter 2 we saw that genre was a moveable feast; this chapter focuses on ways of challenging literary genres more radically. Genre divides literary texts into categories such as poem, play or story, but an experimental approach often breaks down this categorisation. We will look here at four types of writing which transgress generic norms. They are the synoptic novel, discontinuous prose, mixed genre writing, and fictocriticism: a hybrid of creative and critical writing.

The title of the chapter alludes metaphorically to transformed and transgressive sexual identities. The invert (at least in psychiatric discourse) assumes the identity of the opposite sex, and the cross-dresser enjoys dressing up in the clothes of, and identifying with, the opposite sex. This analogy is appropriate because much postmodern writing mischievously subverts generic identities. It turns them upside down (inverts them) as in the synoptic novel and discontinuous prose, or mixes (cross-dresses) them as in mixed-genre writing and fictocriticism. But the title also suggests how bending and blending genres may have desirable and provocative cultural consequences. It can be a way to explore, formally as well as thematically, nonconformist modes of behaviour and alternative identities. When we subvert genre we splice what we regard as whole; mix things that don't match; and turn hierarchies upside down. This process may give us new ways to think about sexual or racial identity, power or disability.

Genre itself has a strong historical dimension. Genres have transformed over the centuries, and their forms and content have been shaped by, or developed in resistance to, historical pressures. Popular fiction has also evolved its own genres such as romance or science fiction, and these too have mutated over time. For example the digital world has brought about the sub-genre known as cyberpunk.

Many writers like to be stay-at-homes within a particular genre, because it gives them limits within which to generate and control ideas. Writing persistently within a particular genre, however, can be restrictive, because it imposes limits and norms, and produces rather predictable results. Historically it has been the case that most innovative writers have pushed the boundaries of the genre in which they were writing. Emily Bronte, for instance, working within narrative realism, engineers characters and situations that constantly exceed that framework. Heathcliff, in *Wuthering Heights,* often seems more like a projection of forces, than a 'rounded' character in the conventional sense.

Even genre-based writers often stretch the forms they work within. British popular novelist Barbara Vine, for example, has made the crime novel much more elastic by displacing the tension in the story, so that it does not necessarily become reduced to the solving of a crime. Instead, her novels often set up ambiguities in the way the story is resolved, and involve considerable psychological development of the characters beyond their function as part of the genre. In a completely different way, Margaret Atwood often stretches the boundaries of narrative fiction with multiple focalisations or complex time shifts. However, this is only taken to a certain point in her work, and is never pushed to the extent where narrative totally breaks down.

Postmodernist writing has played a double game with genre: both paying homage to it and yet pulling the rug from beneath its feet. In the following sections we will enter that game with the synoptic novel, discontinuous prose, mixed-genre writing and fictocriticism. Once you have tried some of these approaches, you may want to play with genre in ways which are not represented here, or have not been attempted by other writers.

exercises

1. Write a synoptic novel.
2. Write some 'notes on the life of a student' using the form of discontinuous prose.
3. Create a mixed-genre piece which 'cross-dresses' a number of literary and cultural genres.
4. Create a fictocritical text.

INVERSIONS, INVENTIONS

The synoptic novel

The 'synoptic novel' (Exercise 1) draws on the novel form but also inverts it. It radically compresses the novel while giving us a strong impression of the overall content. Finola Moorhead is an Australian writer whose 'Novel in Ten Lines' we will use as a model:

> **Example 9.1**
> Leone's room is not near the left bank of the river where she drowned. Harold walked by the park bench, thinking. Thoughts of how and when and guilt were his and we are interested, also, in the clothes he wears, the trench coat with *Giovanni's Room* by James Baldwin in the pocket. Leone came from the country with blond hair that turned dark in the city—her cotton print dresses turned to brown pleated skirts. Leone was lonely. And Harold felt sorry, that's all. He had other friends, and lots of nights with other men: his own problems.
>
> 'Novel in Ten Lines' (Moorhead 1985, p. 142)

This text poses the question: can you really write a 'novel in ten lines' when a novel is by definition lengthy? Isn't this text a complete inversion of the novel, the opposite of what we expect the novel to be? In fact Moorhead's text is both a compressed version and parody of the novel form—usually a synopsis precedes, rather than substitutes for, the writing of such a work. And unlike most novels it draws our attention to the creative process: its improvisational and sketchy beginnings. It includes the author's reflections on the writing process: 'Thoughts of how and when and guilt were his and we are interested, also, in the clothes he wears, the trench coat with *Giovanni's Room* by James Baldwin in the pocket.'

Although the 'Novel in Ten Lines' subverts the novel genre, it does so by exploiting its conventions but to different ends. The realisation of character, plot and setting in such a small space is entirely different from how it would be in a novel, because the brevity requires compression rather like poetry. Complex situations have to be alluded to in passing, so the piece is highly elliptical and fast moving. It gives us, in a very short space, an overall impression of the novel, and hints at developments which would appear in detail in the longer form.

The piece uses a surprisingly wide range of the fictional techniques which were discussed in Chapters 5 and 7. For example, it focalises the story through Harold, Leone and the author, and sketches in a number of locations. It suggests character through a sprinkling of traits: Leone seems to be the sensitive type, perhaps a naive country girl who can't take the complexities of city life. It hints at a plot line: Leone's suicide, and Harold's homosexuality as a possible causal factor, and gives us a brief insight into the impact of past events on present happenings. And it is not arranged in chronological order: it starts with what seems to be the end of the story, Leone's suicide.

Most importantly, the 'Novel in Ten Lines' uses its generic subversion to cultural ends. It captures strongly, if briefly, the plight of those who feel, or are, socially marginalised. Leone seems to be an example of a country girl who found it difficult to survive the pressures, loneliness and exploitation of the urban environment. Harold, though implicated in Leone's problems, is also struggling with his own sexual (non-normative) identity, and has in his pocket the work of James Baldwin, African-American and gay novelist. It also raises the problem of the relationship between art and culture: in the novelist's notebook social problems become reduced to fictional ones.

To create your own synoptic novel try these strategies:

- Create a bird's eye view of the action which conveys an overall impression of what the novel is about. It is easy to fall into the trap of simply writing a scene, rather than conveying a sense of a whole work. Remember that the piece is an overview, so ideally you will need to imply multiple characters, scenes, times and locations.
- Decide on at least one catastrophic or climatic event on which the 'plot' hinges. Hint at events that lead up to, or fall away, from the main event.
- Create a fruitful balance between being detailed and elliptical. You need to give enough information to arouse interest and make certain essentials clear; the rest is up to the reader.
- Compress the time sequence. You will need to cover a large span of time but reduce it to a few sentences. Also play with the order of the story; it may be more racy if not chronological.
- Suggest character traits without developing them.
- Move between different locations and times. This is essential in the synoptic novel to give an overview of the action.
- If you can, use the form as a way of exploring marginalised or unaccepted identities in our society.
- Make sure that you keep the synopsis short. Giving yourself a ten-line limit may be a good way of ensuring that.

In the student example by Joshua Lobb below, time and place keep changing most effectively. Also note how the love scenario builds up but is ruptured by the sentence, 'So he threw those plates'. This acts as a very striking metaphor. It compresses into an image, a whole series of incidents that lead to the breakdown of the relationship:

Example 9.2
He couldn't decide if a tear or a raindrop had splashed on his cheek. Early on, she seemed to have hidden herself away in the darkness, her spring sprung tight. Then there was the moment they kissed— she cried 'kiss me on the eyelids!'. He once said hello to her on a rattling bus but no sound had come out. When she smiled, her eyes always flashed uncertainly. He mistrusted love, it reminded him of long, boring movies set in dark rooms; wet eyes and wet kisses. So he threw those plates. Years later, he saw her crossing the street, her lips middle-aged and shrivelled. It rained all night, splashing blackly against the window.

'synoptic novel' (Lobb 1994)

Now try the synoptic novel for yourself, and look out for similar or related examples, such as 'A Radically Condensed History of Postindustrial Life' by American writer David Foster Wallace (2001).

DISCONTINUOUS PROSE

Discontinuous prose (Exercise 2) is a versatile form which breaks up narrative or expository writing: it is the bread and butter of experimental prose writers. Discontinuous prose is written in sections, and breaks up any continuous narrative flow. Each section can enter a topic in a different way, and can be written, if desired, in a different style. Sometimes in discontinuous prose each section has its own subheading, marking it off from the previous one. A good example of this type of writing is by an Australian, Inez Baranay. It is called 'Living Alone: The New Spinster (Some Notes)':

Example 9.3
When I began to live alone, long-ago, I'd stay up all night, so excited. Your own space! Everything stays the way you left it. The good chocolate you've been saving for the next craving remains in the fridge. You can be obsessively neat or disgustingly messy and no-one cares. You can watch TV at 3am, sleep at 7pm, red wine in the morning and breakfast at night and no-one cares. You don't have to put clothes on, you can cry for no reason and talk out loud to

yourself and no-one's offended, there's no-one to mind, no-one cares. How modern to love living alone for that. For no-one to care.

Maybe I should get a cat, become one of those cat people.

"The politics worries me. You really like living alone?" Helen asked me; she was really asking, too; she was about to try it for the first time, pushing 40. My reply would have been the New Spinster's orthodoxy: your own space, the freedom blah, blah. "It sounds unnatural" she confessed "not" she added hastily, for she had postmodern orthodoxies of her own "not that there's any such thing as 'natural' of course."

Some time after, we talked again about living alone. She doesn't like it. I was trying to explain why, after all (loneliness etc notwithstanding) I still prefer it. Saying things about the demands of writing, the jealous guarding of privacy ("not that I have any secrets") and the commune's demand for the priority of the communal good, whereas my priority is myself. All the roundabout and complicated ways I was really saying "I am obsessive, moody, self-indulgent. I do not wish to change nor to see anyone put up with that."

Living alone is about not living with men. People tell me:
—We were talking about you. We can't understand why you're alone.
Usually they say, the trouble with you. The trouble with you, they say:
—You haven't met your match in a man yet.
—You want something that doesn't exist. You want too much. You have to make allowances.
—You appear so remote and unapproachable.
—You obviously don't want a relationship.
—You want a good relationship but there are far too many other women like you.
—You meet a good man then you act like a smart-arse, a real pain. I've seen you. It makes me sick.

My greatest secret is that I'm really happy, doing just what I want to. This is a secret from myself just about all the time. Well, I get gloomy and it's like all the time. Other times my thoughts delight me dreadfully. Most of the time what I'm thinking is how things could be better.

I get exhausted. I think I do not want to "work" or to be self-reliant any longer. I think about how I'm not alone in feeling this. I don't think men ever think quite this the way women do. You get to an age and you think it was meant to be better than this. Maybe that is what you're "meant" to feel.

Pamela says she doesn't look in the mirror any more. I do. I stare in the mirror and watch my wrinkles deepen and wonder if philosophy is consolation. Pamela says "I'll be 40 in 6 months." See, everybody cares. You think other people don't stoop to this.

Look in the mirror. (As women do: self as object.) Good bones, don't smoke cigarettes, don't drink much, get lots of rest, eat well, do yoga, go for walks, it all helps, it doesn't help. I thought something would stop this from happening, it wouldn't happen to me. I'm not even meant to think of this til I'm 39. You get to an age and you think it was meant to be better than this. This isn't the way I'm meant to be. I'm meant to be younger, and richer.

I'd really like to turn this into a deep and poignant and wise pre-mid-life assessment. I want to sum up, and look forward. I want to have realisations and plans.

If I were a man this would be about how I'll now let myself cry and let myself love children and understand women and smell the roses. It would be about putting my achievements in perspective and being ready to do the mature works and be serious about sex and not waste time and value the moments.

A new spinster can only say about having to make up your own way to be, all the wisdom that cannot make her wise.

You don't want to age and you don't want to die, and then you realise this is not startling and extraordinary but only banal. At some time in your life you have the mortality experience: you realise you're only a human being and you're going to die. You have the immortality experience too, you realise you're more, and you're not.

Then the phone rang. Joy keeps in touch with a phone call every few months. Your life could end up a matter of knowing only the people who kept on calling. We talked about living alone and related matters, such as men. She said "You think deeply when you're on your own.

There are times you do get lonely. You need a network of friends. You need to look after your friends. You need to do work that keeps you in touch with people. I've reached a watershed and I want to change my whole life. There's a rumour in this building that with these real estate prices it'll be sold. For 12 years I've never had a decent relationship. The clincher is that Roger has separated from his 2nd wife and is being a really good companion." "Does this mean after all this time he is beginning to appreciate you?" "Apparently. I had [friends—long detour about the friends] over here and Roger came in and Pat said, he's nice. She wanted him. So I looked at him again." "Are you telling me after all this time you are going to end up with your ex-husband?" "If I don't end up with him some other woman is going to grab him. Right now he is talking about how ideal it would be to get two semi's side-by-side. I think that would be civilised. I would become a part-time step-mother. His ex-wife-soon-to-be never wanted to meet me." "You mean women know these things?" "There are all these variables and I have to make a decision. I don't want the decision to be caused by this building being sold."

'Living Alone: The New Spinster (Some Notes)' (Baranay 1988, pp. 15–18)

This is not a story in the conventional sense. It calls itself 'notes' to imply a loose form which embraces reflections and philosophical musings. However, it does include narrative elements: there are passages of dialogue and quotation, short scenarios and 'flashbacks' to previous incidents or conversations. The writer also dramatises and narrativises herself, for example, sometimes talking to herself in the second person. So the piece uses some fictional techniques, but is a collection of fragments which circle round a topic, rather than a directional plot-orientated story. The fragmented note form allows the writer to create a constellation of ideas which do interconnect. They all relate to rethinking the notion of the spinster in terms of the liberation a woman might feel from living on her own. In a bygone social climate, where marriage and children were supposed to be the solution for all women, the term 'spinster' was entirely negative, even pejorative. It used to imply rejection: a woman who no man had wanted to marry, marriage being the ultimate goal. Again the inversion/ subversion of form is a means to explore an alternative identity.

This piece also breaks up genre because it exists halfway between fiction and autobiography: it is a semi-fictionalised version of the diary form. The writer is negotiating the contradictions which make up her personal and social situation. The main contradiction seems to be that she wants to live alone and be independent, but also fears loneliness and becoming old. But the piece is not simply about personal experience. The author is exploring what feminist ideology means to her (women not defining themselves in terms of relationships with men, enjoying and making meaningful their own space, and so on).

In Exercise 2 I've suggested that you might make this model relevant to your own experience and social situation, and write 'notes on being a student'. One of the keys to making a success of this exercise is to introduce formal variety, for example, chunks of dialogue or lists, so it doesn't become monotonous. You can also employ what you have learned about narrative technique (such as changing between first, second and third person) if you wish.

Although the exercise is attractive because it is quite expansive, it is important to keep it reasonably tight: it is very easy for the writing to start to ramble.

GENERIC CROSS-DRESSING

A multi-genre piece (Exercise 3) combines and 'cross-dresses' various types of writing. It may mix fiction and non-fiction, the literary and the non-literary, and different literary genres. It is neither entirely prose nor poetry (just as a cross-dresser assumes an identity which is neither entirely male nor female). The strength and interest of multi-genre or cross-genre writing is that it creates considerable variety, and brings together different voices, attitudes and ways of approaching the same idea or complex of ideas.

The piece below is a short extract from the piece, 'The City and The Body', which is an example of mixed-genre writing. The piece can be viewed in its entirety, and in a hypertext version, on *The Writing Experiment* website (Smith, Dean & White republished):

Example 9.4

Welcome to the city and the body hotline: arms and legs are flying round us here at an enormous rate and so are cars and street lamps. At the moment we are not anticipating the end of the world or the demise of reproductive organs. But who knows now that sound is only time warps? Schools are going half-speed and universities are closing. Elections will only be held on racial issues. Young women may die from stress unless we treat them for their age. Whatever happened to socioeconomic solutions? Are we going to write poems until all heaven is let loose?

WANTED
A BODY WITHOUT ORGANS
THE PAGE NUMBERS FOR THE ENCYCLOPEDIC CITY
A BODY THAT MAKES MUSIC
ONE SECOND-HAND REPRODUCTIVE SYSTEM
A MIND WITHOUT THOUGHT
A STORY LINE THAT DOESN'T GO ANYWHERE
A MAP WITHOUT A MIRROR

She dreams that the streets are empty and she is standing alone naked in the middle of a square. Her arms are outstretched, her palms turned upwards. On one hand there is a bird, on the other a kettle.

She never really read the map, but half read and half guessed at it. She would walk down a street and only then would she check that she was walking the right way. Sometimes she had to turn the map upside down. It was good this balance between freedom and control, though it meant walking further than was really necessary. She didn't want to check herself too much.

Novels do not merely represent the urban: they produce it.

Cities are under siege from aberrant *readings.*

the place that is everywhere and nowhere

a no-place a non-made a no-man a knot-place

the place that is where in the not that is when

a bare-legged hunch

a star that is sun

a faceless

unplaceable

space

ARE YOU A POST-TOURIST?
DO YOU LIKE TO TRAVEL TO PLACES THAT ONLY EXIST AS MYTHS?

DECONSTRUCTION
a way of taking a position

The Greek city was small (almost village-like) and worked on a democratic principle that nevertheless excluded women, slaves and foreigners. At the core of Greek urbanisation was the concept of polis, sometimes defined as 'city-state'. This was both a community and a sense of community. The Greeks' social life centred on the public marketplace.

Who is policing the body politic?

he puts his hand through the computer screen and grabs the words insert, format and view. Then he saunters through the cityscape and pins them up on crowded billboards.

Are you good at female geography?

Locating the womb linguistically?

Please write your name here in menstrual blood

WELCOME TO THE INTERNET SLIMMERS GROUP THIN DOWN YOUR MESSAGES MAKE YOURSELF MORE ATTRACTIVE TO OTHER USERS

She throws down her eye into the middle of the road. Passers-by walk over it and squash it, unconcerned, unnoticing, uncaring. But the eye winks at her as she bends down, picks it up, and returns it to its socket.

a signpost streaked with undecipherable *desires*

From 'The City and The Body' (Smith 2001, pp. 170–1)

In this piece there are many different kinds of genre: both literary and non-literary. So there are not simply poems and narratives, but also signs, advertisements, warnings and theoretical interjections. Many styles of writing emerge in the piece: there are surreal scenarios such as the woman standing naked in the middle of the square, or the woman throwing her eye down into the street; satirical and futuristic interjections, factual, documentary-like passages and so on. The fragments are separate but they are interwoven by recurring images, such as the references to maps and mirrors. There are also many common concerns: many of the texts refer to the marginalised and oppressed in our and former societies, particularly those subject to sexism or racism, for example:

Example 9.5

SUNDAY MAY 6TH 1243
CITIZENS!
WASH YOUR HANDS OF MENSTRUAL BLOOD!
STAND CLEAR OF UNCLEAN
MENOPAUSAL WITCHES

Medieval hospitals were often situated at city boundaries. They regularly housed lepers, who were stigmatised since leprosy was thought to be caused by sexual sin. The prominence of hospitals at boundaries attracted prayers and alms from travellers and pilgrims.

ATTENTION CYBORGS! WE ARE LOOKING FOR A PRE-
POSTHUMAN BODY: CAN YOU WALK, SPEAK AND EAT?
DO HUMDRUM THINGS? APPLY NOW, DON'T WAIT.
YOU MAY BECOME A SLAVE TO CYBER-CITY CHANGE.

a hyperscape—a heterogeneous, global, constantly changing site characterised by difference. The hyperscape occurs when the body and city are dismantled and reconstituted. *In 1981 British Home Office research estimated that Asian people in the United Kingdom were fifty times more likely to be attacked on racial grounds than white people, and black people thirty-six times more likely.*

Black People's Time
Greenwich **mean** time

From 'The City and The Body (Smith 2001, p. 173)

Almost all the textual fragments refer to either the body or the city, or both, in medieval, modern and future times—but there is no unified body or city which permeates the whole piece. What we see is parts rather than wholes, glimpses and snatches rather than complete entities. The piece in its full version moves between disparate times, places and forms of society: shifting between Kuwait, Siberia, Greece and England. Consequently, the generic mix reflects and transmits **cultural hybridity** between diverse ethnicities, sexualities and perspectives. This relationship between generic mix and cultural hybridity is one that can be seen in a number of authors such as Theresa Hak Kyung Cha (2001).

One of the advantages of this kind of writing is that you can put together fragments of writing, which is something we have been looking at throughout this book. Any tiny fragment you write can be revitalised through the generic melting pot!

For Exercise 3 assemble your own mixed-genre piece. Choose a topic and then start writing fragments. The fragments can be in any genre: you can traverse the realms of prose and poetry, and draw in non-literary forms too. Arrange the bits and pieces in any way you like on the page. A striking visual arrangement can not only increase the impact of the words, but encourages readers to move over the page in a multidirectional, rather than purely left-to-right manner.

FICTOCRITICISM

Fictocriticism (see Exercise 4) is a fusion and exchange of critical and creative writing. Again, therefore, it cross-dresses different types of writing, a point previously made by Anne Brewster (1996) in her excellent article on fictocriticism. Fictocriticism, sometimes known as the paraliterary or postcritical, attempts to bring together academic discourse and creative practice, and overcome the division between them. Such work is very important in universities today, where we are undertaking creative writing within an academic environment. In fact, fictocriticism, which arose sharply in Australia in the 1990s, was largely a response to the growth of creative writing teaching and learning within the university environment, where—as Brewster points out—creative writing is taught in conjunction with other intellectual disciplines, including subjects about post-structuralist theory (Brewster 1996). In the context of the university, and with the rise and popularity of creative writing courses, the question has repeatedly arisen: how do we bring together the different worlds of learning and research, and creative work? In fact theory and creative writing usually address similar intellectual issues, though through different methods. On the one hand, creative texts often fictionalise philosophical and political issues, which are in turn theorised by critics. On the other hand, many well-known theoretical texts engage with creative writing strategies such as puns, the construction of new words, poetic metaphor, multiple voices or extensive use of the first person to develop ideas.

Fictocriticism or paraliterature has also arisen because of an increase of writers who wanted to transmit their own poetics as well as presenting their creative work. Generic experimentation inevitably led to a breaking of boundaries between theoretical and creative work. This was true, for example, of the Language Poets in America. Some of these poets wrote essays about poetics as well as writing poetry, and it became inevitable that sometimes they would fuse the two together. Such an approach is also common in new media work where hyperlinking provides a very good means to link the theoretical and the creative (see Chapter 11).

Ideally fictocriticism creates a symbiotic relationship between theory/ criticism and creative work, so that they feed into, and illuminate, each other. In fictocriticism, critical/cultural theory and creative writing are juxtaposed or merged. As Anne Brewster points out, these endeavours are often thought of as opposed to each other, but fictocriticism seeks to challenge this opposition:

> If there is a generic division or opposition which fictocriticism seeks to mediate, it is the demarcation inscribed in academic production of the genres of high art (fiction, poetry, drama) and the essayistic modes which purport to study them (commentary, criticism, analysis, theory). The opposition between these two genres is figured in the way we characterise criticism, for example, as neutral and disinterested and literature as expressive of a personalised subjectivity. Another figuring of this opposition is the notion that criticism trades in ideas; literature in states of emotion and feeling.
>
> (Brewster 1996, p. 29)

A fictocritical approach to creative writing tends to make intellectual ideas rather more overt than in much fiction or poetry. Obviously, complex literary texts usually have intellectual depth. But the conventional view of writing would tend to be that the intellectual dimension had to be fiction-alised or poeticised, and that its sources should be covered over and hidden. In fictocritical work, intellectual ideas are often addressed more directly and within academic frames of reference.

In common with other types of experimental writing, fictocriticism tends to be an open rather than a closed form. It embraces mixed-genre writing, discontinuous prose and linguistic play. Quotations (often from theoretical texts) are also common in this type of work. However, such fea-tures may not characterise all fictocritical writing. This is a variable and developing field: you should create your own models, and draw together theory and creative work in any way you find productive.

Fictocritics sometimes strive to revivify and rethink the essay form in a more creative way. Although its scope for logical argument and analysis is invaluable and irreplaceable, at times the essay can seem a stiff and inflex-ible form. A fictocritical approach to writing an essay is less formal and linear than the normal academic essay. Fictionalised, poetic and anecdotal elements may be introduced, and the presence of the author may be made more overt. The use of the first person can be extensive and may be used as a way of breaking out of the more depersonalised essay form.

An example of a fictocritical approach to the essay is Charles Bernstein's poem–essay, 'Artifice of Absorption':

Example 9.6

The reason it is difficult to talk about
the meaning of a poem—in a way that doesn't seem
frustratingly superficial or partial—is that by
designating a text a poem, one suggests that its
meanings are to be located in some "complex" beyond an accumulation of devices & subject matters.
A poetic *reading* can be given to any
piece of writing; a "poem" may be understood as
writing specifically designed to absorb, or inflate
with, proactive—rather than reactive—styles of
reading. "Artifice" is a measure of a poem's
intractability to being read as the sum of its
devices & subject matters. In this sense,
"artifice" is the contradiction of "realism", with
its insistence on presenting an unmediated
(immediate) experience of facts, either of the
"external" world of nature or the "internal" world
of the mind; for example, naturalistic
representation or phenomenological consciousness
mapping. Facts in poetry are primarily
factitious.

From 'Artifice of Absorption' (Bernstein 1992, pp. 9–10)

In this opening extract, Bernstein starts to map out ways in which to talk about a form of poetry which breaks through conventions of realism and self-expression. The piece is in many respects prosaic because it expounds ideas in full sentences. But the line breaks give it a more poetic feel, and accentuate certain rhythmical qualities which would not be palpable in the same way if it was written in prose. This poem–essay also mixes informal and theoretical language. So phrasing like, 'The reason it is difficult to talk about/the meaning of a poem—in a way that doesn't seem/frustratingly superficial or partial' is informal, and has a strong speaking quality. On the other hand, from the sentence '"Artifice" is a measure of a poem's/intractability to being read as the sum of its/devices & subject matters', to the end of the passage, the language is much more theoretical and technical.

In other types of fictocritical writing there may be an alternation or negotiation between creative writing and academic discourse, in which different sections of the text gesture towards different types of writing. For example 'Learning to Drive: Reading the Signs' by Australian writer Moya Costello is written in short fragments (it is another example of discontinuous prose). It contains theoretical allusion (for example to Virilio and Lacan); literary allusion (for example to Murray Bail, Helen Garner and Annie Proulx); short narratives; reflective fragments; and quotation. It uses driving as a metaphor for combining change with 'staying on track', and interweaves driving and psychological 'breakdown' with the processes of writing and reading. In the following passage Costello moves, in a deft associative sequence, from literary allusion, to thoughts on the process of driving, to a quotation about the activity of writing. The quotations are from Annie Proulx and Nicole Bourke respectively, and are annotated in footnotes:

Example 9.7

In her novel *Postcards*, E. Annie Proulx has a chapter called 'The Driver' (it is almost a complete short story in itself). After her husband dies, Jewell, the oppressed wife and mother of the backwoods Blood family, gains both freedom in her house—though she narrows down the space she inhabits in it—and freedom in the outside world when she learns to drive and buys a car.

> When she turned the ignition key and steered the car out of the drive, the gravel crunching deliciously under the tires, she went dizzy with power for the first time in her adult life.

One of the hardest things to do, I find, is to get a sense of the space of the car: how much space it fills up, its length and breadth. There will be some days, I am thinking, when perhaps I should not drive. These will be days when I occupy no space.

> When I write, it is a peculiar thing . . . I plunge in, having lost my way, having never had a way, and begin to navigate absen(s)e.

From 'Learning to Drive: Reading the Signs' (Costello 1999, p. 23)

In Anne Brewster's 'sucking on remembrance: encounters with the vampire and other histories of the body', the text alternates between passages of creative writing and theoretical quotations. Again full references are given at the end of the piece. Here is a short excerpt:

Example 9.8

vampire

vampires and strange creatures walk everywhere. i used not to notice them. but once you have seen one you see them everywhere. between this world and the next, half in life and half out of it. they prowl, watching, biding their time. they make no hurried moves, having lived for centuries in slow time. they conserve their energy; a little goes a long way. watching through the cracks in the everyday they wait. in their suits and large cars they inhabit our days like asphalt, like noise, like daily pictures of starvation and atrocity. we have grown accustomed to them. on street corners, in lounge rooms, at receptions with silk ties. we learn to live with them. if it's your neck their eyes alight upon, you practise the art of merging with the wallpaper, of slipping into the crowd. there's safety in numbers and there's no shortage of sweet blood: young women, old women, black women, pale women, women of indiscernible ethnicity; demure women, feisty women, thin women and voluptuous women; willing women, angry women, sacrificial women; naive women, jaded women, elusive women and dwarf women. one can lose oneself in this cornucopia. like wildebeests in the mob, we run together and watch as one falls, her body opened and flowing out across the tongue of the vampire.

vampires are everywhere. even those you cannot escape are seldom fatal. you may find your flesh shrinking. sometimes the taste of disgust is almost unbearable. sometimes the image of death smirks in the mirror. these horrors fade under the glare of day and you go about your business. after all there's no escape when the door opens each morning and closes each night behind you. even vampires you learn to tolerate, like incest or corruption or disease, which are, after all, part of life and part of the death that creeps through the veins of the ghouls that couple in the mysterious ways of their choice with the living.

If the body is not a 'being', but a variable boundary, a surface whose permeability is politically regulated, a signifying practice within a cultural field of gender hierarchy and compulsory heterosexuality, then what language is left for understanding this corporeal enactment, gender, that constitutes its 'interior' signification on its surface?

Judith Butler

i just want to speak. i want to tell you. how it happened. i didn't know how to tell you. i didn't know how to step out of that magic circle an event inscribes around you. the circle that binds you to the spot, the moment. i wanted to tell you. i wanted you to know. what you do with these words is of small import. words travel. change shape. visceral. a gesture. a movement. the stomach of the world. to spin out, to weave. spellbound i watch the conjuring of utterance. tattoo of the gaze. i was trying to tell you. i needed to speak. your eyes missed a beat. the circle wavered. i fell into speech. i moved into darkness. listening is dampness. the word touching. the warm body nurses restlessness into speech. enchanted i was in the world again. there were lights and the music was spinning. there were bodies fully opaque. everywhere words were weaving their spell.

sentience takes us out of ourselves ... images ... engage not so much with mind as with the embodied mind

Walter Benjamin

From 'sucking on remembrance: encounters with the vampire and other histories of the body' (Brewster 1998, pp. 209–11)

Brewster's prose poems, and the accompanying quotations, are symbiotic. The creative writing takes up some of the ideas from the theory, while we are likely to read the quotations differently because of the prose poems which accompany them. At the same time this is not a simplistic relationship, and the connections between quotation and creative writing are diverse and fluid. We will read the theory against and with the creative work, and the two will resonate with each other. But the theory does not 'explain' the prose poetry, and the creative writing is not simply an illustration of the theory. Rather, Judith Butler's formulation of the body as a variable and politically regulated surface resonates with the evocation of vampirism to produce ideas about vulnerability, exploitation and the regulation of gender and sexuality. Similarly, the theme of the third section—the ways in which language is inadequate, but is also embodied and felt—rubs well together with the Walter Benjamin quotation. The symbiosis is also stylistic: the theory uses language creatively and imaginatively, and the creative writing draws energy from theoretical ideas, blurring the distinction between the two.

To write a fictocritical piece, Exercise 4, you may find it productive to employ a discontinuous prose form so you can write in sections. Choose a theme which has some theoretical mileage in it, and then write poems and short narratives in response to it. Also interject quotations from, and/or passages about, theoretical issues. If possible do not simply state a theoretical idea but develop it, or give your own 'take on it'. Alternatively take a theoretical text (or several) that you really like, and use the theory to trigger the writing of fictional or poetic texts. How overt the theory is in a fictocritical piece is a matter of taste. Fictocriticism can be both 'explicit' and 'implicit', and a number of pieces in this book could be construed to be fictocritical while not overtly positioning themselves as such. The theory may be very prominent in the final text; alternatively it may form the basis for the piece but be no longer overtly present in the final text. Fictocritical texts of many different kinds appear in *The Space Between* (Kerr and Nettelbeck 1998). Lesley Stern's *The Smoking Book* (2001) is also a good example of sustained fictocritical writing, as is Rachel Blau DuPlessis's *The Pink Guitar* (1990).

Fictocriticism can also parody itself. The American novel *House of Leaves* includes a pseudo-academic critical commentary which is made up of partly spurious, partly real references (Danielewski 2001).

CONCLUSION

This chapter has encouraged you to adopt an irreverent and subversive approach to genre. Other ways of challenging generic boundaries have been followed through at various points in the book, for example, in Chapters 6 and 7. You will probably now be able to think of your own ways of bending and blending genres. A generic mix will be useful to you in developing your cyberwriting in Chapter 11, and may help you to write the city as a site of difference in Chapter 12. You may be able to pull together fragments you have already written in response to previous exercises to create a cross-genre piece, or you may wish to return to Chapters 5 and 7 to find other ways of inverting fictional norms. Hopefully you can also use these processes to question ways in which we encode identity and power relations and to invert cultural norms. In fact, the subversion of genre is central to an experimental approach, and the textual and cultural norms it questions. As such it can be seen to be pivotal to many of the aims and purposes of this book.

REFERENCES

Baranay, I. 1988, 'Living Alone: The New Spinster (Some Notes)', *Telling Ways: Australian Women's Experimental Writing*, (eds.) S. Gunew and A. Couani, –Australian Feminist Studies Publications, Adelaide.

Bernstein, C. 1992, 'Artifice of Absorption', *A Poetics,* Harvard University Press, Cambridge, Massachusetts, pp. 9–89.

Brewster, A. 1996, 'Fictocriticism: Undisciplined Writing', *First Conference of the Association of University Writing Programs,* (eds). J. Hutchinson and G. Williams, University of Technology Sydney, Sydney, pp. 29–32.

—— 1998, 'sucking on remembrance: encounters with the vampire and other histories of the body', *The Space Between: Australian Women Writing Fictocriticism,* (eds). H. Kerr and A. Nettelbeck, University of Western Australia Press, Nedlands, Western Australia, pp. 209–16.

Cha, T.H.K. 2001, *Dictée,* University of California Press, Berkeley. Originally published in 1982 by Tanam Press.

Costello, M. 1999, 'Learning to Drive: Reading the Signs', *Meanjin,* vol. 58, no. 3, pp. 22–32.

Danielewski, M.Z. 2001, *House of Leaves,* 2nd edn, Doubleday, London.

DuPlessis, R.B. 1990, *The Pink Guitar: Writing as Feminist Practice,* Routledge, New York.

Kerr, H. and Nettelbeck, A. (eds) 1998, *The Space Between: Australian Women Writing Fictocriticism,* University of Western Australia Press, Nedlands, Western Australia.

Lobb, J. 1994, 'synoptic novel', unpublished.

Moorhead, F. 1985, 'Novel in Ten Lines', *Quilt: A Collection of Prose,* Sybylla Co-operative Press & Publications, Melbourne.

Smith, H. 2001, 'The City and The Body', *Meanjin: Under Construction,* vol. 60, no. 1, pp. 170–5.

Smith, H., Dean, R.T. and White, G. K. republished, 'Wordstuffs: The City and The Body', Multimedia work. www.allenandunwin.com/writingexp. Originally published in 1998 and also available at http://www.abc.net.au/arts/stuff-art/stuff-art99/stuff98/10.htm.

Stern, L. 2001, *The Smoking Book,* University of Chicago Press, Chicago.

Wallace, D.F. 2001, 'A Radically Condensed History of Postindustrial Life', *Brief Interviews With Hideous Men,* Abacus, London, p. 0.

CHAPTER TEN
Tongues, talk and technologies

This chapter explores writing for performance, and encourages you to increase the oral dimension of your writing. It is about the various ways in which you can make your text 'talk', explore different voices and untie your tongue. At the same time it takes you from performance poetry into intermedia work (which combines words, sounds and images), improvisation and theatrical presentation. However, it does not encourage you to construct conventional plays, and is not about writing drama.

Although we tend to think of writing as words on the page, there is no particular reason why verbal texts should always be written. Most of our daily communication occurs through conversation rather than the written word. As far as artistic and literary traditions are concerned, most were originally oral. The persistence of that oral tradition is powerful in many cultures, and is a strong presence in, for example, Jamaican dub poetry or Hawaiian pidgin poetry.

Most writers are called upon on occasion to publicly read or perform their own work, but not all texts which are designed for silent reading are necessarily enhanced when 'read out'. So it can be useful to create some pieces which are particularly designed for this purpose.

In this chapter I will be suggesting, however, that the importance of performance extends far beyond this kind of utility. An awareness of the possibilities of performance can give us a whole new and exciting perspective on writing. Performance radically changes the author–reader dynamic: it creates a live situation in which the writer and audience interact in the same space. Performance creates the possibility of unique forms of communication which are sometimes more immediate and malleable than those offered by the page alone.

The degree to which any piece takes on the challenges of performance will vary enormously. For example, at one extreme, the term performance poetry may simply be used to describe forceful and effective communication of a page-based poem. At the other extreme, it may mean a poem which only exists in an oral form. In addition, the concept of performance is becoming more and more enmeshed with technology. Some of the strategies in this chapter combine a performance and technological approach, and can be used in studio-based work or writing for radio.

This chapter is accompanied by examples on *The Writing Experiment* website at www.allenandunwin.com/writingexp. You will gain most if you listen to them in conjunction with reading the chapter. These works are referred to within the chapter and listed at the end of it.

exercises

1. Create a performance text which is:
   a) a speech-based poem
   b) a sonic poem.
2. Construct a performance text which has a mixed media or intermedia aspect.
3. Create an improvised text.
4. Create:
   a) a performance 'score' which has to be completed by performers, or
   b) a piece which requires audience participation.
5. Create a text which explores the relationship between performance and gender and/or performance and ethnicity.
6. Create a piece which experiments with different uses of the microphone.

ANGLES ON PERFORMANCE

There are many different ways of approaching writing for performance. These are some general issues and alternatives which you will need to explore as you begin to create performance texts:

• You can perform your own texts, or they can be performed by others. If you perform the texts yourself you can directly communicate with your audience. Also your physical presence, and such factors as your gender or ethnicity, will have an effect on the words spoken, though you may also wish to find ways of inverting or transforming this effect. If you write texts to be performed by others, on the other hand, there will be the additional interest of seeing how they interpret your work.

- If others perform your work you can give them a very tight script to work from, or a lot of freedom to have a creative input. For example, you can write a script which allows the performers to partly improvise so that there is no totally written-out script: this is a strategy employed by Jackson Mac Low (1986) and discussed later in this chapter. In fact you may have no script at all, or it may consist only of written instructions.
- You can create any kind of relationship between the performance and the written word. You can write a piece which is transformed or only fully realised in performance. Or you can create a piece for perform- ance which does not exist in written form and then transcribe it for the page afterwards. Sometimes there may be no way of transcribing the work, or you may have no wish to do so. On other occasions you may wish to produce a print version for the purposes of documentation, even if you do not feel that it adequately conveys the full aura of the performance. More ideally there might be print and performance ver- sions: these might have a symbiotic relationship, but also exist as independent entities. American performance poet Steve Benson uses his own texts as a basis for his improvised performance, but also some- times transcribes his performances as texts, with striking verbal and visual results. On occasion, as in his work 'Back', the original and improvised texts sit side by side in the published text (see Benson 1989, pp. 77–93). It is also possible to partly translate the performance aspect of a text into visual markers, through the use of different font thick- nesses and sizes, and spacing on the page. The result can be a text which bears the traces of the performance, but is also a striking visual entity in its own right.
- Through the medium of performance you can interconnect verbal language with non-verbal languages such as gesture, visual images, sound and lighting to create what is known as 'intermedia' or mixed- media work.

PERFORMANCE POETRY

Performance poetry is a very general term which has been used to describe many different types of orally based work. It includes sound poetry, ethnopoetics, dub poetry, and what is sometimes known as slam poetry. Performance poetry therefore ranges from avant-garde practices which often involve linguistic experimentation, and extreme uses of the voice, to work which has strong connections with hip hop, popular song, entertainment and ethnic oral traditions.

Performance poetry spans a wide range of Caucasian and non-Caucasian poetries. It includes the work of numerous European, American and Australian poets. But it also includes powerful African-American performance poets such as Harryette Mullen, Wanda Coleman, Scott Woods and Patricia Smith; Hawaiian dub poets and musicians and the Japanese-American performance poet Richard Hamasaki, known as 'Red Flea', who lives in Hawaii (Flea 1996); and Caribbean poets such as Linton Kwesi Johnson, Benjamin Zephaniah or Jean 'Binta' Breeze.

Performance poetry has to be experienced through live events, but is also represented on a growing number of CDs, CD-ROMs and print anthologies. See *Future Poesia Sonora* (Lora-Totino 1978) *Text-Sound Texts* (Kostelanetz 1980), *Homo Sonorus* (Bulatov 2001), and *Short Fuse* (Swift & Norton 2002). One of the best points of access now is websites such as The Wordsmith Press (The Wordsmith Press Ongoing) and UbuWeb (UbuWeb Ongoing). (For discussion of poetry in performance, see also *Sound States* (Morris 1997), *Close Listening* (Bernstein 1998), and *Homo Sonorus* (Bulatov 2001).)

Performance poems range from those which are complete on the page but are given a heightened dimension through performance, to those which are incomplete on the page and require performance for their fruition. Here I will be exploring that continuum, though mainly concentrating on types of performance poetry which present an experience distinct from, and provoking beyond, simply reading a poem on the page. Performance poetry can be divided into **speech-based** and **sonic** performance poems (see Exercises 1a and 1b), though there are many overlaps between the two.

SPOKEN WORKS

In this section we will explore different types of **speech-based** performance poems: sometimes this kind of work is known as 'spoken word'. The language in such poems ranges between the highly colloquial and the highly poetic, sometimes within the same poem. In all cases performance is used to give another dimension to the poem, mainly through the projection of the voice. Dynamics, pitch and accentuation of the voice, as well as rhythmic delivery, are all ways in which the poem can be transmuted in performance.

On *The Writing Experiment* website you will find two examples of such performances by Taylor Mali and Scott Woods. They are both known as slam poets, because of their participation in Poetry Slam competitions. In a Poetry Slam the judges—who are audience members chosen at random—score poets in performance. The poet with the highest score wins: excellent presentation skills and the ability to communicate well with the audience are paramount. Mali and Woods probably would not identify with experimental poetry movements such as Language Poetry, and their formal and linguistic preoccupations. Rather they experiment with the dimension of performance—the voice, projection and the relationship with the audience—to exciting effect.

Taylor Mali is an American poet whose performances often contain musical and theatrical elements. Mali's *Undivided Attention* (republished) on *The Writing Experiment* website is less obviously performance-orientated than some of his poems, which contain more pronounced musical and theatrical elements. But I have included it here because of the subtlety and elegance of the delivery, and to show how a poem can be effectively heightened in performance, even when it already seems relatively complete on the page. The poem mixes poetic and 'talking' language, and the delivery is both direct and subtle. Mali sometimes breaks the poem into short phrases, but at other times scoops up a few phrases together into a longer breath. He also slightly speeds up and slows down his delivery, and lowers and/or raises the dynamic level of his voice. The result impacts very effectively on the meaning. For example, the line 'Who can teach when there are such lessons to be learnt?' is given particular emphasis by a slightly slower pace and softer voice, particularly on the word 'such'. Similarly, the repetition of 'the edge of the seat, the edge of tears, the edge of eight stories up going over' is emphasised by a slight accelerando, raising of the voice and accentuation. All these effects help to emphasise the questions raised in the poem about education and the forms it can take. It is also interesting to note that Mali does not perform the poem exactly as it appears on his website in the written version. Rather he makes a number of cuts and changes, possibly suggesting that there is an improvisational element in his performances. He seems to use the performance situation to render the poem slightly differently each time, not only in terms of delivery but of actual words.

African-American poet Scott Woods's *Elevator Dreams* (republished) is extremely ebullient and feisty. The use of repetition in the piece is most effective, and this is enhanced by the highly rhythmic, jazz-like delivery of the poem. Again Woods uses speed, dynamics and pitch. Most of the poem is delivered in a fast, punchy and loud manner, making it particularly effective when Woods lowers his voice on the word 'safe' near the beginning of the poem, and on the word 'escape' right at the end. Volume, speed and dynamic come together to create long phrases and considerable build-ups of verbal tension. These contrasts within the performance emphasise the tension between reality and dream, the urban and rural, freedom and imprisonment implicit in the words. But there is also an African-American voice and presence in the performance. This evokes the jazz tradition, and has many other cultural resonances. Despite its humorous aspect, the poem echoes Martin Luther King's 'I have a dream' speech, not only in its subject matter but also in its rhetorical and heightened delivery.

Some spoken-word poems particularly emphasise the patterns of speech rather than written language. Such poems may focus on colloquialisms, local or class-based dialects, or ethnic speech patterns.

An example of such a piece is the poem and sound recording *The Six O'Clock News* by Scottish poet Tom Leonard (1984), which satirises the notion of the once omniscient (white, upper-class) BBC accent, and the idea that words spoken in a dialect are regarded with suspicion. It is spelt in dialect and spoken in his inimitable Scottish accent. It can be accessed from his website (see p. 235).

Speech-based work may explore the intersections between different languages, or the impact of bilingualism or polylingualism on uses of language. Such exploration is central to the work of performance artist and poet Caroline Bergvall who lives in England and writes in English, but is of French and Norwegian extraction (French is her first language). For Bergvall 'mis-translations' and 'mis-spellings' are part of the process of writing (1999).

Technology can also give us quite a different take on the idea of 'spoken word'. In the interactive work by American David Knoebel, *How I Heard It* (republished), on *The Writing Experiment* website, clicking on the circles in the visual display creates multiple overlaid voices talking about the same incident, though in fragmented ways, and with additional environmental sounds. The interactive element means that the reader can constantly shift the voices and the way they relate to each other. We will explore more about how to use technology in the following section.

Some possible strategies for Exercise 1a, creating a speech-based performance poem, are:

- Write a poem with a view to giving shape to the words through dynamic, speed and rhythm. Bear this performance aspect in mind while you write the poem, and let it, in some respects, dictate its direction. Choose a theme, or set of themes, which will be responsive to such a performance dimension.

- Write a performance poem which uses your voice to either emphasise or question your own cultural background, e.g. with regard to nationality, gender or ethnicity.
- Write a performance poem which is highly colloquial and uses 'talking language'.
- Write a performance poem which problematises standard English, for example, by employing a dialect.
- Write a performance poem which is a hybrid of two or more languages, or which shows the impact of one language upon another.

SONIC POETRY, SONIC WRITING

A **sonic poem** works at the interface between sound and language, and emphasises the sonic properties of language. Sonic poems exist along the continuum from poetry to music, and from speaking to singing. Nevertheless they are distinct from songs, which set pre-existent words to music. Sonic writing (I use both the terms sonic poetry and sonic writing which is slightly broader) usually creates an interactive relationship between sound and music, so that each modifies the other.

Sonic poetry/writing was preceded by the movement known as sound poetry, which began in the early experiments of the dadaists and futurists, but became much more prominent in the sound-poetry movement of the 50s, 60s and 70s. This is sometimes known as the Text-Sound movement and is documented in *Futura Poesia Sonora* (Lora-Totino 1978) and in *Text-Sound Texts* (Kostelanetz 1980). A sound poem coheres through sound rather than semantics. It might focus on permuting phrases, mantric effects, constructed languages, the breakdown of words into syllables or phonemes, or manipulation of the voice.

Sonic poetry/writing has developed out of sound poetry but takes more diverse forms: it can involve any combination of words, sound and voice. The results may relate to jazz, hip hop, rap, contemporary or classical music, or ethnic traditions. Sonic writing can also take large-scale forms such as 'sound technodrama': these are pieces which are simultaneously dramatic, poetic, narrative and discursive, sonic and technological, (see Smith & Dean 2003).

Technology has impacted very heavily on sonic writing. When sound poetry was at its height, analogue technologies—such as the tape recorder— were used to splice material and multitrack the voice. Increasingly, however, digital technologies have taken over, from keyboard samplers to computer software. You can either use a very basic technology such as the cassette recorder, or sophisticated software programs such as ProTools, the sound-mixing-editing software which is available free on the Internet.

The sound section of the UbuWeb website (UbuWeb Ongoing) is very extensive and is an outstanding collection of sonic poetry/writing (as well as an archive of historic sound poetry material). You can find pieces there by most of the poets mentioned in this section. Try also the ethnopoetics section of UbuWeb for fascinating recordings of contemporary renderings of traditional songs and sound poems from a wide range of different cultures.

To create a sonic poem (Exercise 1b) try some of the following strategies:

- Use parts of words (phonemes and syllables), make up your own words, distort words and construct sounds that seem like words, thereby emphasising the sonic properties of the words as much as their meanings. For examples of this kind of sonic poetry see the work of Maggie O'Sullivan, Bob Cobbing, Trevor Wishart (UK), Amanda Stewart (Australia), Phil Dutton (Canada), and many others in *Homo Sonorus: An International Anthology of Sound Poetry* (Bulatov 2001); and also on UbuWeb: sound (UbuWeb Ongoing). Also see the work of Canadian poet Christian Bok (republished) whose 'Motorised Razors' and 'Mushroom Clouds' (both from a longer ongoing piece called *The Cyborg Opera*) are represented on *The Writing Experiment* website. These pieces use whole words, parts of words, and word- and syllable-like sounds (as well as throat and mouth sounds).

- Use repetition or permutation (see also Chapter 1) to draw attention to the sonic aspect of the work. See the work of Brion Gysin (1962a; 1962b). See also the work of American musician and sound poet Charles Amirkhanian whose *Church Car, Version 2* (republished-a) and *Dot Bunch* (republished-b) are on *The Writing Experiment* website. Amirkhanian's pieces are as much a product of technology as performance, though made in the days of analogue rather than digital technology. Words such as 'church car' and 'bang' are recorded, cut up and then spliced, reassembled and multitracked. Notice, for example, how the words 'church car' blur into many others words such as 'churchyard' or 'cha cha', and also into sounds which are not actual words.

- Exploit the range of the voice through accentuation, dynamic and pitch (without necessarily turning the poem into a song). Write down a phrase and say it in many different ways. In order to do this, vary your pitch, accentuation and dynamic. Alternatively, or in addition, make the sound support, or even represent, the meaning. For example, Ania Walwicz when performing her poem 'bells' (1989, pp. 143–5) accentuates the words in a cyclic way which seems to suggest bell sounds. Try also to exploit the range of the voice, from whispering to shouting,

beyond the normal parameters of the poetry reading. To hear sophisticated manipulation of the voice, listen to Trevor Wishart (2001) or
Christian Bok (republished) on *The Writing Experiment* website.

- Enunciate words rhythmically. This has been popular from avant-garde
poetries to rap: it is likely, however, to require musical expertise to be
maximally effective. Make sure that you pursue syncopated and irregular rhythms as well as regular ones: move against the beat as well as
with it. Again see the work of Charles Amirkhanian on *The Writing
Experiment* website. But also see the work of Caribbean poets Linton
Kwesi Johnson and Benjamin Zephaniah (Tuma 2001)—the rhythmic
content is noticeable even on the page. See also my own work which is
rhythmically notated on the page (Smith 1991) and realised on CD
(Smith 1994); and my collaboration with Roger Dean, *Poet Without
Language,* represented in an extract on *The Writing Experiment* website
(Smith & Dean republished).

- Speak with a musical accompaniment. This could be a rhythmic
backing, a musical composition, or a soundscape consisting of environmental noises. Music and words may be closely related to each other, or
run in parallel with each other, with relatively little interaction.

- Explore the interface between singing and speaking. The poet Amanda
Stewart has created poems which move dexterously between popular
songs, anthems and lines of poetry (sometimes speaking, sometimes
singing) to create this kind of oral mix. For example, her delivery of the
poem *.romance (1981)*—the written text of which is included in Chapter
4—involves abrupt shifts in tone, dynamic and speed. Listen to her performance of this on *The Writing Experiment* website (Stewart republished).
Other poets, like the Canadian, bp Nichol, have explored a continuum
from speaking to singing in their work. See his *Pome Poem* (1972).

- Explore your tongue, lips and throat and the way they can affect how
you speak or make vocal sounds. Push your tongue into different parts
of your mouth or try to make sounds with your mouth closed. You will
find such experiments will enrich your oral delivery though sometimes
in bizarre ways.

- Use a tape recorder or computer technology to multitrack the voice,
creating the speaking equivalent of polyphony in music. Multitracking
can create many different relationships between multiple versions of
the same voice. See Charles Bernstein's *My/My/My* (1976) or an extract
from *Poet Without Language* (Smith & Dean republished), on the *The
Writing Experiment* website.

- Use a keyboard sampler or computer to digitally record words and
manipulate them. A sample is a digital recording of a short sound or
word which can then be manipulated with respect to timbre, pitch

or rhythm. When a word is sampled it can be chopped up, played backwards or repeated in a loop. As a result a word can be transformed into another word, or manipulated up to the point where it is unrecognisable as a word. Words can be superimposed upon each other, or turned into sound textures. Sampling has very important ramifications for the concept of voice in poetry, because it can radically alter the voice and its cultural implications with respect to gender, ethnicity and age. Samples may be used in recordings or as part of live performance. Sampling can be found in *Poet Without Language* (Smith 1994), an extract of which can be found on *The Writing Experiment* website (Smith & Dean republished). This explores the continuum between words and words which are turned into sounds. See also my collaboration with Roger Dean, *the writer, the performer, the program, the madwoman*, on the same website. Here the words are sampled in performance and then manipulated in real time, creating many transformations and much multilayering of the voice (Smith republished). Sampling is now a standard part of sonic writing (though used to many different ends).

- Use a digital delay system (in which anything you say echoes several times over afterwards): you can build up powerful associative sequences and multitrack the voice. Listen to American poet John Giorno (1972; 1978).
- If you have access to sophisticated hardware equipment, treat the voice through reverberation, or spatialise it using different points in the stereo system. If not, you can achieve a related effect using the software Pro Tools, playing the sounds through a domestic or computer stereo recording system.
- Create a tape collage which can, if wished, be combined with live performance: this can be useful as a low-tech strategy which nevertheless reaps interesting results. You can make the collage out of recorded material, or you can combine it with live performance. You can use material from the radio, recordings of music, and performances of your own texts to make the tape. You can then, if you wish, interweave live material with the collaged and taped extracts. You can write a script for this, or you may improvise with the tape, picking up on some of the ideas that the soundtrack triggers. It is important to consider the structure, and to arrange the pieces in an interesting way. If you record snippets of material one after the other without considering the structure, the results may be tedious to listen to.
- Explore the traditional songs or sound poems from your own or another culture, and see how you can work with this material to create your own sonic poem. On the UbuWeb ethnopoetics site, you will find

many exciting examples which include Celtic mouth music and Inuit throat music (UbuWeb Ongoing).

MIXING THE MEDIA

Performance can form a site for intersections between the verbal, visual, sonic and gestural, which result in a mixed-media (or intermedia) event. These intersections greatly enlarge what language can do: they make language speak more rather than less. Furthermore, we live within a culture where the supremacy of the written word is diminishing, and the visual and aural are increasingly important. Videos, advertisements, TV, radio, CDs and the computer dominate our lives. In this section we will explore how you can extend your writing into other media.

Traditional drama involves the integration of words, visual images, gesture and lighting: in this sense mixed-media work is nothing new. However, in drama the relationship of language to the visual, sonic and gestural is usually subordinated to, and subsumed within, the development of plot and character. In intermedia performance work, the juxtaposition of words with visual images or gestures is highly interactive and constantly changing. This creates a complex interweaving of sign systems, what I call 'semiotic exchange': a continuous modification by, and of, the different elements (Smith & Dean 1997; Smith 1999). In such work there will not necessarily be a strong storyline or identifiable characters, though there may be elements of both. Some performance works may be large scale, but they can arise out of simple juxtapositions of words and visual images, or words and physical gestures. A student in one of my classes, for example, created a piece in which she changed hats to signal changes in identity, context and mood. It was a simple device which, nevertheless, modified and counterpointed the spoken text in an engaging way.

Performance work of this kind may benefit from professional performers, but you may be able to write the material in such a way that it does not require this kind of training. Of course, some readers of this book may have theatrical experience, and be able to capitalise on it most effectively in this context.

Making intermedia work

Below are some possible ways of exploring language in an intermedia and performance context (see Exercise 2):

- Present words and letters as visual objects, either on paper, slides, video or computer. The words can appear in colour, in different fonts, and, if desired, at irregular angles. If video or computer are used, the words can move around the screen.

- Create a text and combine it with strong visual images. These images may work with or against the semantic implications of the words. They can appear on paper, slides, video or computer.
- Combine words and physical gestures. The gestures can be quite simple ones, such as stamping your feet or making facial expressions. You should also consider whether the gestures reinforce or move in a contrary direction to a particular word or set of words. A student in one of my classes produced a piece in which a friend read out a series of words from a list (the order of the words could change). Each time a word was read out, the performer made a gesture to go with that word. Sometimes the gesture illustrated the word, for example, the reader would call out 'look', and the performer would make a spectacles sign. But sometimes she made a gesture which contradicted the word, or seemed to have very little direct connection with it. The gestures can relate to the meanings of the words, but they can also relate to their sounds. Again the relationship might be one of contrast: if you perform a very rhythmic text, the gestures could be smooth and continuous. For *TranceFIGUREd Spirit,* a performance work in which I was involved in 1991, I composed rhythmically notated texts with a strong musical element (Smith, Karl & Jones 1990). Bodyworks designed by the artist Sieglinde Karl were worn by artist and dancer Graham Jones. Graham sometimes moved synchronously with my rhythms, but sometimes worked asynchronously against them. Also, when the rhythms were jagged, his movements might be smooth and vice versa. For pieces which bring together dance and words, see the work of Richard James Allen and Karen Pearlman documented in *Performing the UnNameable: An Anthology of Performance Texts* (1999).
- Combine text and objects. Choose an object (it can be quite simple) and consider how integral the object will be to the performance. For example, take a chair, place it in different, possibly unorthodox positions, and also adopt poses in relation to it. Invert the chair, tilt it on its side, place it with its back to the audience, and move it about the space. Place objects on or over it. Position your body on it, at a distance from it, or underneath it. Keep the relationship between body and chair fluid and kinetic. Compose a text which interrelates the words and the movements so they become inseparable. There is a huge range of ideas that you would be able to express through this kind of interaction between text and object. I saw a stimulating performance piece some years ago by the writer Anna Gibbs. It was called 'Running

Out of Words' and she performed a very rhythmic poem consisting entirely of clichéd similes while she worked out on a treadmill. After each short bout of the similes she would pause and one phrase from a longer linking sentence (also full of clichés) would be projected on a slide. The clichés and the breathlessness of working out, though seemingly disconnected, were brought together in this context by the title. But the text and treadmill were also physically linked by Anna's rhythm as she strode on the treadmill and the rhythmic propulsion of the text.

- Combine music and sound. Some of these possibilities have already been explored in the section on sonic poetry, sonic writing. But you might also work with a musician in such a way that you both respond to each other. For example, the musician might find musical equivalents to some of your verbal ideas. Or you might adopt musical structures created by the musician to organise your text. Working interactively with a musician may produce the most unusual and exciting results if the relationship between the sound and the words is not 'fixed' but allows for mutual interactiveness. One of the ways in which you can increase this is through an element of improvisation.

THE IMPROVISOR, TALK-POET, STAND-UP STRATEGIST

One of the many exciting possibilities which performance provides is improvisation (see Exercise 3). I am not concerned here with the huge and fertile field of theatrical improvisation, but more with the specific capacity to generate verbal texts. Improvising means literally writing in performance. It involves generating text within the time-frame of the performance, in front of an audience, and without revision: this is 'pure improvisation'. Improvisation can also take place in private if revision is minimised: this is 'applied improvisation' (Smith & Dean 1997).

Improvisation is a technique which has been current in all the arts in the last 50 years, but is particularly prominent in both music and theatre. Improvising writers are more difficult to find, but Jack Kerouac, for example, used to write novels continuously and without revision. American 'talk' poet, David Antin, on the other hand, improvises in performance. His improvisations proceed through narrative, anecdotes, philosophical musing, association of ideas, and recurrent metaphors. Highly articulate, he is the intellectual equivalent of the stand-up comic. His work exists in written transcriptions (Antin 1976; 1984) and recordings of some of his talks are also available on his homepage at the

Electronic Poetry Centre (Antin Ongoing). The work of Spalding Gray (1987; 1991), also American, who partially improvises highly entertaining monologues is also relevant here. For more about Antin, Gray and improvisation in the arts, see Smith and Dean (1997).

Improvisation has many advantages. 'Pure improvisation' allows for interaction between performers, and potentially with the audience and environment. Also, not being able to revise, and having to work at speed, may result in different kinds of effects and results. Although editing is an important part of the creative process, it can also bring with it certain dangers. When we are working at speed we may sometimes find ourselves blocking out rational thinking. Once we are in editing mode, the rational mind tends to take over, and may censor some of the more striking but intransigent elements of the text.

Improvisation is often confused with spontaneity, but it is in fact a skill which has to be learnt. Improvisors do not revise, but they draw on methods of working which they have acquired over a long period of time. Improvisors also need techniques for developing their material: these can be quite similar to those used in writing texts, but it takes great skill to implement them at speed and with no 'going back'.

Improvising strategies

You may be excited by the idea of improvising but not know how to set about it. The following strategies for Exercise 3 give you a working base so that you do not feel totally at sea, but have some initial material to work with. This approach is known as **referent-based improvisation**: it provides a starting point for your improvisation to which you can 'refer' back . Here are some possibilities:

- Return to the word pool exercise in Chapter 1. Create a word pool on a page, and then combine the words aurally. Improvise fragments instead of trying to think in terms of a whole piece, and don't worry about making overall sense or integrating the disparate phrases. Keep going even if you feel the improvisation is not very inventive or fluent initially. It's all a question of practice.
- Return to the word association exercise in Chapter 1. But instead of writing down the words, associate orally. Again try to keep going, using association by both sound and sense. If you feel that you are drying up, say anything that comes into your mind until you are back on track, and then start to associate again.
- Record a track of yourself improvising, and then lay down one or two

more tracks in which you dialogue with yourself: that is, multitrack your own voice. Once one track is down it is easy to 'converse' with it. Again you might want to start with words, or phrases, or sentences on a piece of paper, and use these as a base. It's usually beneficial, if you are building up a multitracked improvisation, to leave some gaps on the first track you put down. That way the recording does not become too dense, but this does depend on what kind of effect you want to create.

- Improvise largely by changing the dynamic, accentuation and volume of your voice, and exploring extremes of vocal delivery, to create effects other than those purely of meaning. Try to improvise freely, allow the words and sounds to form and reform, and do not be too burdened by the pressure to make sense.

- Develop your capacity to monologue or 'talk' in the style of David Antin or Spalding Gray. The monologue approach to improvising does not commit you to pursuing one topic endlessly for 20 minutes or so. Rather you can move, as Antin does, from story to conjecture to anecdote, freewheeling from one idea to another. You can also draw on ideas which are triggered by the environment or the audience, and weave them into the text.

- Improvise with others. In musical or theatrical contexts improvisation is usually collective and collaborative, and this helps to trigger and sustain the development of the piece. So you might want to improvise with friends or within the classroom. For example, a group of people can improvise from a word pool: they can speak together or independently, associate from each other, and maintain independent streams. Your fellow improvisers may be writers or theatrical performers, but they may also be musicians or actors. The improvisation may be even richer if it is intermedia and involves working with creators from other disciplines. Alternatively, if you do not want to improvise yourself, but feel this is an exciting area, you can work with improvising musicians. Your contribution can be non-improvised text, and the musicians can improvise in response to it. An improvisation can have a range of elements, some of which may be preconceived.

Whatever your strategy, you need to develop the capacity to listen to yourself while you are improvising, and to remember what you have created. Then you can refer back as the improvisation develops, and you will also have a better sense of the shape and direction of the piece. If you retain what has happened, you will be able to let ideas, words and phrases drop out and be picked up again later: this integrates and structures your material. Also consider recording yourself so you can listen to the results: it will help you become aware of any limitations in your approach to this kind of work. You may find when you listen to it that the text is more interesting than it seemed when you were actually inventing it!

PERFORMANCE SCORES

Performance can radically reconfigure the role of the author by shifting some of the responsibility for creation of the work onto the performers. For example, a writer may produce a score which has written instructions or prompts for the performers. This score is not a complete script, but acts as a trigger and constraint. In such a piece the responsibility partly falls on the performers who become co-authors. At the same time, the author is setting up strict and stimulating parameters within which the piece can be created. No performance of the work will be exactly the same, though different performances are likely to have some features in common.

In poet/composer Jackson Mac Low's scores there is a very subtle balance between control of the compositional concept and creative opportunity for the performers. Sometimes performers are given particular words, letters and notes which they must implement, but with considerable freedoms about how to combine and transmute them (Mac Low 1986). For an example of a Mac Low score, which balances authorial control with performer improvisation, see Example 10.1 (p. 228). Notice also the emphasis on performer interaction:

> Each performer must listen intently to all sounds audible, including those produced by other performers (if any), by the audience, or by elements in the environment. Performers must relate with these sounds in producing their own, exercising sensitivity, tact, & courtesy, so that every performance detail contributes to a total sound sequence they would choose to hear.
>
> (Mac Low 1977–78)

Some of the scripts by American poet and playwright Kenneth Koch are more theatrical in intent, but unlike a conventional drama consist only of instructions, at times of a somewhat surrealist kind. His 'Mexico City', for example, is a set of instructions in which 'An elderly American homosexual tries to describe Mexico City to an illiterate and extremely ugly Finnish farm girl who has never been in any city whatsoever.' The performer must be 'as complete in his description as possible' and the Finnish girl has to repeat his description as precisely as possible. The elderly man then has to tell her how well he feels she 'has truly captured the spirit and mood of the city' (Koch 1980b, p. 215). In 'Coil Supreme' the actors must speak for 30 minutes, but every sentence they speak has to contain the words 'coil supreme'. They can distort or play with the language in anyway they want, and the piece should end on a note of 'unbearable suspense' (Koch 1980a, p. 216).

For Exercise 4a, create a score which gives detailed instructions to the performers, but also gives them some freedom about how to complete the score. In devising the instructions, you will need to exercise some imagination about possible outcomes. You may wish to use the score by Jackson Mac Low, below, as a model, or devise your own.

Example 10.1

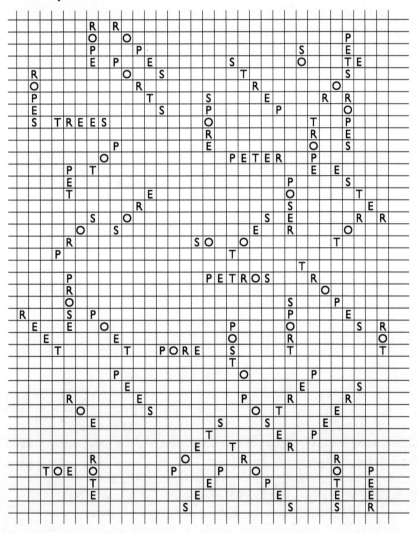

A Vocabulary Gatha for Peter Rose (Mac Low 1977–78)

Performance Instructions for 'A Vocabulary Gatha for Peter Rose'

The Gatha may be performed by a single performer or by a group of any size. Each performer starts at any square & moves from there to any adjacent one, horizontally, vertically, or diagonally, & thence to other squares. Each letter or group of letters (joined in any direction(s)) may be spoken, sung, or played on a musical instrument. All three ways of realizing the Gatha should occur in a performance.

Vocal possibilities include the speaking or singing of the letters' individual sounds (as they are pronounced in any language known to the performer), the letters' English names (e.g., 'oh' or 'tee'), any syllables formed by letters adjacent in any direction(s), & whole words. Any of these elements may be repeated *ad lib.* The name 'Peter Rose' may be spoken or sung at any time, & the performer may then jump to a square not adjacent to the last one realized. In singing, the performer may either sing pitches assigned to letters for instrumental realization (see below) or freely choose pitches in accord with the performance situation. When playing an instrument, the performer moves from square to square as above, but realizes each letter as an instrumental tone, choosing the octave in which each tone is placed. The letters occurring in the Gatha are realized as follows:

P is played as B or B flat/A sharp.
E „ „ „ E „ E flat/D sharp.
T „ „ „ D „ D flat/C sharp.
R „ „ „ A „ A flat/G sharp.
O „ „ „ G „ G flat/F sharp.
S „ „ „ C „ F.

The performer chooses between alternative pitches for each letter, or trills or wavers between them, & connects tones consecutively or simultaneously as their letters lie adjacent in any direction(s). Letter tones may be repeated or reversed. Tones may be connected by *glissandi* as well as being played discretely. Empty squares are rendered as silences of any duration chosen by the performer.

Each performer must listen intently to all sounds audible, including those produced by other performers (if any), by the audience, or by elements in the environment. Performers must relate with these sounds in producing their own, exercising sensitivity, tact, & courtesy, so that every performance detail contributes to a total sound sequence they would choose to hear. Virtuosity is strongly encouraged but must be exercised with consciousness of its place in the total aural situation. Performers must be both inventive & sensitive at all times. '*Listen*' & '*Relate*' are the most important 'rules'.

All parameters not specified above, including octave placement, simultaneous &/or successive grouping, repetition, duration, rhythm, loudness, tempo, timbre, attack, &c., are at the discretion of the performer & are to be chosen spontaneously during a performance.

A performance may be ended at any time within the limits set by the performance situation. A total duration may be set beforehand or arrived at spontaneously. A group may appoint a leader to signal the beginning, keep track of elapsed time with a watch, & signal the end of the performance.

Score and instructions copyright 1978, 1983, and 1996 by Jackson Mac Low. All rights reserved. Actual size of score: 8½ in. x 11 in.

New York, 11/12/77–5/30/78

THE AUDIENCE AUDITIONS

Some pieces may involve an element of audience participation. It is quite common to attend theatrical events where performers address comments to specific members of the audience, or ask them to perform a simple task. In some cases members of the audience are incorporated into the performance to such a degree that the boundary between performer and audience becomes blurred.

It is sometimes fun to try this kind of piece in the classroom. You may ask the 'audience' (your classmates) to suggest words which are integrated into your performance, or give them tasks to do. In doing so you make them 'talk back' to you as writer. This has political ramifications because you are empowering, even democratising, the role of the audience. Note, however, that when it comes to public performance such participation may be irksome, even confrontational, for some members of the audience, particularly if they are shy. Some theatre companies such as The Sydney Front have used such forms of intimidation to explore power relationships, particularly fear of authority, but such experiments need to be approached with skill. So be sure that you consider the type of audience you are dealing with and your purposes: you may wish to avoid compulsory interaction.

For Exercise 4b devise a piece which requires audience participation. Even if you don't encourage audience members to participate directly in the piece, you may be able to affect their interaction with it. For example, you might change your spatial relationship with the audience by standing amongst them rather than separately, or by constantly repositioning yourself in different parts of the performance space.

GENDER, ETHNICITY, MORPHING IDENTITIES

Performance work, because it emphasises the body and the voice, is a good medium in which to explore ideas about gender and ethnicity. As soon as we speak, our gender and ethnicity is revealed in a way it is not when we write words on the page.

Sometimes simply the presence of gendered or ethnic characteristics may be highly effective. Ania Walwicz's texts, many of which deal with immigration, are made even more forceful in performance by her Polish accent. But performance can also be a very good forum for challenging and unfixing 'normal' ways of thinking about gender and ethnicity. For example, a voice can be changed to some degree acoustically, and to a larger degree technologically, to affect perceptions of gender. So it is possible to make a male voice sound female, and a female voice sound male: this is what I have elsewhere called 'sonic cross-dressing' (Smith 1999). Similarly, the way that the body is presented and clothed in a performance can challenge ideas of gender and sexual identity.

Performance, then, can subvert the 'performativity' of gender: the way, as theorist Judith Butler (1990) has suggested, we continuously and repeatedly perform gender to conform with certain social norms. If we are female we play the role of being female through manner, dress, gesture, voice and attitude, and therefore reinforce the idea that we are female. In performance we can subvert these norms by blurring gender characteristics.

Similarly performance, with the aid of technology, can be a way of challenging the idea of ethnic identity as other. A western speaking voice, for example, might be 'morphed' into a Chinese or African-American one. In this way performance and technology can be used in a highly transgressive and confronting way to undermine comfortable assumptions about identity.

For Exercise 5, create a text which explores the relationship between performance and gender, and/or performance and ethnicity, using your voice and body in ways which challenge their normal social construction.

FROM PAGE TO STAGE, PLAYING THE MICROPHONE

When you are performing in public, you will need to prepare carefully for your presentation. Even if it's just a conventional poetry reading, you need to work out exactly what you will be reading, and approximately time the pieces so you do not overrun your allotted time-slot. Some people may prefer to adapt to the situation as it arises, and read what seems appropriate at the time: if you do this you must be confident that you can give as polished and exhilarating a performance as you would if fully prepared.

Make sure that the texts you choose are varied, and that the poems work effectively as oral entities and in a public space. Poems that read well on the page may be less effective under these conditions. It's a good idea to try reading the text at home, possibly several times over, to make sure that you are fluent: some performance pieces may require extensive rehearsal. There is more, however, to reading or performing work than fluency. Think of ways in which you can enliven and enhance the words. The voice is an instrument that you can play: try varying the pitch and the dynamic both within and between different poems. Varying the pace is important too: reading that always moves at the same speed may become very monotonous. Such effects will usually need to be quite subtle. Experience, and listening to yourself on tape, will give you an idea of how to pitch your performance, and help you to develop your own style of delivery whether extrovert or more understated.

Using the microphone (see Exercise 6) is also an important part of reading or performance work. Many poets, especially if they are not very experienced in public performance, do not use the microphone as effectively as possible. Distance from it is crucial: if you stand too far away it will not pick up your voice; on the other hand if you are too close your voice may be overpoweringly loud and could be distorted. If there are a number of readers you may need to adjust the microphone to your own height. Microphones vary a lot, and some are much better than others. However, certain letters are likely to distort: in particular the letter 'p' creates a popping noise which can be very distracting for listeners. The closer you are to the microphone, the more distortion there will be. However, you can largely avoid this by standing slightly sideways on to the microphone. Also try to avoid blowing too forcefully into it when you have to pronounce a 'p': instead slightly swallow/subdue the consonant to minimise the effect. Again practice will help with this: if you are even starting to think about such matters you will be ahead of other poetry readers who often haven't considered them at all.

You can also obtain interesting effects in your reading by 'playing the microphone', that is, by varying your distance from it and by employing it in ways which are contrary to normal use. For example, moving close to the microphone, and then whispering into it, can create a very rich though hushed impact; such a mode of delivery has more presence than normal whispering. On the other hand, moving away from it, but talking louder creates an intriguing combination of forcefulness and distance. Or you can work with two microphones (and a stereo sound system), and move from one to the other as performance poet Amanda Stewart habitually does. These are only a few possibilities, but playing the microphone can make a huge impact on your overall performance, and should be viewed as an important part of your creative work.

CONCLUSION

Different modes of working, such as performance, are very important, because they produce new challenges and can push your work in unexpected directions. The creation of a talk poem, or an intermedia piece, will inevitably create surprises in your writing, because you work with language in ways which are more oral, theatrical or intermedia. The stimulation of performance may also bring changes to your page-based work. For example, when you next write for the page, you could find yourself producing multi-voiced texts, playing with speech patterns, or emphasising the sounds of the words more strongly. In other words you might find yourself adapting performance strategies to the page.

Performance is central to the aims of this book as a whole, because it encourages you to be a chameleon in your writing and embrace different forms of projection and different identities. Similarly, intermedia work encourages you to mix sound, word and image, just as we cross-dressed genre in Chapter 9. In this chapter we have also started to explore the power of technology to take our work in completely new directions, and this will be addressed much further in Chapter 11.

WORKS ON *THE WRITING EXPERIMENT* WEBSITE

Charles Amirkhanian, *Church Car, Version 2*.
Charles Amirkhanian, *Dot Bunch*.
Christian Bok, 'Motorised Razors' and 'Mushroom Clouds' from *The Cyborg Opera*.
David Knoebel, *How I Heard It*.
Taylor Mali, *Undivided Attention*.
Hazel Smith and Roger Dean, *Poet Without Language* (extract).
Hazel Smith and Roger Dean, *the writer, the performer, the program, the madwoman*.
Amanda Stewart, *.romance* (1981).
Scott Woods, *Elevator Dreams*.

REFERENCES

Allen, R. J. and Pearlman, K. 1999, *Performing the UnNameable: An Anthology of Australian Performance Texts*, Currency Press, Sydney.

Amirkhanian, C. republished-a, *Church Car, Version 2*, Sound recording. (P) (C) 1981 Arts Plural Publishing (BMI). All Rights Reserved. www.allenandunwin. com/writingexp.

—— republished-b, *Dot Bunch*, Sound recording. (P) (C) 1981 Arts Plural Publishing (BMI). All Rights Reserved. www.allenandunwin.com/ writingexp.

Antin, D. 1976, *Talking at the Boundaries*, New Directions, New York.

—— 1984, *Tuning*, New Directions, New York.

—— Ongoing, http://epc.buffalo.edu/authors/antin/.

Benson, S. 1989, 'Back', *Reverse Order*, Potes & Poets Press, Elmwood, Connecticut.

Bergvall, C. 1999, 'Speaking in Tongues: John Stammer talks to Caroline Bergvall', *Magma 15*. http://magmapoetry.com/Magma15/bergvallInterview.html.

Bernstein, C. 1976, My/My/My, Sound recording. http://www.ubu.com/sound/ bernstein.html.

—— (ed.) 1998, *Close Listening: Poetry and the Performed Word*, Oxford University Press, New York and Oxford.

Bok, C. republished, 'Motorised Razors' and 'Mushroom Cloud' from *The Cyborg Opera*. Sound recording. www.allenandunwin.com/writingexp. Also on UbuWeb, http://www.ubu.com/sound/bok.html.

Bulatov, D. (ed.) 2001, *Homo Sonorus: An International Anthology of Sound Poetry*, National Centre for Contemporary Art, Kaliningrad, Russia. 4 CDs and book.

Butler, J. 1990, *Gender Trouble: Feminism and the Subversion of Identity*, Routledge, New York and London.

Flea, R. 1996, *Virtual Fleality*, Hawaii Dub Music, Honolulu. CD with accompanying chapbook published by Tinfish Net\work.

Giorno, J. 1972, *Vajra Kisses*, Sound recording. http://www.ubu.com/sound/ giorno.html.

—— 1978, *Grasping at Emptiness*, Sound recording. http://www.ubu.com/ sound/giorno.html.

Gray, S. 1987, *Swimming to Cambodia: The Collected Works of Spalding Gray*, Picador, London.

—— 1991, *Monster in a Box*, Pan Books, London, Sydney, Auckland.

Gysin, B. 1962a, *Junk is No Good Baby*, Sound recording. http://www.ubu.com/ sound/gysin.html.

—— 1962b, *No Poets*, Sound recording. http://www.ubu.com/sound/ gysin.html.

Knoebel, D. republished, *How I Heard It*, Multimedia work. www.allenandunwin. com/writingexp. Previously published in *Cauldron and Net* vol. 3. http://www. studiocleo.com/cauldron/volume3/contents/index.html.

Koch, K. 1980a, 'Coil Supreme', *Scenarios: Scripts to Perform*, (ed.) R. Kostelanetz, Assembling Press, Brooklyn, New York.

—— 1980b, 'Mexico City', *Scenarios: Scripts to Perform*, (ed.) R. Kostelanetz, Assembling Press, Brooklyn, New York.

Kostelanetz, R. (ed.) 1980, *Text-Sound Texts*, William Morrow & Co., New York.

Leonard, T. 1984, *The Six O'Clock News*, Print version and sound recording. http://www.tomleonard.co.uk/sixoclock.htm.

Lora-Totino, A. (ed.) 1978, *Futura Poesia Sonora: Critical-Historical Anthology of Sound Poetry*, Cramps Records, Milan.

Mac Low, J. 1977–78, *A Vocabulary Gatha for Peter Rose*, http://www.thing.net/~grist/l&d/jmlpr.htm. Also published in J. Mac Low 1986, *Representative Works: 1938–85*, Roof Books, New York.

—— 1986, *Representative Works: 1938–1985*, Roof Books, New York.

Mali, T. republished, *Undivided Attention*, www.allenandunwin.com/writingexp. Sound recording. Also at www.taylormali.com. Poem published in 2002 in T. Mali, *What Learning Leaves*, Hanover Press, Newtown, CT.

Morris, A. (ed.) 1997, *Sound States: Innovative Poetics and Acoustical Technologies*, University of North Carolina Press, Chapel Hill and London.

Nichol bp 1972, *Pome Poem*, Sound recording. http://www.ubu.com/sound/nichol.html.

Smith, H. 1991, *Abstractly Represented: Poems and Performance Texts 1982–90*, Butterfly Books, Sydney.

—— 1999, 'Sonic writing and sonic cross-dressing: gender, language, voice and technology', *Musics and Feminisms*, (eds.) S. Macarthur and C. Poynton, Australian Music Centre, Sydney, pp. 129–34.

—— republished, *the writer, the performer, the program, the madwoman*, Sound recording. www.allenandunwin.com/writingexp. Previously published in 2004 in *HOW2: Contemporary Innovative Writing by Women* 2004, vol. 2, No. 2 at http://www.departments.bucknell.edu/stadler_center/how2/current/multimedia/index.shtm.

Smith, H. and Dean, R.T. republished, *Poet Without Language* (extract), www.allenandunwin.com/writingexp. From H. Smith with austraLYSIS, *Poet Without Language*, 1994, Rufus, CD, 005.

Smith, H. and Dean, R.T. 1997, *Improvisation, Hypermedia and the Arts Since 1945*, Harwood Academic, London and New York.

—— 2003, 'Voicescapes and sonic structures in the creation of sound techn-odrama', *Performance Research*, vol. 8, no. 1, pp. 112–23.

Smith, H., Karl, S. and Jones, G. 1990, *TranceFIGUREd Spirit*, Soma, Sydney/London.

Smith, H. with austraLYSIS 1994, *Poet Without Language*, Rufus, CD, 005, Sydney.

Stewart, A. republished, *.romance (1981)*, Sound recording. www.allenandunwin.com/writingexp. Previously published in 1998 in *I/T: Selected Poems 1980–1996*, Here & There Books/Split Records, CD and Book.

Swift, T. and Norton, P. 2002, *Short Fuse: The Global Anthology of New Fusion Poetry*, Rattapallax Press, New York.

The Wordsmith Press Ongoing, http://www.thewordsmithpress.com/content/poets.php.

Tuma, K. (ed.) 2001, *Anthology of Twentieth-Century British and Irish Poetry*, Oxford University Press, New York and Oxford.

UbuWeb Ongoing, http://www.ubu.com.

Walwicz, A. 1989, 'bells', *Boat*, Angus & Robertson, Sydney.

Wishart, T. 2001, 'Tongues of Fire', *Homo Sonorus: An International Anthology of Sound Poetry*, (ed.) D. Bulatov, National Centre for Contemporary Art, Kaliningrad, Russia. 4 CDs and book.

Woods, S. republished, *Elevator Dreams*, Sound recording. www.allenandunwin.com/writingexp. Also on the Wordsmith Press Ongoing at http://www.thewordsmithpress.com/content/poets.php.

CHAPTER ELEVEN
New media travels

The most important change in writing in the late twentieth and early 21st century is the rise of the new media. Writers are becoming cyborgs who are half-human, half-machine: this is the era of the cyberwriter, digital writer or technowriter. Many modes of communication, such as email and blogs, are now screen- rather than page-based, and this changes how we write, and how we think about literature. In this chapter we will explore some of the creative possibilities of the new media, and how you can use these new technologies to experiment with, and change, the way you write.

Text on the screen is organised and produced in different ways from page writing. New technologies can transform textuality through hyper-linking, animation of text and interactivity. The new media also presents unique opportunities for intermedia work, as it gives the opportunity for images, sound and language to be interwoven in the same environment.

New media writing allows us to take many of the ideas in this book even further. It promotes plurality of meaning and style, is fundamentally non-linear, and facilitates ways of writing that are not possible on the page, such as the animation of words. Techniques fundamental to new media writing, such as the use of split screens, animation and hyperlinking, tend to promote a more fluid reading practice. They encourage scanning, reading in directions other than from left to right, and the simultaneous absorption of multiple and fragmented texts. New media writing sometimes exists at the edges of readability, as words transform on the screen, or disappear from view, before we have had a chance to digest them. It also creates different kinds of virtual spaces, distances and topographies where we can 'travel' from one part of the text to another at a single click of the mouse.

237

Putting into action the ideas in this chapter will entail a degree of basic skill in writing web pages, but this expertise does not need to be extensive. Ideally, you will need to learn a WYSIWYG (What You See Is What You Get) interface such as Dreamweaver, which largely writes html (hypertext mark-up language) for you, and an animation program such as Flash, but there are other alternatives. The point of this chapter is not to show you how to use the technology, but give you some idea of directions in which you might take such work (including simple strategies which should not involve too much technological expertise). New media writing (sometimes known as digital writing, cyberwriting, cyberpoetry, hypertext, hypermedia and so on) is a new field, and is quickly evolving as new technologies and approaches develop. What seems trendy and adventurous one year may seem old-fashioned the next.

Many websites showcase new media work. These include *Cauldron and Net*, (Cauldron and Net Ongoing), *Poems That Go* (Poems That Go Ongoing), *Beehive* (Beehive Ongoing), *inflect* (inflect Ongoing), *UbuWeb* (UbuWeb Ongoing) and *Alt-X* (Alt-X Ongoing). These sites mostly have extensive archives which you can look through. The Electronic Literature Organisation's directory (Electronic Literature Organisation Ongoing) will also help you to find interesting work. *Digital Poetics* is a useful book about this developing field (Glazier 2002) and *The New Media Reader* (Wardip-Fruin & Montfort 2003) will also give you much relevant background.

Throughout this chapter are references to a number of very good examples of new media work on the Allen & Unwin website at www.allenandunwin.com/writingexp. These works are referred to during this chapter and listed at the end of it.

exercises

1. Create a hypertext.
2. Create:
   a) an animated text within a single scene
   b) an animated 'movie'.
3. Create a text piece using split screens, frames or layers.
4. Write a piece which incorporates computer code in the text. Use this as a way of considering the effects of computerisation on contemporary culture.
5. Create a hypermedia piece.

THE LINK, THE SCREENER, THE HYPERTEXTUAL

Fundamental to writing on the web is the hyperlink. The most important aspect of the hyperlink is that it is non-linear. Through the hyperlink any piece of text can be juxtaposed with any other (either sequentially or simultaneously). The hyperlink can also take us from text to image, image to text, text to animation, and so on. The link can lead readers or 'screeners' immediately from one text to a second text, which in linear terms might be extremely distant from the first. When we press on a hyperlink, the text we are reading is often replaced by another, but if the screen is divided into a number of frames or sections, pressing on a hyperlink may cause an event to occur in another frame, and consequently in another part of the screen.

One of the main forms of hyperlinking results in hypertext. Fundamental to the concept of the hypertext is the idea of branching and interconnected pathways. These create a web-like structure, in which many different chunks of text are interlinked. In such a structure any two pieces of text can be joined: potentially any text can lead to any other. In a hypertext each individual text (usually known as a lexia) is likely to contain more than one link. For example, there may be three links in a lexia (sometimes detectable through underlined words) all of which take the reader to different destinations. If we click on one of the links, we will arrive at another lexia which also has multiple links, and so on. Links do not always interconnect to a new text, but may take us back to one which we have visited before, making the structure recursive. When we revisit this lexia we may then take another pathway out of it, rather than revisit the one we took on the previous occasion. There will therefore inevitably be many alternative pathways through any hypertext, and each reading will take a unique route.

During the 1990s writers started to experiment with hypertext as a creative medium. This gave rise to a whole new genre called 'hypertext fiction'. One of the classics of hypertext fiction is a work by Michael Joyce called *Afternoon: A Story* (1990) written in a program called Storyspace. Other well-known works are *Patchwork Girl* by Shelley Jackson (1995), and *Samplers: Nine Vicious Little Hypertexts* by Deena Larsen (1996). The central feature of such texts is alternative storylines produced by branching pathways. These pathways are created by multiple links, resulting in a textual constellation. One reading of the novel may leave out huge chunks of text which are predominant in another reading. As a consequence, in hypertext fictions such as Michael Joyce's *Afternoon: A Story,* the concepts of plot, climax or narrator are radically reworked. These parameters are not so much erased as displaced and multiplied, so that there are numerous plots, climaxes and narrators. Hypertext fiction is extensively discussed in George Landow's *Hyper/Text/Theory* (1994).

Hypertext fiction was certainly revolutionary, because it induced a fundamentally different way of writing and reading from that required by on-the-page texts. Cyberwriting is a fast developing field, however, and hypertext fiction is not as prominent as it was. It has been superseded by other forms of hyperlinking: these involve the use of multiple frames, or more freewheeling forms of textual display. However, hyperlinking is fundamental to all writing on the web, and is an important technique to grasp. Creating a hypertext is reasonably simple, and is still an interesting mode of writing to experiment with.

Multiple routes, multiple pathways

To give some impression of the way hypertexts can be interlinked, let us look at some possible initial routes through a tiny extract from my own hypertext *Wordstuffs: The City and The Body* (Smith, Dean & White republished) which is on *The Writing Experiment* website. This text appears in part in a page-based version in Chapter 9. But the hypertext version is very different—not only because in its entirety it consists of far more texts than the page-based version, but because it also offers many more choices and reading pathways (the hypertexts are also in colour and display a variety of fonts and spacings which I have not attempted to fully duplicate here).

Every reader starts with the first text:

Example 11.1
Welcome to the <u>city</u> and the <u>body</u> hotline: arms and legs are flying
round us here at an enormous rate and so are cars and street
lamps. At the moment we are not anticipating the end of the world
or the demise of reproductive <u>organs</u>. But who <u>knows</u> now that
sound is only time warps? Schools are going half-speed and
<u>universities</u> are closing. Elections will only be held on <u>racial</u>
issues. Young women may die from stress unless we treat them
for their age. Whatever happened to <u>socio-economic</u> solutions?
Are we going to write <u>poems</u> until all heaven is let loose?

Within this text there are eight different choices as to how to proceed next. Activating the link 'city' produces a text which suggests the paradoxes of place and identity:

You hold up the <u>map</u> to the mirror.

All the <u>streets</u> have new names that
you cannot recognise or read

You smash the mirror but you cannot erase the <u>inversion</u>.

On the other hand if we activate the link 'poems', we obtain a poem about the relationship between time and space, the verbal and the non-verbal:

Spawning <u>offshore</u> on far-off stars
   caught between nets at the bottom of creeks
     unborn at the rim of the earth

the day spears the night till it dies reveals
   a <u>space</u> where new sounds explode as time
     she strikes words on the sky in looping flames

the untouched paths of the <u>untold</u>

In this new text, the link 'offshore' leads to the following urban but surreal narrative:

Someone you intensely dislike predicts the <u>day</u> on which you will die. You know that he cannot really know. You do not know whether he is serious or joking or both. But you approach the day with a certain fatalistic dread. Beforehand you say good-bye to everyone, friend or acquaintance, just in case. On the day itself you are careful when you cross <u>roads</u>. In the evening you return home, on an effortless high, believing you may survive, ready to pour yourself a drink, and find that your neighbour has committed suicide.

However, activating the link 'space' in the poem takes us to a satirical advertisement for city and body 'parts':

WANTED

a <u>body</u> without <u>organs</u>
the page numbers for the encyclopedic city
a body that makes music
one second-hand <u>reproductive</u> system
a mind without thought
<u>a story line</u> that doesn't go anywhere
a <u>map</u> without a mirror

Here there are again multiple choices, but the link 'reproductive' produces a reminder of historical taboos about the body, at the same time mimicking the form of a medieval public notice:

Sunday May 6th 1243
<u>Citizens!</u>

Wash your hands of menstrual blood!
<u>Stand</u> <u>clear</u> <u>of</u> <u>unclean</u>
<u>menopausal</u> <u>witches</u>

In this text the link 'citizens' produces an aphoristic, linguistically playful text which inverts the discourse of disability:

a <u>city</u> built only for the <u>disabled</u>

are we *<u>crippled</u>*
by
abelism?

However, if we choose instead the link 'unclean' it produces a reminder of some of the racial prejudices which have historically surrounded the body:

<u>Angles</u> on Jews in the Middle Ages?

Christians thought the mind their
dominion

the body a filthy Jewish <u>domain</u>

This is a fraction of the hypertexts in *Wordstuffs: The City and The Body,* and demonstrates only a few of the possible alternatives even for navigating through this small section.

Hypertext as hyperactive

As this example shows, hypertext is a dynamic medium and also an ideal medium for mixing different genres of writing. In hypertext prose, fiction, poetry, criticism, non-fiction and theory can all intermingle.

Hypertext markedly increases the interactivity of the reader. Interactivity is very important because audiences become bored if they are passive. Give people something to do, and they immediately wake up and feel more involved and in control. In hypertext, readers have to trigger links, and their choices shape the contours of the particular readings they retrieve.

In hypertext it is also possible to produce texts in colour: this is normally not possible with on-the-page writing (even visual poetry has tended to be in black and white). Colours can be used in a multiplicitous way, which corresponds to the heterogeneity of the text. Or, alternatively, colour schemes can be carefully controlled, even systematic.

Links can take other forms than underlined words: they can appear in bold, in different fonts or as visual icons. They can be hidden or partially hidden. The pathways through the texts can be tightly fixed, programmed to be random, or weighted towards certain possibilities.

Creating hypertexts: Linking and looping

The following are a number of different ways of creating hypertext for Exercise 1. These strategies can also be combined:

- Write a short piece of text and choose three words that seem particularly interesting: mark them out as potential links. Then write three more texts which will be the destination point for those links. Put three links in those next three texts, and write other texts to which they can be linked. Continue this process until you have a large and elaborate hypertext, though sometimes you may want to link back to previous texts rather than creating new ones, forming hypertextual loops. Think also about the different ways of exploiting the link word. On the one hand it might hint at, or even symbolise, the contents of the text it leads to. On the other hand it might be arbitrary (that is, seem to have very little connection with the text it links to), or be actually quite misleading. These are ways that you can trigger and control the curiosity of the reader. Links can also be made to texts outside the work itself, so the hypertext links up to external sites. Building through linking is a **generative** approach to writing hypertext. The hyperlinking leads the way and suggests the material.
- Alternatively, or in addition, write a number of short texts (possibly on the same theme). Then retrospectively decide how you are going to link these textual fragments in a hypertext (you may, when you put the texts together, find you need to write some extra ones).
- Think of a core story, but instead of narrowing it down to one possible outcome, try and think of alternate possibilities. Construct a hypertext in which the links take readers to different possible outcomes. We have already explored this process in a different context, and with application to on-the-page writing only, in Chapter 7. It means thinking in terms of multiple possibilities. In the process of writing we often think of such alternatives, but reduce them to one option.

As you undertake these tasks, experiment with the type and visibility of the link. If you want to give the reader a clear choice between different pathways, make the links visible. But if you want to make the choices more unpredictable, introduce hidden links which the reader has to search for.

Also experiment with colour, font size and spacing of the hypertext in such a way as to create the most striking impression. Think of the words as visual objects, and keep your readers visually stimulated.

THE ABC OF ANIMATION

Animation is one of the most radical ways in which new technologies can change the way you write. On the page there are no such kinetic possibilities. There are a number of different animation programs you can use, but at the time of writing Flash is one of the most accessible and useful.

Each stage of a Flash animation is called a scene, and several scenes can be gathered together into a movie. Each scene consists of a timeline, which enables you to move words from one part of the screen to another.

Through animation, words can be moved around the screen, split apart and reconfigured. Words, letters or sentences can transform or morph into others. Varying speeds can be used (though a very fast speed can challenge readability). Words may go off the screen and then reappear: in this sense the screen does not act as a reliable/rigid frame in the way that the page does. This allows the meaning to become very fluid, so that a phrase, sentence or word can constantly be changing its configuration. It can also indicate the process of forming meanings.

One of the classics of new media word animation is Brian Kim Stefans's *The Dreamlife of Letters* (republished) on *The Writing Experiment* website. This piece is based on elements of an online roundtable discussion on literature and sexuality (and this background to the piece is explained at the beginning of the piece itself). Each section of the poem hinges on words which begin with a successive letter of the alphabet. Words and letters move around and off the edge of the screen, sometimes with such speed that they evade normal reading habits. They also invert, rotate, and transform. Letters and words appear on the screen and gradually build into linguistic and semantic formations. Words constantly break into segments, and sometimes reassemble in other linguistic formations and as sculptural patterns. Many of these transforming and re-forming words relate to ideas about identity, sexuality, writing and the body. They point to the idea that sexuality and language are both extremely fluid and are constantly 'morphing'. That is, neither language nor sexuality are fixed entities. For example, in the prologue to the piece, the words 'fix-gendered' and 'handsome' are turned upside down. And later in the piece the verbal list 'oedipality, oedipality, oedipality? oedipalized' emerges, slides diagonally upwards, and mutates into a rapid circle of letters.

Also on *The Writing Experiment* website is *beer* by Australian performance poet and cyberwriter, Komninos Zervos (republished-a). This piece morphs the word 'beer' into many other words (for example, 'been' and 'beef', and subsequently 'help', 'yell' and 'tell'): it moves from one word to another by changing some letters and not others. However, the morphing concerns the shape of the letters and words as much as their linguistic import: sometimes the words appear as half-shape, half-word, sometimes as only shape. Zervos's brightly coloured and dynamic *u cannot be programmed* has more elements and combines user-interaction triggered by mouse movements with animation (republished-b). It consists of a whole alphabet that keeps receding, disappearing and rotating, and from which the letter 'u' emerges, changes shape, and repositions itself on different parts of the screen. There are other 'u's of different colours and sizes—some static, some moving—and the visuals are accompanied by a partly verbal soundtrack. By means of animation the piece plays on a number of verbal relationships: between 'u' and 'you'; between the alphabet and individual letters; and between the letters themselves ('u' upside down looks like 'n').

Jason Nelson's piece *this will be the end of you: play6: four variable creation* (republished-a) explores animation in a different way. Here, after an initial textual bombardment, fragments of text suggest an overall, but broken, narrative and are interspersed with a map/diagram and algebraic formulae.

In *soundAFFECTs*, sections of text by Anne Brewster and myself were taken by Roger Dean and treated with programs written by him within the real-time image processing platform Jitter (Dean, Brewster & Smith republished). Each text is treated as a whole image, so the words are not manipulated at a micro-linguistic level as in *The Dreamlife of Letters*. Instead the text is subjected to a number of processes, such as layering, stretching, superimposition and compression, which act in combination: the screen also divides into multiple frames of the same text. The computer manipulation includes a process of 'overwriting' in which a text progressively writes over itself or another text: this disintegration and replacement of text creates intricate visual patterning. The text–image can be continuously processed during any performance of it with different results each time.

Other exciting examples of animated texts can be found in the work of Jim Andrews, Peter Howard and Ana Maria Uribe, as well as other pieces by Komninos Zervos, Jason Nelson and Brian Kim Stefans. The work of most of these web artists can be found on their individual websites, but also in the journals and archives mentioned previously.

A single-scene movie

These are strategies for Exercise 2a, creating an animated text within a single scene:

a) Place two short blocks of text on the web page, and then—using the timeline—animate one of them so it moves to a different location (for example, make it move from the right-hand to the left-hand side of the screen). Try this exercise several times, extending the range of what you do: for example, put three blocks of text on the screen and animate two of them. How does changing the position of the texts transmute their relationship to each other and consequently the meaning?

b) Make one block of text disappear from the screen, and then reappear in a different position. Look at how this affects the meaning and design on the screen.

c) Place a word on the web page and using the timeline, make letters disappear or change in order.

d) Make words, letters or blocks of text invert or rotate on the screen.

e) Combine some of the above strategies so that the meaning of the words is constantly 'on the move'.

f) Using the morphing facility, place two 'handwritten' words on the screen and morph them into each other. Expand this process with larger numbers of words.

A multi-scene movie

Once you have made several individual scenes, string a number of scenes together to create a complete movie (Exercise 2b). You can sequence the screens so they play one after the other, but you can also add hyperlinks so that the reader/screener can jump to different parts of the movie.

As you work with these blocks of text, try to think in a fragmented and fluid way, rather than necessarily in terms of a unified poem or story. Shuffle the scenes in different orders and allow sequences to develop that you would have been unlikely to anticipate before you started. This way you will be fully interacting with, and exploring experimentally, the possibilities of the medium.

SPLITTING, FRAMING, LAYERING

Exercise 3 concentrates on different ways of working with the screen, such as creating split screens, frames or layers. First, you have to decide whether you want the text to scroll or appear within a single frame. If you don't want the text to scroll, then you will need either to write shorter (possibly more aphoristic) texts, or divide longer ones into manageable chunks. Bear in mind that if there are long stretches of text (particularly in tiny font) on the screen, people tend not to read them.

The screen can also be divided into different units, usually called frames. To do this, first of all split the screen in two either horizontally or vertically. There are many different ways that you can organise the split screen: there might be two separate verbal animations running at different speeds in the two frames, or one half might consist of images, the other words. A set of texts in one frame and another set in the other promotes interesting—and often unpredictable—verbal relationships between the two. There are numerous possibilities: for example, there could be a narrative in one screen-half which is commented upon in the other. You can organise the frames so that they interrelate or are independent (even if you treat them separately you will find that relationships seem to arise between them). You can, of course, divide the screen into several frames—though the more you create, the less space for words in each.

Dividing the screen into frames can also be significant for hyperlinking. Activating a link in one frame may make text appear, disappear, move or change in another. Much current cyberwriting engages with this kind of approach, so that the screen appears fluid and transformative: see the work of Loss Pequeño Glazier (1998) and Talan Memmott (2000). See also on *The Writing Experiment* website the work of American Jason Nelson (republished-a; republished-b), and Australian 'netwurker' mez (Breeze republished). Notice, for instance, in Jason Nelson's *this will be the end of you: play6: four variable creation*' (republished-a) how clicking on the arrows makes other fragments of text appear, and how gliding over the screen with the mouse in *this will be the end of you: play9: curious to know* (republished-b) reveals different parts of an underlying text. Notice in mez's piece *_] [ad] [Dressed in a Skin C.ode_* (Breeze, republished) how sliding the mouse over one text often opens up another.

It is also possible to create layers of text or image which can overlap with each other, and which the reader can move to different positions on the screen, sometimes with unpredictable effects. For example, in *The Roots of Nonlinearity: Toward a Theory of Web-Specific Art-Writing,* by American cyberwriter Christy Sheffield Sanford (republished), layers of text— written in Dynamic HTML—can be activated and also shifted around the screen. Sometimes clicking on a text may reveal another underneath; sometimes a second text may pop up within the same spatial environment but without the disappearance of the first; sometimes a text when moved may break into two, creating new spatial effects and meanings.

THE CYBORG WRITES CODE

Cyberwriting sometimes includes linguistic experimentation: we have already seen how animation allows for experimentation with the formation and deformation of language. But computer writers have also negotiated the interface between ordinary language and code language in what is known as 'codework' (Raley 2003). Sometimes, as in Mark Amerika's work *Filmtext* (2003), this means making the use of computer code overt in the piece; sometimes it involves mixing code and ordinary language. Such a mixture is particularly pronounced in the work of mez. Her language is poetic in that it engages with puns, anagrams, neologisms, unusual spellings and constructed words, created by a mixture of code and ordinary language. Mez uses 'found' texts on the Internet, such as email dialogues and network exchanges, then 'mangles' them with computer-programming languages. She makes extensive use of the full stop—or domain separators as in a web address—sometimes to dissect familiar words into parts. She also employs brackets, slashes and hyphens, and numbers and symbols instead of letters. Mez's experiments have a great deal in common with the linguistically innovative/language poetries we explored in Chapter 8, but take on the world of computer programming. This produces a hybrid language which incorporates programming language, network protocols, and mark-up code: mez describes it as 'm[ez]ang.elle'. Her work defamiliarises and interrupts contemporary modes of transmitting information and communication. In an (email) interview mez was asked how she would describe her own work. She replied in 'mezangelle', afterwards providing a translation. Here are the two versions:

Example 11.2
::N I Word: mezangelled
::N I Sentence: the con[nned]flagration B-tween m-mage N text[ual]/ sound N
fr[ott]ag[e].mentation ov breath/lec.tron.ics N flesh
::In Many Wordz: Eye make sever.all versionz of [intra]net [worked].art,
each I par.tic[k].ular 2 mi conceptual n-tent m-bedded within you.knitz/
phone.tick-tock snippettes ... labellez/cat.e.gori[cal]es that somehow get
shrinkwordwrapped ah-round my stuph alwaze zeem som[a]how n-adequate ...

Her translation of this was:

In/using one word, I'd describe the kind of net.artwork I make as 'mezangelled'. In/using one sentence, I'd describe it as a conflagration between image, text and sound + a fragmentation [allusion of frottage as well here] of breath, electronics and flesh. Extended, the description would be that I make several versions of networked art, each one particular to my conceptual intent, which is imbedded within units/phonetic snippets [hence, the audience/'you' actively knit the units/connections together]. The labels and categories that are applied [or 'word shrink-wrapped'] to my artwork/stuff always seem somehow inadequate.

(Breeze 2001)

See also mez's _][ad][Dressed in a Skin C.ode_ (Breeze republished) on *The Writing Experiment* website which includes mezangelle and email text in an actual digital work. Experiments with codework can also be found in the work of Talan Memmott (2000).

In order to incorporate code into your texts (Exercise 4), find ways of making email or other web-based texts/exchanges the basis for creative texts. Write some web-based texts which mix normal and code-based language. Incorporate some of the html code that you are using in making the piece into the text, or alternatively incorporate aspects of code whether or not they are relevant to the piece. Use this as a way of considering the effects of computerisation on contemporary culture.

HYPERMEDIA HAPPENINGS

Cyberwriting is a very rich medium, but can be even more exciting if it is combined with image and sound. Digital technologies make sound, image and word available within the same space—the domain of the computer. Digital work which combines different media is usually called hypermedia or multimedia work. An important consideration in bringing word, sound and text together in cyberspace is negotiating the relationships between them.

As we have already seen in Chapter 10, one of the interests of using different media is exploring how they can interact with, and modify, each other. This interplay between the verbal, visual and sonic is a very important feature of many new media works. For example, in Brian Kim Stefans's *The Dreamlife of Letters* there is constant dialogue between the meanings of the words and the visual designs they are creating. Sometimes the words behave iconically: that is, they visually act out their meanings—the word 'ink' makes an ink-like blur on the screen. Sometimes the movements of the words, as we have seen, point to the fluidity of sexuality and writing. Notice also, in Jason Nelson's two pieces on *The Writing Experiment* website how the music is adapted to the particular ambience and import of the text (Nelson republished-a; republished-b). For example, in his *this will be the end of you: play6: four variable creation* the dynamic music organised in repetitive loops works well with the rapid outbreak of different textual fragments. On the other hand in his *this will be the end of you: play9: curious to know* the more gentle quiet music goes well with the gradual discovery of the underlying text. The soundtrack can, of course, be verbal. Komninos Zervos's *u cannot be programmed* (republished-b) has an interactive soundtrack in which the words 'u cannot be programmed' are reiterated amongst sometimes super-imposed variations such as 'u cannot be erased/hypertexted/cybersexed'.

In new media work there is also the added dimension of interactivity between the elements, since words, images and sounds can all be 'interrupted', creating constantly changing relationships between them. In *Wordstuffs: The City and The Body,* for example, on *The Writing Experiment* website (Smith, Dean & White republished), there are various levels of interactivity. The music was created by composer-improvisor Roger Dean, and was written using the computer program MAX. There are a number of different soundtracks, and it is possible to interact with the music by playing it back-wards, controlling the volume, and activating several tracks simultaneously, while at the same time scrolling through the hypertexts. There is an inter-active feature by Greg White which intermittently replaces the musical controllers: this consists of the image of a body over which configurations of words and sounds change in response to mouse movements. There is also a feature called the 'Word Wired Web' written by Greg White, in which strings of words taken from my hypertexts can be pulled in a number of different directions, with accompanying and interactive sounds. At the same time the hypertext can take the reader on many different routes, depending on which links are chosen. The hypertexts are also linked to word and image anima-tions, again different ones will emerge depending on which links the reader activates. So the interaction between sound, image and word can be contin-uously interrupted and rearranged by the reader.

CREATING HYPERMEDIA PIECES

The following strategies are relevant to Exercise 5 which asks you to create a hypermedia piece:

- Juxtapose words with visual images and animations. For example, create a hypertext with links to visual objects, or an animation which plays with the layering of words and images. Create tensions and colli-sions between the meanings of the words and the visual images in the ways we explored in Chapter 10.

- Turn the words into visual images through spatial arrangement, font and colour. It is also possible to handwrite words on the screen in ways which make them appear more visually idiosyncratic.
- Display words on the screen, and also record (the same or different) words in a sound file, so that the screened and sounded words 'dialogue'. You may also want to refer back to some of the strategies for sonic poetry in Chapter 10: these can be adapted to new media work.
- Accompany or offset words with music or a soundscape. The sound dimension can take many forms: it can consist of speaking, or environ-mental sound, or music. There can be several sound files or spoken files which play at once, and these can be interactive. If you do not have much musical expertise you may want to collaborate with a composer, or use ready-made sound files which are already on the Web. Again refer back to Chapter 10 for ways of integrating sounds and words.

Hypermedia is a very broad area, and includes many works which are not text-based. In order to appreciate the possibilities you need to familiarise yourself with multimedia work which springs from fields other than writing, for example, from the visual arts. However, on *The Writing Exper-iment* website, work by Jason Nelson, Komninos Zervos and Christy Sheffield Sanford, and my own collaborations, demonstrate some of the possibilities of hypermedia work. See also work by Mark Amerika, especially his piece *Filmtext* (2003).

TEXT GENERATION AND CONCLUSION

In this chapter we have explored the way in which new media is changing writing, creating new textual spaces and opportunities. We have also seen how new media is itself an evolving field which is travelling in many dif-ferent and new directions. It is now possible, using a computer program, to generate text according to specific parameters: such software-based gen-eration of text is not within the scope of this book, and would be a tome in itself. However, text generation and transformation is an important aspect of the work of some writers, for example, the poet John Cayley (Cayley Ongoing), and may prove to be one of the most significant ways to implement new technologies in writing. Although this is not our main focus here, many of the exercises in this book—such as phrase permuta-tion or collage—could be carried out very comprehensively by computer programming. If you have an interest in programming, it could be extremely productive to follow up developments in this area.

ITEMS ON *THE WRITING EXPERIMENT* WEBSITE

Mary-Anne Breeze (mez), _][ad][Dressed in a Skin C.ode_.
Roger Dean, Anne Brewster and Hazel Smith, *soundAFFECTs*.
Jason Nelson, *this will be the end of you: play6: four variable creation*.
Jason Nelson, *this will be the end of you: play9: curious to know*.
Christy Sheffield Sanford, *The Roots of Nonlinearity: Toward a Theory of Web-Specific Art-Writing*.
Hazel Smith, Roger Dean and Greg White, *Wordstuffs: The City and The Body*.
Brian Kim Stefans, *The Dreamlife of Letters*.
Komninos Zervos, *beer*.
Komninos Zervos, *u cannot be programmed*.

REFERENCES

Alt-X Ongoing, http://www.altx.com/.
Amerika, M. 2003, *Filmtext*, Multimedia work. http://www.altx.com/mp3/film text.html.
Beehive Ongoing, http://beehive.temporalimage.com/.
Breeze, M.-A. (mez) 2001, Interview with Josephine Bosma, http://www.hotkey. net.au/~netwurker/jbinterview.htm.
—— republished, _][ad][Dressed in a Skin C.ode_, Multimedia work. www.allenandunwin.com/writingexp. Also available at http://www.cddc. vt.edu/host/netwurker/.
Cauldron and Net Ongoing, http://www.studiocleo.com/cauldron/volume4/index1.html.
Cayley, J. Ongoing, http://www.shadoof.net/.
Dean, R.T., Brewster, A. and Smith, H. republished, *soundAFFECTs*, Multimedia work. www.allenandunwin.com/writingexp.
Electronic Literature Organisation Ongoing. http://directory.eliterature.org/.
Glazier, L.P. 1998, *(Go) Fish*, Multimedia work. http://www.ubu.com/contemp/glazier/glazier.html.
—— 2002, *Digital Poetics: The Making of E-Poetries*, The University of Alabama Press, Tuscaloosa and London.
infLect Ongoing, www.ce.canberra.edu.au/inflect.

Jackson, S. 1995, *Patchwork Girl*, Hypertext Fiction. Eastgate Systems, Watertown, Massachusetts.

Joyce, M. 1990, *Afternoon: A Story*, Hypertext Fiction. Eastgate Systems, Watertown, Massachusetts.

Landow, G.P. (ed.) 1994, *Hyper/Text/Theory*, The Johns Hopkins University Press, Baltimore and London.

Larsen, D. 1996, *Samplers: Nine Vicious Little Hypertexts*, Hypertext Fiction. Eastgate Systems, Watertown, Massachusetts.

Memmott, T. 2000, *From Lexia to Perplexia*, Multimedia work in *The Iowa Review Web* at http://www.uiowa. edu/~iareview/tirweb/hypermedia/talan_memmott/.

Nelson, J. republished-a, *this will be the end of you: play6: four variable creation*, Multimedia work. www.allenandunwin.com/writingexp. Previously published in 2003 in *inflect* at http://www.ce.canberra.edu.au/inflect/01/jsonend6/ending6.swf.

—— republished-b, *this will be the end of you: play9: curious to know*, Multimedia work. www.allenandunwin.com/writingexp. Previously published in 2003 in *inflect* at http://www.ce.canberra.edu.au/inflect/01/jsonend9/ending9.swf.

Poems That Go Ongoing, http://www.poemsthatgo.com/.

Raley, R. 2003, 'Interferences: [Net.Writing] and the Practice of Codework', http://www.electronicbookreview.com/v3/servlet/ebr?command=view_essay&essay_id=rayleyele.

Sheffield Sanford, C. republished, *The Roots of Nonlinearity: Toward a Theory of Web-Specific Art-Writing*, Multimedia work. www.allenandunwin.com/writingexp. Previously published in 2000 in *Beehive* vol. 3 issue 1 at http://beehive.temporalimage.com/archive/31arc.html.

Smith, H., Dean, R.T. and White, G.K. republished, *Wordstuffs: The City and The Body*, Multimedia work. www.allenandunwin.com/writingexp. Originally published in 1998 and also available at http://www.abc.net.au/arts/stuff-art/stuff-art99/stuff98/10.htm.

Stefans, B.K. republished, *The Dreamlife of Letters*, Multimedia work. www.allenandunwin.com/writingexp. Originally created in 1999 and also available on UbuWeb at http://www.ubu.com/contemp/stefans/stefans.html.

UbuWeb Ongoing, http://www.ubu.com.

Wardip-Fruin, N. and Montfort, N. 2003, *The New Media Reader*, MIT Press, Cambridge, Massachusetts.

Zervos, K. republished-a, *beer*, Multimedia work. www.allenandunwin.com/writingexp. Also available at http://www.griffith.edu.au/ppages/k_zervos/.

—— republished-b, *u cannot be programmed*, Multimedia work. www.allenandunwin.com/writingexp. Also available at http://www.griffith. edu.au/ppages/k_zervos/.

CHAPTER TWELVE
Mapping worlds, moving cities

In the previous chapters, we have been exploring techniques for writing rather than themes or topics. On the whole, this book has tried not to draw too much of a distinction between form and content, and has been at pains to point out that there is 'a politics of form'.

In this chapter we will take a topic/theme which is central to cultural studies. We will focus primarily on ideas about place and space. We will look at the concept of place itself; different ways of representing place; writing the city as a site of difference; the city as walk poem; and how to shift a text between disparate times and spaces. These are all ways of both mapping and moving place, that is, representing it, making it dynamic and changing our conceptions of it.

This chapter brings theory and practice together in a particular way. In some of the other chapters, theory has been a tool for understanding and articulating the process of writing; in this chapter it is a trigger for ideas.

In order to write about place you may want to research it as a topic historically and theoretically. You may also want to explore literary approaches to the subject (the way writers have written about it), and the way ideas about place have changed over time. Or you may want to research specific places and their histories.

The exercises in this chapter exploit many of the approaches you have learnt in this book, and allow you to draw on many of the genres or techniques which have been the focus of previous chapters. You can, for example, write a poem, prose, discontinuous prose, fictocriticism, a performance piece or hypertext in response to them.

exercises

1. Create three texts:
   a) one based on an explicit sense of place
   b) one based on an implicit sense of place
   c) one which is a mixture.
2. Create a text which has an oblique relationship with place.
3. Create a text which constructs the city as a site of contradiction and difference.
4. Create a series of texts which engage imaginatively with each of the following: the diasporic city, the consumerist city, the under-privileged city, the gendered and sexualised city, the sensory city, the virtual city and the unreal city. Or think of other types of cities and also write about them.
5. Create a walk poem.
6. Create a text which engages the interface between body and city, but breaks down the unity of both.
7. Create a text which pivots on time–space compression (that is, shifts rapidly between different times and spaces).

MAPPING WORLDS

Postmodern geography

The area of cultural studies in which space and place are most discussed is **postmodern geography**. A very important and influential idea in postmodern geography is that a place is never circumscribed, unidirectional or apolitical. Doreen Massey, for example, argues that a place does not have a single identity, and is not contained within physical boundaries. Rather, it always links and merges with other places beyond its apparent limits. Any place consists of constantly shifting social and economic interrelationships between people and institutions, both within that place and with other places (Massey 1994). Place is therefore heavily involved in issues of power and symbolism, and charged by social relations. Places are always hybrids, constantly intersecting, aligned with, or superimposed upon each other. Maps are essential for establishing the position of a place and its relationship with other places. But maps give a very limited impression of the geographical, social and political complexity of places, because they mark them out in a fixed and bounded way.

Mapping worlds in fiction, however, is different because we can produce a much more fluid sense of place, and of the relations between places and people: we can make the map move. The exercises in this chapter encourage you to evoke a sense of place which is never determinate. Place in fiction is sometimes referred to as setting, but this is an unsatisfactory term. The word 'setting' suggests that a place is a backcloth to the action: it also gives a static impression. I prefer to use the word **location** to suggest a more dynamic and interactive relationship between places and people.

An explicit sense of place

In most fiction a sense of location is established through descriptive techniques like those you learnt in Chapter 2 for the person-in-action exercise. When constructing a sense of place, you need to think of a 'place-in-action'.

The following passage by Indian writer Arundhati Roy captures the dynamism of the landscape:

Example 12.1

May in Ayemenem is a hot, brooding month. The days are long and humid. The river shrinks and black crows gorge on bright mangoes in still, dustgreen trees. Red bananas ripen. Jackfruits burst. Dissolute bluebottles hum vacuously in the fruity air. Then they stun themselves against clear windowpanes and die, fatly baffled in the sun.

The nights are clear but suffused with sloth and sullen expectation.

But by early June the south-west monsoon breaks and there are three months of wind and water with short spells of sharp, glittering sunshine that thrilled children snatch to play with. The countryside turns an immodest green. Boundaries blur as tapioca fences take root and bloom. Brick walls turn mossgreen. Pepper vines snake up electric poles. Wild creepers burst through laterite banks and spill across the flooded roads. Boats ply in the bazaars. And small fish appear in the puddles that fill the PWD potholes on the highways.

From *The God of Small Things* (Roy 1998, p. 1)

This passage uses familiar descriptive techniques, but in an extremely effective way. It employs strong sensory images, but does not simply rely on the visual. We are made aware of colours (black crows, red bananas) and sounds (the hum of the bluebottles). But, above all, the countryside is active and changes with the seasons: 'The river shrinks', 'Jackfruits burst', 'black crows gorge' and 'Pepper vines snake up electric poles'. The landscape exceeds its own boundaries, spilling and bursting in all directions.

An implicit sense of place

Roy's description of Ayemenem is very explicit. But sometimes a sense of location is implicit and arises out of the activities, thoughts or feelings which occur within that place. Many of the stories in *The Penguin Book of the City* (Drewe 1997) involve events that take place in the city: they are consequences of urban life. They do not so much evoke the cityscape as its ethos. In the poem 'Taxi', by indigenous Australian writer Lisa Bellear, the urban environment is implicit in the image of passing car drivers who will not stop for a black person. The poem does not describe the city so much as convey the indigenous experience of being marginalised within it, of being excluded from the city community:

Example 12.2
(For Joan Kirner)

splashed by a passing cab,
and another and another
there's rules you see;
don't. stop. for.
black women. accelerate
past black men
and pensioners on pension day
can't trust,
trash
got no cash
we're all *nuisances*
reminders of an unjust
world, where the poor,
people of colour
are at mercy
of even taxi drivers.

'Taxi' (Bellear 1996, p. 70)

For Exercise 1 create three short pieces, one of which creates an explicit sense of place, one of which creates an implicit sense of place, and one of which is a mixture. Which seems to you to be most successful?

PLACE IN QUESTION

Some experimental fiction questions normal categorisations and representations of place. In Bernard Cohen's book *Tourism* (1992), towns and cities in Australia are entered alphabetically under headings: Adaminaby, Adelaide, Alice Springs, Ararat, Armidale, Auburn, Avoca, Batchelor, Bathurst and so on, one page to each town. The layout suggests a tourist manual, but the entries do not describe the town or city in the normal way. They tell us very little about the physical environment, and virtually nothing about its amenities, buildings, restaurants, cultural life or activities. In fact, some of the entries are extremely tangential to the place concerned, and hardly seem to 'belong' to it at all. In this sense the book shifts preconceived notions of place, since locations are non-specific and continually overlap with each other. The first piece, 'Adaminaby', suggests that any place is always spilling over its own boundaries and changing: the spreading ink on the map is a metaphor for this. It also draws attention to the way that place, language and identity are inextricably linked:

Example 12.3
Adaminaby
The nip of an insect is a catchcry; the shriek of the gulls a complicated threading across the sky. The horizon admits everything. As far as I am concerned, this town keeps going and going, changing its name, its colour, its attitude, but continuing. Here it is on the map. Here. A word and a point.

I rest the tip of my pen on the point marked 'Adaminaby' and the ink begins to spread. At first it's quite quick, the growth of the town, but it appears to slow as the area defined by a noticeable change in radius increases. In the end I have to look away for some minutes and then back to discern change. In the end the entire map is marked with the one point.

In Adaminaby I am made up of utterances. Bubbles of speech adhere to the air and follow me about as I arbitrate the next turn. Here we are limited to two types of speech: stories, and slogans. There are no other ways through the language.

And although so much remains hidden, I am always surprised to discover new things. Every minute turns up a bauble to seize. In this place, you take what you can, leave what you will. Oh yes, and in the end, you can still read the names of towns through the page's inevitable inkiness.

(Cohen 1992, p. 1)

Another section, 'Armidale', draws our attention to power relations within the city. Again this does not seem to be only applicable to Armidale.

Example 12.4
Armidale
This is a dirty doubledealing knifeintheback town. This town is costlycostly. The town cannot be trusted by us, alone or in groups. It's a whisperinthegrassinthesleeve wallshaveears town. What is now happening in Armidale has happened, in the course of history, to all thinkers and leaders of oppressed classes fighting for emancipation. This is a town of pyrrhic victories, of the ends don't justify the means, of symbolic goals. This is a place where the wrong word to the wrong person in the wrong place always produces a deviant response.

From *Tourism* (Cohen 1992, p. 5)

Bernard Cohen's *Tourism*, therefore, grapples with generic ideas about place, rather than conveying a realistic and individuated impression of particular locations.

For Exercise 2 create a text with an oblique relationship to place. To do this you might like to write a text with place names as headings, like the Cohen examples, in which the relationship between place and name is oblique. What can you say about place in this way that would be more difficult by more directly representational means?

MOVING CITIES

In poetry, in particular, location has tended to focus on the countryside: in the nineteenth century this was invoked in a romantic pastoral. Many contemporary writers have transmuted writing about nature into writing about the social and environmental problems of rural life from an ecological perspective. Other writers have reacted against the pastoral tradition by focusing on urban environments, and this has been very popular in postmodern literature. In this next section we will focus on writing the city.

CITY SPLITS

One way to write the city is to focus on it as a **site of contradiction and difference** (Exercise 3). The city is a public site of buildings, thoroughfares and institutions. But it is also a private site where we conduct relationships and pursue domestic goals. The private and public aspects of our lives are intertwined, power structures operate in both, and sometimes conflict with each other. The city can also be viewed in utopian and dystopian lights. Cities are cultural and creative places where people meet, live and work together productively. But cities can also be sites of violence, oppression and conflict. Throughout the history of literature, writers have tended to display an ambivalence about the city. They have been moved by it and seen it as a place of excitement, creativity and sensuous experience, but also of terror and repression (see Lehan 1998). Sometimes this difference within the city registers itself geographically: the inner city is evoked as a site of aggression and violence, and the suburbs as peaceful and safe. But such polarities often reverse themselves: there may be domestic violence in the suburbs.

Cities are both physical and imaginative spaces. Life in the city is marked by memories and desires as well as events, buildings and activities. As Jonathan Raban has said, 'The city as we imagine it, the soft city of illusion, myth, aspiration, nightmare, is as real, maybe more real, than the hard city one can locate in maps and statistics, in monographs on urban sociology and demography and architecture' (Bridge & Watson 2003, p. 14). The city expresses and embeds both the conscious and unconscious aspects of our lives: visible emotions and repressed memories and desires.

In writing the city as a site of difference (Exercise 3), try to engage with the contradictory emotions, impressions and thoughts that the city stimulates. You might like to think in terms of opposites, such as vertical and horizontal, violent and creative, friendly and impersonal, and build your city text from there. Perhaps you can activate several of these oppositions at once. Perhaps you can also show how these polarities are constantly reversing themselves. For example, in Paul Auster's novel 'City of Glass' (1988) the beggars turn out to be the kings of the street.

CITIES RATHER THAN CITY

The city, then, has many different faces: in fact there are many cities within the city. Let's consider some of these and the way they relate to urban power structures (Exercise 4).

The diasporic city

As the concept of the nation-state breaks down, people migrate and borders shift. The modern western city has become a mixture of nationalities and ethnicities: this has transformed food, clothing, customs, art and language.

It has produced cultural hybridity: a city such as London includes people from India, Pakistan, Africa and many other locations. Some of these people, like Karim Amir, the central character in Hanif Kureishi's *The Buddha of Suburbia* (1990), were born in England, but are from families where at least one parent is Asian or African. Consequently, they do not feel they belong entirely to one culture or the other. The diasporic city contains within it ethnic micro-cities: the most obvious of these is the Chinatown we see in most urban centres. An important aspect of the diasporic city can be the experience of immigration into a new and strange environment with radically different cultural values, religion and language. Problems can also result from growing up in a family which abides by fundamentally different values from others in the community. Most serious is the experience of racial discrimination, and the difficulties of socially and legally rebutting it. The diasporic city is as much about displacement as about place.

The consumerist city

Cities are also sites of intensive consumerism. Consumerism is, in many ways, the new religion. Shopping malls are more popular places to frequent than parks or gardens. Consumerism can be viewed negatively as rampant materialism and commodification: an elitist sport only available to those who are affluent. The violence, greed, selfishness and madness which can ensue when consumerism in the city reaches extremes is graphically evoked in Bret Easton Ellis's *American Psycho* (1991) and Don DeLillo's *Cosmopolis* (2003). But consumerism can also be viewed more positively as a creative endeavour, an opportunity to make choices and develop tastes.

The underprivileged city

Whenever we walk through the streets of the city we are likely to see homeless people. The city is also the site for drug trafficking and prostitution: on the streets we are as aware of the disadvantaged as we are of the affluent. In many cities around the world, unemployment problems and low incomes have impacted on the urban environment. Ethnic minorities and indigenous people are often among the low paid and underprivileged. Within any city there is an underbelly: a side of life that many people would like to ignore. There are many sites in the city, such as prisons, orphanages or hostels, which are signs of the underprivileged.

The gendered and sexualised city

The city is a site of conflicting demands for some women between work and motherhood. Whereas more and more women are working in the city, they are often at risk of physical and sexual violence. Consequently, there may be places where women cannot, or do not want to, go. Such places may be unsafe, or they may be intimidating because they are predominantly male environments. While diverse sexual identities are much more accepted than they used to be, gay people are often subject to homophobic attacks, and may gravitate towards gay pubs, bars or other meeting places, where they are more readily accepted.

The sensory city

The city is a site of strong sensory stimulation: it is not only a landscape, but also a smellscape and a soundscape. Theorists have pointed out that sight has often been prioritised over the other senses. But smell, touch and hearing can be as important in the way the city is culturally constructed.

Henri Lefebvre, for example, has pointed out how smell (often associated with disgusting rather than pleasant sensations) has been reduced and controlled in modern life through the use of substances and technologies which remove smells (discussed in Bridge & Watson 2003). Yet one of the strongest associations we have with a place is how it smells. Similarly, the city is a soundscape which intermingles the noise of traffic, talk, footsteps and musak.

The virtual city

There is now considerable tension between the city as a specific and visible location where people live and communicate, and the growth of telecommunications and computer networks which work across space–time barriers and create a virtual city. In other words technology is moving us into what has been called a 'post-urban' age, where the physical city will be much less important than it has been in the past (Bridge & Watson 2003). The consequences of this can be viewed in an optimistic or pessimistic light. Technology, for example, is taking us into an era in which information, in theory, will be available at all times to all people. However, digital information is increasingly commodified by giant corporations. Critics claim that technology polarises because it is in the grip of a wealthy elite, and is not accessible to the poor.

The unreal city

The unreal city is one which only exists in your imagination. An unreal city may have a name: you may feel that it exists, but it does not. An unreal city might be constructed of roads that are dead ends, or have bridges made from sheets of music. The unreal city is made of desires and memories, but is as important as the physical city. There are many unreal cities in Italo Calvino's *Invisible Cities* (1978), an example was given in Chapter 7, Example 7.7.

Above I have used headings to talk very briefly about some aspects of each of these 'cities within cities'. For Exercise 4 use these headings to write a series of creative short texts, one for each heading. For example, under the heading 'the diasporic city', you could fictionalise a migrant's first impressions in a strange city; under 'the consumerist city' you might want to chart the ups and downs of a shopping expedition. You might also wish to add your own headings such as 'the non-western city' or 'the intellectual city'.

THE POEM STRIDES OUT

Exercise 5 (create a walk poem) further situates the idea of the city as a site of difference, but mobilises it as a walk poem. When you walk the city you are in some senses *writing* it. The advantage of the walk poem is that it retains a sensation of mobility, the impression of place never ossifies. The walk is in some respects representative of contemporary life, because it is improvised, transient and ephemeral. A walk may be planned out, but often it changes as different directions suggest themselves, and is shortened or lengthened according to circumstances. In a walk poem you write from a position of active involvement, situate yourself as a point of reference, and interface with the environment.

Walking involves a unique mixture of observing, thinking and feeling. Memories, desires and extraneous thoughts are constantly obtruding onto the more immediate perceptions of the surrounding events. In fact, it is possible to walk and not notice what is going on in the outside world: to be totally engrossed in thought.

Nevertheless, to walk in the city is to encounter the marginalised and disadvantaged: the beggar, the prostitute and the homeless. The walk may traverse districts that sharply contrast in economic wealth. In some cities certain areas may have to be avoided because it would be unwise to walk there. Walking through the city means confronting and disturbing normally hidden aspects of city life.

When we walk in the city we write it in our own way. Cultural theorist de Certeau (1984) believed that walking was a creative act in which pedestrians write (but are unable to read) their own texts. He suggests that in walking the city we create texts that subvert its hegemonic power structures. We take whatever routes we desire, and fragment and transform spaces as we move, making social patterns through our walking. Whereas the nineteenth century 'flaneur' was somewhat detached and elitist, de Certeau's walker is one of the masses, and the walk is a form of resistance.

The archetypal walk poem is 'A Step Away From Them' by New York poet Frank O'Hara. Although this poem was written in the 1950s, it can tell us a lot about the pleasures and possibilities of walking in the city:

Example 12.5

It's my lunch hour, so I go
for a walk among the hum-colored
cabs. First, down the sidewalk
where laborers feed their dirty
glistening torsos sandwiches
and Coca-Cola, with yellow helmets
on. They protect them from falling
bricks, I guess. Then onto the
avenue where skirts are flipping
above heels and blow up over
grates. The sun is hot, but the
cabs stir up the air. I look
at bargains in wristwatches. There
are cats playing in sawdust.
                              On
to Time Square, where the sign
blows smoke over my head, and higher
the waterfall pours lightly. A
Negro stands in a doorway with a
toothpick, languorously agitating.
A blonde chorus girl clicks: he
smiles and rubs his chin. Everything
suddenly honks: it is 12:40 of
a Thursday.

            Neon in daylight is a
great pleasure, as Edwin Denby would
write, as are light bulbs in daylight.
I stop for a cheeseburger at JULIET'S
CORNER. Giulietta Masina, wife of
Federico Fellini, è bell' attrice.
And chocolate malted. A lady in
foxes on such a day puts her poodle
in a cab.
            There are several Puerto

Ricans on the avenue today, which
makes it beautiful and warm. First
Bunny died, then John Latouche,
then Jackson Pollock. But is the
earth as full as life was full, of them?
And one has eaten and one walks,
past the magazines with nudes
and the posters for BULLFIGHT and
the Manhattan Storage Warehouse,
which they'll soon tear down. I
used to think they had the Armory
Show there.
          A glass of papaya juice
and back to work. My heart is in my
pocket, it is Poems by Pierre Reverdy.

'A Step Away From Them' (O'Hara 1979, pp. 257–8)

The poem charts the movement of the walk, 'First, down the sidewalk',
'On/to Time Square', so that the location is constantly shifting. It embraces
a changing environment. It is not only about what is happening now
(though it is very immediate, an impression which is reinforced by the use
of the first person), but what will happen in the near future: 'the Manhattan Storage Warehouse, which they'll soon tear down', or has happened in
the past, 'I/used to think they had the Amory/Show there'. But there is,
nevertheless, a very strong sense of time and place: the poem is punctuated
by the clock, 'It's my lunch hour' and 'it is 12:40'.

At the same time the poet's walk is overlaid with memories and associations from other times and places. He remembers his deceased friends
Bunny, John Latouche and painter Jackson Pollock. A café reminds him of
Juliet of the Spirits (directed by Fellini and starring Giulietta Masina). The
experience of the city is both a piecemeal affair of variegated impressions,
and also a welter of activity in which everything is interconnected. Notice,
too, how the poem pulls different ethnicities, genders and classes—African
Americans, Puerto Ricans, the workers and the affluent, 'lady in foxes'—
into this network.

We see here how the poem is about the interaction of the self and city,
and how one moulds and changes the other. It is also about how historically and geographically times and places are always simultaneously
present: as the poet walks he also thinks of those who are no longer
alive. The poem tells us as much about the poet's thinking as it does about
the city.

For Exercise 5 write a walk poem which either takes a trajectory through the city you are familiar with, or invents one. Be specific about place and time, and include sensory impressions of the city. But also use the city to trigger thoughts, memories and ideas which take you into other spaces. You may want to try some contemporary variations on the walk poem, such as driving or taking a bus through the city.

BODIES AND CITIES

As the previous exercise has shown, a very important aspect of our experience of the city is the way our bodies interact with it. In this section I want to take that idea even further. Exercise 6 asks you to create a text which engages with the interface between body and city, but breaks down the unity of both.

Cultural theorist Elizabeth Grosz outlines three different models for the relationship between city and body (1995, p. 108). In the first, the self and city are in a causal relationship, that is, subjects build cities which are manifestations of human projects, desires and achievements. The second is one of parallelism or isomorphism between the body and the city, so that the two are congruent with each other and mirror each other's characteristics. In the third model, which Grosz suggests is her preferred one, both city and body are broken down and realigned. Grosz argues that this is a model of bodies and cities that sees them 'not as megalithic total entities, but as assemblages or collections of parts, capable of crossing the thresholds between substances to form linkages, machines, provisional and often temporary sub- or micro-groupings'. Seen in this light, the interrelations between body and city 'involve a fundamentally disunified series of systems, a series of disparate flows, energies, events, or entities, bringing together or drawing apart their more or less temporary alignments' (Grosz 1995, p. 108).

Each of these models can be a stimulating starting point for writing. The first might lead to texts about building communities, but also to the creation of imagined and allegorical cities. The second might lead to texts in which the city is a metaphor for the body, and vice versa. However, the third model particularly interests me here, because it allows for a discontinuous and cross-genre approach to writing. It projects neither body nor city as unified entities, but as multiplicitous and fragmentary parts which interact with each other in continuously changing ways.

An example of such a text is *The City and the Body,* part of which was included in Chapter 9, and which can be viewed in full as a hypertext and hypermedia piece and entitled *Wordstuffs: The City and The Body* (Smith,

Dean & White republished). I wrote this partly in response to Grosz's essay, and also to reading more widely about the city. I have attempted to imagine many different kinds of bodies or cities in the individual texts, and sometimes their interaction. In the piece, there is no unified city or body. The emphasis is on parts rather than wholes, glimpses and fragments rather than totalities, moments rather than sustained stories.

This assemblage is also highly politicised: societal regulation of the body is fundamental to the piece. The body can be policed in its relationship to the city, hence the reference to 'docile bodies/indoctrination' and the 'policing' of the 'body politic'. The piece draws our attention to this kind of regulation through governmental repression (the law that prohibits kissing in public in Kuwait and the use of the vaginal speculum to examine women's bodies in the fourteenth century). But it also suggests ways in which regulation can be transgressed by walking, dreaming, writing and other creative acts. This tension between regulation and transgression permeates the piece and is never resolved. The transgression does not necessarily 'win', and cannot always be sustained, but the potential to break through the repression is always there.

In responding to Exercise 6, try to break down the body and the city as totalities. Include many different cities and bodies; focus on parts rather than wholes, and a variety of interactions between them.

GLOBALISATION GOVERNS

Exercise 7 asks you to create a text which pivots on time–space compression (that is, shifts rapidly between different times and space). Postmodern theorists, such as Edmund Soja or David Harvey, see **time–space compression** (a consequence of globalisation) as absolutely fundamental to the postmodern world (Harvey 1990). Time–space compression means that in our global world distant points tend to converge on each other. First, many of us are able to make links with places which seem to be very distant culturally, electronically and physically through commerce, travel, the media, the Internet and migration. Second, we are also more able to connect with past time in history through, for example, the media (so we constantly see replays of World War II). That time–space compression is a feature of modern life is widely accepted in postmodern thought. But whether it is productive or destructive has been hotly debated in cultural theory. On the one hand, it can be argued, we have an increased awareness of different cultures and the historical events which have shaped us. On the other hand, shorthand ways of experiencing times and spaces, such as tourism and the media, can result in a blunting and debasing of our awareness. On the TV, for example, we are constantly fed what Jean Baudrillard has called **simulacra**—that is, copies or imitations of events, rather than the events themselves—to the point where the copy becomes indistinguishable from the original.

In many novels, different times and places are juxtaposed with each other, often through a process of alternation. In Margaret Atwood's *Cat's Eye* (1990), for example, the past is projected and anchored through the consciousness of the narrator, Elaine, who remembers her relationship with her friend and tormentor Cordelia. Structured around flashbacks and flashforwards (or analepses and prolepses), the novel projects back into Elaine's relationship with Cordelia, and forwards into her fantasies about what Cordelia might be like now. Most importantly for our purposes here, the past city (the one they knew as children) is juxtaposed with the present one. The text refers to the fact that time is actually a space, 'Time is not a line but a dimension, like the dimensions of space' (Atwood 1990, p. 3). But there is no confusion about what has happened in the past, and what is happening in the present—the novel keeps them quite separate. They are anchored through Elaine's memory, and held together in a storyline which relates them unequivocably to each other.

Some experimental texts, however, emphasise time–space compression, and represent several times and places simultaneously. In such texts there may be rapid, and abrupt, transitions between different temporal and spatial dimensions. Such expressions of time and place often powerfully convey how perception and memory superimpose events and impressions without necessarily 'sorting them out' into a linear narrative. They can demonstrate, at a formal level, the historical depth of any place, and the way disasters, wars, power struggles, achievements, migrations and departures accumulate (like layers of rock) over the years. They also demonstrate how globalisation has produced an intricate web of relationships between places, both economically and culturally, beyond the boundaries of the nation-state.

Let's look at some examples of this kind of time–space compression.

Examples of time–space compression

My piece 'Secret Places' Figure 12.1 (Smith 2000; see p. 272) resulted from a collaboration with artist Sieglinde Karl. It was featured as part of an installation in a number of art galleries, was included as a visual image, and was also featured in a recorded version in the gallery space (a recording of the piece can be heard on my website, Smith Ongoing). The text refers to a larger-than-life figure of a woman made from casuarina tree needles by Sieglinde. It also alludes, through images of threading and weaving, to the process of her creation.

In the text I try to convey a number of different times and places simultaneously, and to intertwine disparate psychological, historical and geographical realities, without cohering them into a single overall narrative. In order to do this I've invented three women, Cass, Cathy and Casuarina, all of whom might be the same or different people. This gives me the freedom to position them in different times and spaces. The text itself, when published, was accompanied by some brief notes which indicated the sources of some of the ideas.

In the first section a sense of place is not explicit, but in the section beginning 'When Casuarina was a child' we are projecting into a fantasy past: the world of myth. In the next section 'Cass loves the simple things in life' we are in present-day Australia. There are references to Australian current affairs, but Cass's thoughts travel into many other spaces including Sarajevo, Rwanda and Siberia. Different places are also superimposed on each other: the 'Rooms sealed with red wax' refers to the door of the laboratory where the ice-maiden's body was being treated (which I read about in an article in the *Sydney Morning Herald*). But it also refers to the red seal which was to be found, in the Stalinist era, on the doors of the homes of purge victims who were taken away in the middle of the night by the secret police (also in the *Herald* article).

In the third section we are in a casuarina grove, the site of Casuarina's origins in the present, and after that we move to Yuendumu, an Aboriginal community in central Australia. The 'paintings on doors at Yuendumu' mentioned here refers to the doors of the local school, which were decorated with paintings of the dreaming as part of a collective Aboriginal artists' project in the 1980s. When I saw the doors they were overlaid with graffiti, though parts of the original paintings were still to be seen. Again there is a superimposition of the 'blood red door' of the second section, and the Yuendumu doors, compressing different types of historical oppression. In the penultimate section we find ourselves at the site of a holocaust massacre (taken from a survivor story I heard on television).

So in this text a sense of time and place is conveyed by:

- A combination of real and unreal spaces. These spaces are sometimes determinate, sometimes indeterminate.
- Superimposition of a number of different historical events and geographical spaces. Although there is some sense of linear time within the individual narratives, the links between different sections are not 'spelt out' or contained within an obvious narrative framework.

Time and place take the form of juxtapositions, they are not folded into a continuous narrative: the piece is written in discontinuous prose. This discontinuous form emphasises the continuities of oppression, massacre and totalitarianism between individual eras and locations.

- Floating contexts which are not pinned down or mutually exclusive in the piece. There is a much less explicit sense of time and place than in the Atwood novel.
- A number of micro-narratives rather than one macro-narrative.
- Mixed genres (the fairytale, the dialogue, the poem, the narrative, the performance) which emphasise different aspects of these historical and geographical realities.
- Recurring ideas/images which bind the piece together. These work across normal temporal or spatial connections. Examples are the images of sewing, journeys and references to the red door.
- The interweaving of three closely connected women who never become fully-fledged characters.
- A variety of voices and subject positions which creates different degrees of distance from, and perspectives on, the story. For example, the third person narration in the third section which is lightly satirical, 'Cass loves the simple things in life', contrasts with the first person narration in the holocaust section, which is much more intense.

This superimposition of times and places is a way of conveying how similar (and often tragic) ideas and events echo, repeat and transform themselves in vastly different historical and geographical circumstances. However separate some of these events may seem, everything is linked to everything else, and the past continually re-creates itself in the present, through individual and collective memory.

In a completely different way, Australian novelist and poet John Kinsella superimposes different times and spaces in his novel *Genre*. At the beginning of the novel 'the Renaissance Man' thinks about all the people who are inhabiting flats in the block in which he is living. They are in different spaces, but all co-exist simultaneously within his mind in an associative monologue:

Example 12.6
The Renaissance Man is writing an essay on an exhibition and thinking about his latest book on aesthetics. He gets up and washes his hands. His thoughts are interrupted by the video machine in his head which keeps

replaying *Blue Velvet.* His thoughts are interrupted by an idea for a play, by his child rolling on the floor and complaining of boredom, by the likelihood that his wife is reading the letters he's left intentionally on top of the filing cabinet. They are photocopies of his original letters to publishers, writers, artists, academic colleagues . . . even movie stars. There are also other documents—drafts of essays, notes, private thoughts and so on. He wonders if the sin of reading them is greater than the sin of constructing such a temptation. He thinks of the letters to '. . .' he's inserted at regular intervals. He knows they'll annoy her. His wife, the novelist, is working on her *Ghoul* manuscript. The student in flat five is preparing to leave, he is reading Descartes, in English translation, and intermittently returning to a draft of his first book—a science fiction novel with the working title *Lens.* He's quite handsome, one might let oneself think, in a stray moment. Though he watches your every step. It's best to pretend to keep your eyes averted. It's best that way. The 'girls' are getting dressed. One of them is thinking how much she hates sex. They've both just snorted a line of speed. The bitter taste is just entering the back of their throats and they both, occasionally, snort like pigs. The steroid-hungry guy in flat six is frustrated and starting a journal on the advice of his therapist, his girlfriend is writing up her case study notes; the woman whose child has been removed by the Department is frantically trying to prepare a vase of flowers for possible visitors/intruders over the weekend while her boyfriend, the addict, is reading *Slide Show*—a cult drug novella; the Indonesian couple are arguing.

From *Genre* (Kinsella 1997, pp. 9–11)

It is also common in much contemporary poetry to move quickly from one moment or scenario to another, often implicitly disrupting a strong sense of time and place and creating time–space compression. Such time and space shifts have been apparent in a number of examples in this book, such as in the prose poetry of Lyn Hejinian and Ania Walwicz, and are also to be found on a larger scale in the work of experimental novelists such as Sabrina Achilles (1995). They are apparent, too, in the word association on travel by Michele Sweeney in Chapter 1, Example 1.8.

For Exercise 7 create a text which pivots on time–space compression. Move between different centuries and continents: the transitions between the locales and time zones can be very swift and abrupt, or slower and smoother. Whatever type of text you produce, try to capture a sense of how disparate times and places are geographically and historically interrelated.

Figure 12.1: 'Secret Places' (Smith 2000, pp. 22–5)

This is the story of Casuarina, but it is a story with several speakers.
This is my voice, not Casuarina's.

This is a story of separation, but also a tale of threading lost needles.
Breaking to be, bleeding as healer.

> This is a story of forests and flight-paths, songlines and
> shellfire, cross-pollination of time-warps and mind trails.

This is a story which speaks for itself through mummified skins,
secrets as peeling.

Cathy, what is the thought you were dreaming?

A man leaving a room with a blood red door

When Casuarina was a child she grew the most beautiful
wings. They were white with purple spots. And the spots
were ringed round with gold. But her father cut them off,
so she could never fly. But later she decided she could
move just as well on foot. So she went on her travels
where she met a man who promised her eternal life.
Casuarina was fairly discerning so she said, if you give
me eternal life what do you want in return? And the man
said, I will extract my price, but you must agree in
advance without knowing the terms. You have everything
to gain and nothing to lose. *Look* at what I am offering you.
This chance will never come again.
Casuarina did not hesitate. She said, I certainly will not
agree to *that*. I never pay for anything up-front.

Cass loves the simple things in life, coffee and cakes, skimming the newspaper without taking anything in. This morning she reads about the Siberian ice-maiden, undisturbed for 2,500 years, they think she may have been a shaman. The dead in Sarajevo and the slaying in Rwanda. The Hindmarsh affair. She's pleased they are legalising euthanasia. She likes TV and trash too, there's a woman on Donahue who thinks she's reincarnated. She walks in the woods and finds a shady spot to lie down. It's great to be alive! Most of all she loves secrets. To be able to think anything and nobody will ever know. All those forbidden thoughts, those veiled acts, those hidden faces.

Yet things trouble her, they knock but she never quite knows who they are. Rooms sealed with red wax. Planes dropping bombs. Wounds like tattooes. She thinks of the ice-maiden in her wooden coffin roused from eternal sleep. Faces come back to her, like the links from a spreadout, recalcitrant sequence.

Casuarina's broadminded and reads both Freud and Jung without feeling there is any competition between the two. She likes to imagine herself lying in a grove with all her clothes off. Faces appear from above and stare down at her but she doesn't mind. She likes the way they look at her, she likes the way they stare at *it*.

Casuarina what's needling you?

I just realised when I'm enjoying myself, it's always at someone else's expense.

the silent slit from which voices erupt
the threading of a needle with nerves
a word-web spun from the wildest text

THE PAINTINGS ON DOORS AT YUENDUMU
GHOSTS INTERLACED WITH GRAFFITI

    a book which stirs out of crinkled skins
    a story made by a woman from stones
    a sign composed of ambiguous dots

    THE PAINTINGS ON DOORS AT YUENDUMU
    GHOSTS INTERLACED WITH GRAFFITI

        the hollow cry of the hidden costs
        a journey towards a land beyond loss
        the purple light on the reddest rocks

        THE PAINTINGS ON DOORS AT YUENDUMU
        GHOSTS INTERLACED WITH GRAFFITI

a place which is every and no place you know
a wish that is never the want that you will
a meaning that moves as memory unpicks

Cass, which wastes do your thoughts inscribe?

which songs does your silence kill?

which secret sites are buried in blood?

We have travelled a long way but the

        worst

        is yet

        to c

We stood in line at the edge of the pit. They started to shoot. My daughter kept saying "mummy
they are shooting people, let's run away". They shot my mother and father, in front of my
eyes. My sister was a beautiful woman, with dark eyes and hair. She begged to be
saved. She met the guard's gaze and said "let me live". But he took no heed. My
daughter kept imploring me "let's run away". She was five years old. He told
me to give her up, but she would not go. A shot was fired, I did not see, I
could not look. Then he fired at me. I fell into the pit.
I knew nothing.
When I awoke I thought that this was the land of the dead. Then
I knew I was still in the world and maybe I had a chance to
live. The pit was corpse-full. There were limbs on top
of me, over my face. There were other bodies helping
me push. But I had not the strength and if I had
risen I would have been shot again. It was
still light. I waited till night, I waited for
hours, I could not breathe. Then
when it was dark, I climbed
out, crawled away. Now
I know the guilt that
survives.

These are the stories of Casuarina, but these fables leap
from several seedlings. These are my words, not Casuarina's.

This is a story of places and people but also the intertwining of spindles.
Blinding to see, wounding as weaving.

This is a story of pine-groves and pistols, bright sun and dark shade, links between
lines and rites beyond living.

This is a story which pleads for itself through dread and delight,
secrets which listen.

Cathy, whose is the death you are grieving?

CONCLUSION

In this chapter a range of formal strategies has been used to explore ideas
about place, and to raise issues of identity and power within places. We
have seen how writing about place is often a subtle combination of
mapping and moving: describing places and yet dissolving the boundaries
within and between them. Furthermore, the exploration of place and
space could be seen to be central to this book which has itself tried to mark
out and cut across territories, pull down boundaries, and bring together
spaces which are usually kept well apart.

REFERENCES

Achilles, S. 1995, *Waste*, Local Consumption Press, Sydney.

Atwood, M. 1990, *Cat's Eye*, Virago, London.

Auster, P. 1988, 'City of Glass', *The New York Trilogy*, Faber & Faber, London, pp. 3–132.

Bellear, L. 1996, 'Taxi', *Dreaming in Urban Areas*, University of Queensland Press, St Lucia, Queensland.

Bridge, G. and Watson, S. (eds) 2003, *A Companion to the City*, Blackwell, Oxford.

Calvino, I. 1978, *Invisible Cities*, Harcourt Brace & Company, New York and London.

Cohen, B. 1992, *Tourism*, Picador, Sydney.

de Certeau, M. 1984, *The Practice of Everyday Life*, (trans.) S. Rendall, University of California Press, Berkeley.

DeLillo, D. 2003, *Cosmopolis*, Picador, London.

Drewe, R. 1997, The Penguin Book of the City, Penguin Books Australia, Ringwood, Victoria.

Ellis, B.E. 1991, *American Psycho*, Picador, London.

Grosz, E. 1995, S*pace, Time and Perversion: The Politics of Bodies*, Allen & Unwin, Sydney.

Harvey, D. 1990, *The Condition of Postmodernity: An Enquiry into the Origins of Cultural Change*, Blackwell, Oxford UK and Cambridge USA.

Kinsella, J. 1997, *Genre*, Fremantle Arts Centre Press, South Fremantle, Western Australia.

Kureishi, H. 1990, *The Buddha of Suburbia*, Faber & Faber, London.

Lehan, R. 1998, *The City in Literature: An Intellectual and Cultural History*, University of California Press, Berkeley.

Massey, D. 1994, *Space, Place and Gender*, Polity Press, Cambridge.

O'Hara, F. 1979, 'A Step Away From Them', *Collected Poems*, (ed). D. Allen, University of California Press, Berkeley.

Roy, A. 1998, *The God of Small Things*, Flamingo, London.

Smith, H. 2000, 'Secret Places', *Keys Round Her Tongue: Short Prose, Poems and Performance Texts*, Soma Publications, Sydney.

—— Ongoing, www.austraLYSIS.com.

Smith, H., Dean, R.T. and White, G.K. republished, *Wordstuffs: The City and The Body, Multimedia work*, www.allenandunwin.com/writingexp. Originally published in 1998 and also available at http://www.abc.net.au/arts/stuff-art/stuff-art99/stuff98/10.htm.

CONCLUSION
The ongoing editor

One of the ideas implicit in this book is that writing is a gradual process of transformation. Any text can grow from the most humble beginnings into a complex and sophisticated work. In such a view, editing work is part of creating it. This questions the idea that there is inevitably a specific stage towards the end of the creative process which is dedicated to editing.

Although it has been commonplace for writers to talk about drafting their work, writing is just as likely to be a continuous process of transformation, particularly in the era of word processing. Editing-as-you-go is fundamental to the way we write on a computer, since procedures such as cutting and pasting are available to help us shape and edit text as we write. This means that the text tends to change continuously, rather than in visible discrete stages. Most of the processes you have been learning about in this book (such as the amplification and substitution in Chapter 2, or narrative shaping in Chapter 5) are also editing techniques, because they are ways of organising and structuring your material.

Having said that, writers will approach the creative process in a wide range of ways, and the same writer may engage with it differently at different times. Sometimes you may find yourself writing freely and copiously as the first stage, and then moving into editing mode as the second; sometimes there will be no absolutely clear point at which editing starts. The editing mentality requires an awareness of what language can do which should be with you all the time, but which it may be appropriate to apply with more discipline at some times rather than at others.

Although the ability to shape and cull your own work is very important, and involves considerable self-discipline, editing should also be treated with caution. The most interesting elements of a creative text are often irrational, the ones which stick out from the rest and which are tempting to cut away. Make sure when you edit that you don't simply conform to what you think the text ought to look like, or how it might be most acceptable to others, rather than how you would like it to be.

Some books on writing stress the idea of writing as a craft. This book certainly focuses sharply on the technical features of writing, but does not use the word 'craft' which can suggest the careful assembly of known elements, the polished rendering of recognisable forms, rather than a more open-ended approach. However, this does not mean that experimental work will be, or should be, messy or badly made. The strategies outlined will help you produce work which is technically rigorous and meticulously shaped, whatever its objectives.

Most university courses include workshops in which student work is discussed by the class. This can sometimes result in a very productive form of joint editing. Remarks about any particular piece of work will be of many, and often of opposing, kinds. This should alert you (yet again) to the arbitrary and subjective nature of the creative process. You will probably find many of the comments very illuminating. Since members of the class are not familiar with your material, they are likely to read it in a different way. You may find, for example, that ideas that you thought you had transmitted effectively do not come across to your readers. On the other hand you may find that some ideas are more obvious than you intended. Listen to what everyone has to say and try not to be defensive if the comments are critical. But remember that this is ultimately your own text, and in the end only you can decide how it should develop. Bear in mind also that comments from other people may on occasion tend towards conformity rather than innovation. Some members of the class may be uncomfortable with experimental pieces because of lack of familiarity.

The editing process will also vary enormously in accordance with the type of writing. A piece of realist fiction will require a very different editing mentality from that required for an experimental poem. A realist narrative may need to be tidied up while an experimental poem may need to be opened out. If editing takes place in the workshop, these matters need to be discussed openly, so work is discussed in its own terms, rather than in the light of irrelevant criteria.

Having voiced the above reservations, there are certain strategies which writers call on when they are editing and which can be systematically categorised. These are related to processes we have looked at throughout this book, and can be employed at any stage in the writing process.

Cutting

Less is often more in writing: you should be ruthless about cutting out irrelevant words, sentences and phrases. Look at every word to see what function it is really fulfilling, though that function does not always have to be strictly semantic; it may be sonic or visual. Cutting—like all editing strategies—must be related to the writing style you are adopting: some styles are more florid than others. Some writers, like Gertrude Stein, have used repetition and redundancy to remarkable effect. However, over-writing and over-explaining are errors that writers tend to make, even when they are very experienced.

Amplification

This involves expanding, developing or highlighting an interesting idea which is scantily treated in the first instance. In Chapter 2 amplification was introduced as a strategy for building up a passage, but it can be used at any stage of the writing process.

As you write and edit you will probably find that you are constantly juggling between cutting and amplification. Knowing how much to put in, and how much to leave out, is a very subtle aspect of writing and one to which there are no hard and fast answers. You may find yourself sometimes being more explicit, sometimes less explicit, in different types of work.

Substitution

Finding alternatives (sometimes synonyms) for weak words and phrases is a major task in editing. We sometimes put words on the page because we cannot think of any others, and this is fine in the early stages. But it is then easy to leave the words, and to become so familiar with them that they become acceptable by default. When we edit we must try to become more critical again, and in such cases find substitute words which are linguistically stronger. Again substitution was a strategy we started to use as early as Chapter 1.

Concretising and abstracting

In some types of writing, for example descriptive writing, it may be important to substitute concrete imagery for abstractions, to give a more immediate and vivid impression. This can also help to create a context for your work (for example, give a strong sense of location). In some of the more experimental types of writing, however, you may want to make the concrete aspects of the text more oblique and abstract. When we built up a person-in-action in Chapter 2, we were making the description more concrete. In Chapter 8, however, we tended, especially in the section on 'the new sentence', to make the text more abstract.

Rearrangement

Changing the order of a text can often improve the structure and make the material much stronger, even if it is otherwise unchanged. Think of your work as if it were in moveable segments. Is your structure progressive or repetitive, varying, multilayered or numerical? Is it several or none of these? What is the structural rationale behind it? Look back to Chapters 3 and 5 for more guidance on this.

Shaping

Look at the fine detail such as punctuation, spelling and grammar (whether you are working with or subverting these conventions). This book assumes familiarity with these conventions, but many books are available for consultation if you feel you are not familiar with them. Shaping also involves, where relevant, playing with the visual effect. Remember that, especially in poetry, there is no reason to stick to the left-hand margin.

Overall, treat the idea of a final (and perfect) text with scepticism. Remember that the final text is usually only the place where the author decides to stop. Behind every final text are many other routes that the text could have taken. In fact it is perfectly reasonable to create several versions of a work rather than only one (as many musicians/writers/artists have done). We have also seen in this book how it is possible to adapt a particular text for different media (a hypertext or performance text, for example, may be rewritten for the page) so that the work itself is constantly transforming. The creative process always consists of forking paths from which it would be possible to move in many other directions. And experimentation is about taking risks, trying different alternatives, not searching for absolute perfection. Creativity lies in having the courage to make choices, but the paths that were not taken are still open, and can be explored another day.

Good luck with your experiments and enjoy your writing!

Acknowledgments

I would like to thank the following people for giving me permission to publish or republish their work: Richard James Allen, Inez Baranay, Lisa Bellear, Charles Bernstein, Anne Brewster, Maxine Chernoff, Sophie Clarke, Tom Clark, Bernard Cohen, Wanda Coleman, Alice Coltheart, Moya Costello, Elizabeth Crawford, Alison Croggon, Laurie Duggan, Steve Evans, Ben Garcia, Isabelle Gerrard, Lyn Hejinian, Yunte Huang, Elizabeth James, John Kinsella, Yuriya Kumagai, Emma Lew, Joshua Lobb, James Lucas, Richard Lunn, Greg Lyons, Myron Lysenko, Jackson Mac Low, Rhyll McMaster, Geraldine Monk, Finola Moorhead, Maggie O'Sullivan, Gabrielle Prendergast, Frances Presley, Denise Riley, Susan Schultz, Ron Silliman, Amanda Stewart, Mohammad Tavallaei, Bryoni Trezise, Robert Wilson (through his archivist Aaron Beebe), Johan de Wit and Ian Young.

I would like to thank the following people for allowing me to publish their work on *The Writing Experiment* website: Charles Amirkhanian, Christian Bok, Mary-Anne Breeze (mez), Roger Dean, David Knoebel, Taylor Mali, Jason Nelson, Christy Sheffield Sanford, Brian Kim Stefans, Amanda Stewart, Greg White, Scott Woods and Komninos Zervos.

All individuals' works are fully referenced in the book.

Other acknowledgments:
Charles Armirkhanian (*Church Car* [P] [C] 1981 Arts Plural Publishing [BMI]. All rights reserved; *Dot Bunch* [P] [C] 1981 Arts Plural Publishing [BMI]. All rights reserved); extract from *Who's Afraid of Virginia Woolf?* by Edward Albee published by Jonathan Cape, used by permission of The Random House Group Limited; 'A Step Away from Them' from *Lunch*

Poems copyright 1964 by Frank O'Hara, reprinted by permission of City Books. Thanks to John Kerrigan, executor of the Hugh Sykes Davies estate, for publication of 'Poem "In the stump of the old tree . . ."' and to Karen Koch, executor of Kenneth Koch's estate, for giving me permission to quote from 'Mexico City' and 'Coil Supreme'. My thanks also to ex-students Michele Sweeney and Amy Tan who I was unable to trace, and to Lynda Walker for her original graphic design of *Secret Places*.

Index

absent narrator, 95
abstracting text, 279–80
acrostic structure, 39–40
Adaminaby (extract), 258
addition of words, 13, 30
adjectives, 33
advertising style, 60–1, 63
'afterwardness', 103
allusion, fictocriticism, 207
alternation, fictocriticism, 207
Amalgamemnon (word
    association example), 10–11
ambiguities
    crime novels, 193
    focalisation, 98
    lineation, 38–9
    multiple focalisations, 107–8
America, avant-garde poetics,
    167–9
American Psycho (novel), 142
*American Woman in the Chinese
    Hat, The* (extract), 93
amplification of text, 30–1, 279
'An All-time Favourite Motto'
    (multiple focalisation), 101–3
analepses, 86, 104, 268
animated texts
    new technologies, 244–6
    person-in-action, 29–34
anthologies
    concrete poems, 182
    experimental poetry, 170
    performance poetry, 215
anti-hero, 142
anti-narrative, 184
antonymy, 175
apologies website, 60–1
Armidale (extract), 259
arrow of time, 103–7
'Artifice of Absorption'
    (poem–essay), 206
As I Lay Dying (novel), 99
Ash Range, The (collage), 68–9
assassination of JFK, rewritten,
    145
audience participation, 230–31
Australia, avant-garde poetics,
    168
'authoritarian' narration, 86
autobiographical experience,
    x–xi

avant-garde poetics, 167–70
Ayemenem (place), 256–7

'Back' (performance poem),
    214
backwards
    dialogue, 116–17
    time movement, 149
Ballad of Narayama, The (film),
    150
'Balloon, The' (short story
    extract), 34–5
beer (word animation), 245
'bells' (sonic poem), 219
Beloved (novel), 103, 143
'Bent' (poem), 166
bias
    narrator, 88
    personal experience, 143–4
'Bloody Chamber, The' (story),
    77–9
Bluebeard fairytale, 77–9
bodies, interaction with cities,
    263–7
Body Artist, The, 22
body movement, intermedia
    work, 223–4
Book of Illusions, The (novel), 32

'cantilevering' process, 30
Cat's Eye (novel), 268
central character narrator, 89–90
centrifugal/centripetal poems,
    171
characters
    intermedia work, 222
    loosely differentiated, 140–1
    marginalised, 143–4, 195, 257
    names, 141, 269
    non-human, 143
    one-trait, 141–3
    postmodern, 135, 140
    reborn, 140–1
    traditional view, 139–40
    'types', 36–7
chatting/chat shows, 123–4
Chimney Sweeper's Boy, The
    (novel), 95
chronology
    out of order, 195
    structuring, 104–7

Cinderella tale rewritten, 80–2
cities
    bodies' interactions, 263–7
    multiple faces of, 260–3
    split focus, 259–60
    walk poems, 263–6
'Cities and Memories' (extract),
    152
'City and The Body, The'
    (extract), 200–203
'City of Glass' (postmodern
    fiction), 137, 140–1
clichés, 4
closed narratives, 107–8
codework, 248–49
'Coil Supreme' (script), 227–8
collaboration
    dialogue, 125–8
    improvisation, 226
collage
    creating, 72–4
    examples, 68–72
    exercises, 66
    explained, 67–8
    sonic poems, 221–2
communication, rise and fall,
    120–2
concrete poetry, 40, 182
concretising text, 279–80
consumerist city, 261, 263
contemporary images, 166–7
contemporary perspective
    comment on values, 76
    rewriting classic texts, 77–82
contradictions, focalisation, 98
control, knowing narrator,
    94–5
conversation, satirised, 121
crime genre, 193
critical theory, 165
cross-dressing
    fictocriticism, 204–10
    generic, 200–204
    literary analogy, 192
    'sonic', 231
'Crossing the Bar' (poem),
    172–3
cultural barriers, crossing, 144
cultural hybridity
    diasporic city, 261
    mixed genres, 203

cultural viewpoints, opposing, 99
culturally specific text,
  exercise, 50
*Curious Incident of the Dog in the
  Night-time, The* (novel), 121–2
cutting text, 279
cut-up method, collage, 72–4
cyberwriting, 240, 248–9

dance, performance work, 223
death, mirror images, 21–2
Death of a Salesman (play), 114,
  115
decontextualised dialogue, 124–5
defamiliarisation, 38, 180
'Defence of Poetry, A'
  (poem–essay), 180–1
'democratic' narration, 86
destabilised subject position, 92–4
detail, inclusion of, 33–4
dialogue
  authorial comment, 111
  chatting and chat shows, 123–4
  collaborative, 125–8
  conception methods, 111,
    112–13
  decontextualised, 124–5
  exercises, 111–12, 119–20
  function, 112–13
  improvisation, 117–18
  non-communicating, 120–2
  non-realist, 114–17
  power relationships, 117–20
  progressive, 120
  realist, 113–14
  thought processes, 116
  unconventional, 121–2
  written backwards, 116–17
  written forms, 110–11
dialoguing
  across genres, 124–5
  breakdown of, 110
  interactive process, 127–8
  social forms, 123–4
diary entries in fiction, 60
diary form, semi-fictionalised,
  199–200
diary slips as poetry, 75–7
diasporic city, 260–1, 263
disabled people, dissident lyric,
  165–6
discontinuity
  bodies and cities, 266–7
  fictocriticism, 207–9
  postmodern poetry, 178–9
  prose, 196–200
discontinuous prose, 270
discourse-related approach, 86
dissident lyric, 165
dissociation
  word building, 8
  word list, 7
door
  imagery use, 269
  metaphor development, 41–4
  word as hook, 39–40

Dreamlife of Letters, The
  (hypermedia), 244–5,
  249–50

editing process, 277–80
'Elevator, The' (postmodern
  story), 139
Elevator Dreams (poem),
  216–17
'Empty Lunch-Tin, The', 105–6
England, 'linguistically
  innovative poetries', 168
essays, fictocritical, 205–6
ethnicity, performance work, 231
exaggeration, 37
expectations of plotlines, 137–9
experimental movements
  concrete poetry, 182
  poetry, 167–9
  Text-Sound, 218
experimental strategies, ix–x
extension technique, new worlds,
  153
external action, interior thought,
  98

fairytales, rewriting, 77–82
far-past, 104–7
fibonacci series, 58
fictocriticism
  exercises, 193, 209–10
  explained, 204–10
first person
  focalisation, 96
  multiple focalisations, 101
  narrator, 88–91
flashbacks, 104, 199, 268
flashforwards, 104, 268
'flat' characters, 141–3
focalisation
  child's viewpoint, 100–101
  components, 97
  constructing, 96–8
  cultural identification, 143–4
  differences, 98, 100
  exercise, 85
  explained, 95–6
  multiple viewpoints, 98–103
  new world, 153
  third person narration, 96
foreshadowing, narrative, 85,
  94–5
found text, 74–7
frames, screen, 246–7
free-verse tradition, 169
Freytag Pyramid, 136
friction
  as fantasy, 147–53
  histories, 144–7
  as writing strategy, 133–4
  see also postmodern fictions
games, linguistic play, 173
gender, subverting, 231
gendered city, 261–62
generic experimentation, 204–5
Genre (novel), 270–71

genres
  cross-dressing, 200–204
  different modes within, 27
  explained, 27
  hypertext fiction, 239–40
  postmodernist fiction, 135
  transgressing norms, 192–3
  writing exercises, 193, 200
  see also mixed genres;
    narratives
geography, postmodern, 255–7
globalisation, effect of, 267–71
God of Small Things, The
  (extract), 256
grammar
  exercises, 178
  functions, 175–6
  poetry, 45–6, 175–8
  subversion of, 176–8

Heart is a Lonely Hunter, The
  (novel), 21–2
heterodiegetic narrator, 87–9
historical events
  postmodernism, 134
  rewriting, 144–7
  time–space compression,
    103–7, 269–70
'historiographic metafiction',
  144–5
*History of the World in 10 1/2
  Chapters, A* (novel), 145
'Holes and Stars' (poem), 162–3
homodiegetic narrator, 87, 89–91
homonyms, 173–4, 175
hook phrases, 52
Human Document, A (novel),
  66
human voice
  improvisation strategies, 225–6
  sonic poems, 219–22
  spoken word, 215–18
  taped voice comments, 111
*Humument: A Treated Victorian
  Novel, A* (novel), 66
hyperlinks, 239
hypermedia
  exercises, 238
  technique, 240–51
hypertext
  creating, 243–4
  exercises, 238
  explained, 239–40
  interactive, 242–3

'I am Marion Delgado' (poem),
  176–7
'I Am Told' (poem), 160–1
ideas
  fictocriticism, 205
  lack of, xi–xii
  recurring, 270
  word association, 5–11
identities, morphing, 231
imagery, contemporary, 166–7
impartiality, narrator, 88

improvisation
  collective, 226
  dialogue, 117–18
  origins, 224
  performance texts, 214
  practice, 224–5
  scores, 227–8
  strategies, 225–6
  words/gestures, 223
'In Parallel' (visual poem), 182,
  187
indigenous marginalisation,
  257
indigenous writing, 169
information, controlled release,
  94–5
interactivity
  hypermedia, 250
  hypertext, 242–3
intercutting, textual, 70–1
intermedia work
  explained, 222
  making, 222–4
intertextuality, xi, 65
'Interviews for the Freedom of
  Dreams' (prose poem), 15–16
inversion technique
  new worlds, 153
  synoptic novel, 194–6, 199
Invisible Cities (novel), 152
Isidora (fictitious place), 152
isomorphism, body and city,
  266–7

Jane Eyre (novel), 77, 120
'Jouissance' (visual poem), 183,
  188–9
juxtaposition
  collage, 70, 72–3
  hypermedia, 249–51
  hypertext, 239
  intermedia work, 222
  literary collage, 67
  new worlds, 153
  past/present, 105–6
  of textual chunks, 68–9
  time–space compression,
   268–70

'Klupzy Girl, The' (poem), 163–4
knowing narrator, 94–5

Lacanian mirror stage, 158
Lady Oracle (novel), 32
landscape description, 256–7
language
  avant-garde poetics, 168–70
  bilingualism, 217
  code-based, 248–9
  constructed, 179–82
  creating, 181–82, 248–9
  fictocritical approach, 206
  futuristic, 151–2
  making up, 150–2
  morphing, 244–5
  polylingualism, 217

self-expression, 157
  see also words
'Language Poetry' (movement),
  167
Language Poets, The, 167–9, 183,
  204–5
language-based strategies
  exercises, 4
  fundamental approach, 3–5
  poetry, 37–46
  phrase manipulation, 11–17
  word association, 5–11
  word games, 4–5
  word pools, 17–18
'Last to Go' (short revue), 120–1
layers, hypertext, 247
leapfrogging, word building, 7
'Learning to Drive: Reading the
  Signs' (fictocritical writing),
  207
Left Hand of Darkness, The
  (novel), 149, 151
'Left' (poem), 159–60
'Lesson from the Cockerel, A'
  (poem), 179–80
Letter for Queen Victoria, A
  (play), 114–15
letter ommission, 174
letters in fiction, 60
lexical experimentation, 179–82
Libra (novel), 145
' "Like Musical Instruments . . ." '
  (poem), 172
linearity, 49–50
lineation, poetry, 38–9
linguistic experimentation
  cyberwriting, 240, 248–9
  discontinuity, 178–9
  games and systems, 173–5
  grammar, 175–8
  lexical experimentation,
   179–82
  metaphor/metonymy, 171–3
  prose poetry, 182–6
  syntax, 175–8
  visual poem, 182–3
'linguistically innovative
  poetries', 168
links, hypertext, 239–44
lipograms, 174
'listenspread' (new word), 151
literary transformations, 59–62
'Living Alone: The New Spinster
  (Some Notes)' (prose), 196–9
location see place
loops, hypertextual, 243
Lost in Thought (extract), 127
Love, etc, (novel), 22–3, 99
lyric, postmodern see
  postmodern lyrics
lyrics, postmodern see
  postmodern lyrics
Magic Toyshop, The (person-in-
  action), 31–2
'Make-Up' (poem), 177–78
mapping worlds, 255–7

marginalisation, character,
  143–4, 195, 257
mesostic structure, 39–40
metafictional narrator, 88–9
metaphors
  city/body, 266–7
  developing, 41
  and metonymy, 171–2
  'mixed', 172
  morphing, 172–3
  poetry, 40–5
metonymy, 171–2
'Mexico City' (script), 227
'mezangelle' language, 248–9
microphones, use of, 231–3
mid-past, 104–7
mimesis, 139
mimicry, 163–4
minor character narrator, 90–1
mirror
  images, 19–25
  Lacanian stage, 158
  possible aspects, 20
  rear-view, 22–3
  'Mirror, The' (poem), 20–1
  'Mirror' (poem), 23–4, 46
  'Mirrors' (short story), 24
mixed genres
  exercises, 193
  time–space compression, 270
  writing, 200–204
  see also hypertext
modernist fictions, 147
monologue, 226
movement, sense of, 31–3
movements see experimental
  movements
movies, animated text, 246
multicultural writing, 169
multilayering, 50, 56–7
multiple focalisations, 98–103,
  107–8
multiplicity, collage, 73
multi-scene movie, 246
multitracking, vocal, 220, 226
music
  accompaniment, 220
  hypermedia, 249
  intermedia work, 224
  sonic poetry, 220
musings, philosophical, 199
My Life (prose poem), 58–9,
  184–6

Nachträglichkeit, 103
names, character, 141, 269
narratee, 91–2
narratives
  closed, 107–8
  definition, 86
  developing, 97–8
  as genre, 84
  open, 107–8
  power dynamics, 86
  restructuring, 103–7
  writing exercises, 85

narratology, 85–7
narrator
  absent, 95
  heterodiegetic, 87–9
  homodiegetic, 87, 89–91
  hypertext fiction, 239–40
  identity withheld, 91
  intrusive, 88–9
  knowing, 94–5
  multiple, 99
  new world, 153
  subversion of voice, 162–5
  use of narratee, 91–2
  using various types, 85
nature poems, 178
near-past, 104–7
Neither the One nor the Other
  (collaboration example),
  16–17
Neuromancer (novel), 149
new media writing
  creation exercises, 238
  cyberwriting, 240, 248–9
  hyperlinks, 239
  hypermedia, 249–51
  screen creation, 246–7
  technologies, 237–8
  on websites, 238
  see also animated texts;
    hypertext
new worlds
  creating, 147–53
  techniques, 153
  triggers, 153
  writing exercises, 255
Noah's flood, rewritten, 145
non-human characters, 143
non-literary forms, 59–62
note form, fragmented, 199
nouns, 33
'Novel in Ten Lines' (synoptic
  novel), 194–5
novels, dialogue, 111
numerical structures, 57–9

object referents, 19
Oedipal complex, contemporary,
  97–8
'Of Time and the Line' (poem),
  173–4
'official verse culture', 169
one-trait characters, 141–3
open narratives, 107–8
orientation *see* focalisation
Oulipo (Ouvroir de Littérature
  Potentielle), 59, 174–5

palindromes, 175
*Pandering to the Masses: A
  Misrepresentation* (play), 111
paraliterature *see* fictocriticism
parallelism, body and city, 266–7
passport details, 61–2
past *see* historical events
past tense, use of, 90
Paterson (collage), 68

'Pause' (poem), 51–2
performance
  delivery of poems, 216–17
  exercises, 213
  intermedia work, 222
  morphing identities, 231
  poems, 214–15, 217–18
  scores, 227–30
  spoken word, 215–18
  subverting gender, 231
  *A Vocabulary Gatha for Peter
    Rose* (score), 228–30
  writing for, 212–14
permutation *see* phrase
  permutation
person-in-action construction
  animation, 29–34
  exercise, 28
  satirical, 36–7
  surrealistic, 35
phrase manipulation
  examples, 11–17
  exercises, 4
  using, 11–17
'phrase manipulation' (example),
  14
phrase permutation
  examples, 12, 14–15, 183, 188–9
  sonic poetry, 219
  technique, 11–12
place
  explicit sense, 256–7
  implicit sense, 257
  new worlds, 152–3
  postmodern geography, 255–7
  questioning sense of, 258–9
  writing about, 254–5
  writing exercises, 255
  see also time–space
    compression
plays, dialogue, 111
plots
  broadening concept, 137
  hypertext fiction, 239
  influence, 136
  over-determined, 138
  postmodern fictions, 135–9
  subverted, 136–9
  traditional structure, 136
  see also storylines
'P.M.T.' (poem), 167
'Poem: i.m. John Forbes'
  (poem), 158–9
'Poem: "In the stump of the old
  tree . . ." ' (poem), 53–4
'Poem Found in a Dime Store
  Diary' (found poem), 75–6
poems
  concrete, 40, 182
  performance delivery, 216–17
  single sentence, 37
  sound, 218
  visual, 182–3
  walk, 263–6
  see also poetry
poetic acrobatics, 167–70

poetry
  experimental, anthologies, 170,
    182, 215
  experimental movements, 167–9
  free-verse tradition, 169
  grammar, 45–6, 175–8
  lineation, 38–9
  location focus, 259
  metaphors, 40–5
  metonymical, 171–2
  numerical systems, 57–9
  for performance, 214–15
  from prose, 37–46
  repetition, 51–2
  similes, 40–5
  simultaneity, 55–56, 183
  spacing, 39–40
  split self, creating, 161
  syntax, 45–6, 175–8
  time–space compression, 271
  typography, 39–40
  variation, 52–5
  word forms, 5
  see also poems; sonic
    poetry/writing
Poetry Slam competitions, 216
point of view *see* focalisation
polyloguing, 123
polysemic language, x, 5, 38, 175
postmodern fictions
  characteristics, 135
  characters, 135, 140
  epistemological dominant, 147
  exercises, 133–4
  ontological dominant, 147
  plot structure, 135–7
  rewriting the past, 144–7
postmodern geography, 255–7
postmodern lyrics
  dissident, 165–6
  exercises, 157
  explained, 156
  split self, 157–61
  subversion of voice, 162–5
postmodernism, definition, 134–5
post-structuralist theory, 134–5
power relationships
  audience participation, 230–1
  chat situations, 123–4
  dialogue, 112–13, 117–20
  dialogue exercise, 119–20
  narrator, 86, 91
  present, time sequence, 103–7
Prince Charming/Cinderella
  rewrite, 80–2
procedural writing, 58
prolepses, 104, 268
prose
  discontinuous, 207–9
  fictocriticism, 206
  realist, 28–34
prose poems
  as a dialogue, 124–5
  'Interviews for the Freedom of
    Dreams', 15–16
  the new sentence, 183–6

'ProseThetic Memories'
    (collaboration), 60–1, 70, 127

questions, different responses,
    112–13
quotations, inclusion of, 205,
    207–9

racism
    dissident lyric, 165
    slavery fictions, 103, 143
radio pieces, dialogue, 111
rap, 5
readerly texts, 108
realism
    characters, 139, 141–2
    described, 28–9
    dialogue, 113–14
    examples, 29–34
    exercises, 28
    inclusion of detail, 33–4
    sense of movement, 31–3
    visual aspect, 31
rearrangement of text, 280
recombination technique, new
    worlds, 153
recycling texts
    described, 65–6
    exercises, 66
    found text, 74–7
    strategies, 66
    see also collage; rewriting
'Red Wheelbarrow, The' (poem),
    37–8
referent-based strategies
    exercises, 4
    explained, 3–4, 18–19
    improvisation, 225
    mirror as medium, 19–25
refinement, 30–1
reflections, 199
reiteration, 76–7
Renaissance man extract, 270–1
repetition
    exercises, 49–50
    non-linear structure, 51–2
    sonic poetry, 219
representation, word use, 27
restructuring narrative, 103–7
'Revolution in Poetic Language'
    (essay), 169–70
rewriting
    approach to, 79–80
    changing perspective, 77–82
    Cinderella tale, 80–82
    historical events, 144–7
    satirical, 36
    surrealist, 35
rhyming verse, 5
rhythms
    intermedia work, 223–4
    sonic poetry, 220
Riddley Walker (novel), 151
'Riting of the Runda, The'
    (constructed language),
    180–1

Robber Bride, The (novel), 100
'.romance (1981)' (performance
    poem), 71, 220
Runda language, 181
'Running Out of Words'
    (intermedia work), 223–4

sampling, sonic poetry, 220–1
satire
    about conversation, 121
    advertising style, 60–1, 63
    apologies website, 60–1
    exercises, 28
    explained, 36–7
'School of English' (non-literary
    form), 61–2
science fiction, 147–8
scores, 227–30
second person
    narrator, 91–2
    split self, 158–9
'Secret Places' (performance
    work), 141, 268–70, 272–5
self-expression, language, 157
semantic flexibility, 177
semiotics, x
sensory city, 262
sentences, prose poetry, 183–6
sexual identities, gendered city,
    261–2
sexualised city, 261–2
'Shantung' (poem), 162
shaping text, 280
'shifgrethor' (new word), 151
short stories, dialogue, 111
signified/signifier relationship
    explained, 4–5
    word association, 6–7
similes
    rhythmic poem, 224
    use in poetry, 40–5
simulacra, 268
simultaneity, 50, 55–6, 183
single-scene movie, 246
Six O'Clock News, The
    (poem/sound recording),
    217
slam poets, 216
slavery
    marginalised characters, 143
    narrative restructuring, 103
smell, sensory stimulation, 262
social interaction, alternative
    dialogues, 112–13
social organisation, new worlds,
    149–50
sonic poetry/writing
    creating, 219–22
    exercise, 213
    explained, 218
sonic relationship, words, 6
Sophie's story
    central character narrator,
    89–90
    destabilised subject position,
    92–3

intrusive narrator, 88–9
knowing narrator, 94–5
minor character narrator, 90–1
multiple focalisations, 99
open/closed narrative, 107–8
second person narration, 91–2
third person narration, 87–8,
    96
time structure, 106–7
sound, intermedia work, 224
'Sound, The' (prose poem), 124–5
sound poem, 218
soundAFFECTs (animated text),
    245
spacing, poetry, 39–40
'spinster' term, 199
splintered self, 160–1
split life, 159–60
split screens, creating, 246–7
split self
    changed subject position, 93
    mirror images, 19
    poem, 161
    postmodern lyrics, 157–61
    psychoanalytic theory, 158
    second person, 158–9
spoken word, 215–18
stage, performance presentation,
    231–3
*Stein, Sturken and Thoreau: A
    collage,* 70–1
'Step Away From Them, A' (walk
    poem), 264–5
'Stillborn' (poem), 171
storylines
    alternative, 139
    conflicting, 138–9
    hypertext fiction, 239
    intermedia work, 222
    see also plots
structuralist movement, 49
structure
    linear, 50
    multilayering, 56–7
    numerical systems, 57–9
    principles, 48–9
    repetition, 51–2
    simultaneity, 55–6
    variation, 52–5
    writing exercises, 49–50
subject positions, 92–4, 270
subjectivity, xi
substitution, word, 12–13,
    14–15, 30, 279
subtraction, word, 13
subversions of plot, 136–9
'sucking on remembrance:
    encounters with the vampire
    and other histories of the
    body' (fictocriticism), 207–9
'Sunset Debris' (prose poem),
    184
'surface' characters, 141–3
surrealism
    exercises, 28
    explained, 34–5

synoptic novel, 194–6
'synoptic novel' (example), 196
syntax
  exercises, 178
  poetry, 45–6, 175–8
  systems, linguistic play, 173–5

taboo subjects, 166–7
talent, writing, ix
'talk' poet, 224
'Taxi' (poem), 257
technology
  sonic writing, 218–19, 220–1
technology in future worlds,
  149
text generation, computer, 251–2
Text-Sound movement, 218
'the ISM' (poem), 165
The Sydney Front, 230
third person
  focalisation, 96
  narrator, 87–8, 91
  two perspectives, 100
*this will be the end of you: play9:
  curious to know* (animated
  text), 247, 250
*this will be the end of you: play6:
  four variable creation*
  (animated text), 245, 247,
  250
thought processes in dialogue,
  116
time
  building new world, 148–9
  past/present sequence, 90,
    103–7
  shifts, 149, 193
  types of pasts, 104–7
*Time's Arrow or The Nature of
  the Offence* (novel), 107,
  116–17
time–space compression
  examples, 268–75
  exercise, 271
  explained, 267–8
  method, 269–70
  postmodern fictions, 134–5
'Tofu Your Life' (visual poem),
  182, 188

topography, new worlds, 152–3
Tourism (novel), 60, 258–9
TranceFIGUREd Spirit
  (performance work), 223
'types', 36–7
typography, poetry, 39–40

u cannot be programmed
  (hypermedia), 250
UbuWeb website, sound section,
  219
Unconsoled, The (postmodern
  fiction), 137, 141
'Under The Tree' (poem), 12
underprivileged city, 261
Undivided Attention (poem), 216
unreal city, 262–3
'Untitled' (Cinderella rewrite),
  80–2
'Untitled' (non-literary form),
  61, 63

vampire (extract), 208
variation
  exercises, 50
  technique, 52–5
verbs, strong, 30–1, 31–2
'Viola's Quilt' (postmodern
  fiction), 141
Virginia Woolf Poems, The, 66
virtual city, 262
visual poems, 182–3
visualisation, 31
*Vocabulary Gatha for Peter Rose,
  A* (score), 228–30
voice
  alternative, 163–4
  notion of, exercise, 164–5
  subversion of, 162–5
  variety, 270
  see also human voice

walk poems, 263–6
Wanderground, The (novel), 151
'Waste Land, The' (poem), 67–8
web pages, writing skill, 238
websites
  apologies online, 60–1
  Smith Ongoing, 268

'White Christmas Eve' (phrase
  manipulation), 14–15
White Noise (novel), 36–7
Who's Afraid of Virginia Woolf?
  (play), 118–19
Wide Sargasso Sea (novel), 77, 99
women, gendered city, 261–2
'wonderful' (prose poem), 10,
  171
word association
  examples, 8–9
  exercises, 4
  improvisation strategies, 225
  by meaning, 6–7
  multisyllabic word play, 7–8
  by sound, 6, 10
  techniques, 5–11
  variation, 52–3
word play, 173–5
word pools
  creating metaphors, 41
  creation, 17–18
  improvisation, 225
'Word Wired Web', 250
words
  addition, 13, 30
  changing function, 176–7
  choice of, 179
  constructed, 151, 180–1, 219
  grammatical function, 176–7
  new media animation, 244–5
  new-world concepts, 153
  playing with, 4–5
  substitution, 12–13, 14–15, 30
  subtraction, 13
*Wordstuffs: The City and The
  Body* (hypertext), 240–2, 250,
  266–7
'World, A Girl, A Memory: act
  one, A' (short prose), 54–5
worlds, new
  creating, 147–53
  techniques, 153
  triggers, 153
writerly texts, 108
writers, frequent questions,
  viii–xii
'writing through' process, 66

Printed in Great Britain
by Amazon